Virginia at War, 1864

VIRGINIA
AT WAR
1864

Edited by William C. Davis
and James I. Robertson Jr.
for the Virginia Center for Civil War Studies

THE UNIVERSITY PRESS OF KENTUCKY

Editorial and Sales Offices: The University Press of Kentucky
663 South Limestone Street, Lexington, Kentucky 40508-4008
www.kentuckypress.com

ISBN 978-0-8131-2562-6

Manufactured in the United States of America.

Book Club Edition

Contents

Preface

For Virginians, 1864 brought the war home as never before. Indeed, for the first time, for the bulk of Virginia's forces, the war was fought entirely in the Old Dominion. Never before had the conflict taken such a toll on the landscape and the civilian population, while for the men under arms it was a story of unrelentingly diminishing numbers and resources. Under any other army commander in the Confederacy, Virginia likely would have been lost in 1864. It was only the brilliance and determination of Gen. Robert E. Lee that kept the Commonwealth's military forces intact and able to retard, if not stop, the relentless advance of the Union. Yet the men of Lee's army, and those other Virginia soldiers spread from northern Virginia to the most southwesterly reaches of the state, were a minority of the Virginians involved in and affected by the war. All of them combined had endured more than two and one-half years of intermittent warfare on home soil by January 1864, and unknowingly they were about to enter a phase in which the war would be with them all day, every day, until the end.

This current volume of *Virginia at War* casts a special focus on vital home front matters in the Commonwealth during the war. Subjects such as politics, patriotism, transportation, agriculture, education, literature, emancipation, and journalism may not carry with them the allure of campaigns and battles, generals and regiments, but they were the vital raw materials both of the war effort and of the civilian infrastructure necessary to keep armies in the field. In a democracy, and in an American democracy perhaps most of all, it is these nonmilitary matters that help to distinguish between a militaristic state at war and a fully developed society in conflict. After this book sets the context in a general essay on military operations in the state in 1864, essays on these subjects reveal the full breadth of the impact of the war on the entire polity as well as the influence on the war effort of things as diverse as professors and poems, potatoes and potholes, canals and cabbages, and much more. As in earlier volumes, while this one is titled *1864,* in fact the essays cover their topics for the entire war period, though the subjects have been selected for this volume with a view to the special impact of this particular year. The Fourth of July, for instance, was important to Virginians throughout the war, but in 1864 it had special poignancy as a reminder of the disasters at Gettysburg and Vicksburg that marked the day in 1863, and as the last wartime patriotic holiday for Confederate Virginians.

Operations in the state in 1864 are detailed with eloquent thoroughness by Dr. Richard J. Sommers, for more than thirty years a friend to researchers at the U.S. Army Military History Institute, now a part of the U.S. Army Heritage and Education Center at Carlisle Barracks, Pennsylvania. Sommers is the author of the landmark *Richmond Redeemed,* one of the most distinguished works ever written on phases of Virginia's 1864 war, and in 2007–2008 was Harold Keith Johnson Visiting Professor of Military History at the Military History Institute. In his essay here he reveals the full complexity of a war on many fronts, offering articulate testimony to the fact that Virginia was beset from many sides, and that much of its war was hundreds of miles from Lee and Grant, in faraway places with forgotten names that still cast their influence on the course of the conflict in the Commonwealth.

It has been said that warfare is merely politics by another means. Certainly, in the Confederacy and in Virginia, politics could not be separated from what happened on the battlefields. Indeed, the two were mutually dependent. The political Confederacy could not hope to survive without its military to protect it, while the armies in the field would be helpless without political backing in Richmond. Aaron Sheehan-Dean's essay on Virginia politics reveals just how interdependent they were, and how fragile was the democracy that relied on both. Sheehan-Dean, who took his doctorate at the University of Virginia, is associate professor of history at the University of North Florida and the author of several distinguished works, including *Why Confederates Fought: Family and Nation in Civil War Virginia.*

There was another prop necessary to sustain both Virginians in the field and Virginians at home, and that was a regular press. From its earliest days, even before the Revolution, Virginia depended upon a vigorous and unfettered press. The rigors of war severely strained Virginia's newspapers from 1861 to 1865, and yet they continued to operate in spite of hardship of every kind, from shortages of newsprint and ink to decline in readership to the difficulty of getting reliable information. Dr. Ted Tunnell, for more than twenty years a professor of history at Virginia Commonwealth University, looks at the trials of Virginia's newspapers during the war, as they both served and represented the interests and apprehensions of the people of the Commonwealth. Tunnell is a keen student of Reconstruction in particular. His publications include *Crucible of Reconstruction: War, Radicalism, and Race in Louisiana, 1862–1877,* but recently he has done distinguished work on the history of journalism.

One of the functions of the press was to sustain morale and patriotism, and the ceremonial forms that patriotism in Virginia took are an interest of Jared Bond, who recently received his M.A. in history from Virginia Tech. In particular, he looks here at how Virginians clung to the great national holiday for which Northerners, too, felt an ancestral reverence, the Fourth of July. The ways in which Virginians celebrated that day, while at the same time trying to separate themselves from Yankees also revering the day, and the ways in which Virginians sought to assert their preeminent claim on the celebration, reveal much about the nature of patriotism in the Commonwealth during the war.

It is often forgotten that wars depend on so much more than just armies. Indeed, armies themselves depend on many of the same things required to keep a civilian population functioning, and on nothing more than transportation. This was a mobile war, especially in Virginia. Virginia had experienced the canal boom of the 1830s, followed by the more revolutionary coming of the railroad. Virginia had the oldest roads in America and also one of the most modern macadamized routes in the pike that ran through much of the Shenandoah Valley. Armies needed those avenues to move and to supply themselves, while farmers, travelers, and civil officials used them almost as much to keep the infrastructure of the state functioning in wartime. Dr. Bradford A. Wineman of the Department of Military History, United States Army Command and General Staff College at Ft. Leavenworth, Kansas, addresses Virginia's overtaxed transportation system during the war, appraising its impact on the conduct of military operations as well as its ability—or inability—to meet civilian needs. A graduate of the Virginia Military Institute and Texas A&M University, Wineman is a specialist in the military history of the war.

Transportation was inextricably intertwined with the agriculture of Virginia during the war. Farmers needed to get their produce to markets. The government needed to get food and livestock to the armies in the field. If the two did not work together, neither could meet its wartime demands.

Virginia was a fertile place in 1861, but going onto a wartime footing very soon placed burdensome demands on the output of the soil. Dr. Ginette Aley, assistant professor of history at the University of Southern Indiana, is a specialist in midwestern and agricultural history. Her essay on Virginia reveals the extent to which Virginia growers and livestock raisers were able to support both civilian and military needs, the spreading devastation that the war caused to agriculture, and the impact that farmers' ability to feed both civilians and soldiers ultimately had on the war effort. Aley has published extensively in agricultural history and has three forthcoming books on nineteenth-century women and the Civil War home front in the Midwest.

Virginians needed to feed the mind as well as the body. Education is always one of the first casualties of warfare, and nowhere more than in a civil war. With the conflict raging on their doorsteps, and with the insatiable demands of armies for young men, schools are hard pressed to find either pupils or teachers to instruct them. It was no different for Virginia, as revealed by Dr. Peter Wallenstein, professor of history at Virginia Tech. His works on civil rights, the Civil War, and most recently his *Cradle of America: Four Centuries of Virginia History* establish him as one of the Commonwealth's most distinguished historians. In particular, he looks at how the war caused the erosion of higher education, always the pride of the Old Dominion in antebellum days. With such schools as William & Mary and the University of Virginia, among others, Virginia had been a leader in Southern education. The war threatened to change that irrevocably. Only through extraordinary effort did a few schools manage to keep their doors open, and the impact of the war years on the postwar education of Virginians would be dramatic.

Like education, arts and literature are often among the early casualties of war. William C. Davis, coeditor of this series and professor of history and director of programs of the Virginia Center for Civil War Studies at Virginia Tech, explores the literature of wartime Virginia. What he reveals is a constant struggle for artistic creation amid the scarcity of mundane industrial plants and raw materials. At the same time there was a war within Virginia's writers, an internal struggle between the impulse to produce lasting works of creativity and temporal works addressing the war at hand, the need for patriotic writing, memorialization of the dead, and sustaining the spirit of the people. Politics, religion, poetry, even humor and satire, all attracted the pens of Virginians, but a great war literature failed to emerge. What did come from the war in Virginia, of course, was a searing experience that would inspire and inform generations of Virginia—and Southern—writers to follow.

And one more thing that came from the war, undeniably, was a new freedom for thousands of Virginians previously kept in bonds. Union authorities began tinkering with social reconstruction years before official Reconstruction came into play, and one of the earliest testing grounds was Fort Monroe, which remained a Union enclave in Virginia throughout the war. J. Michael Cobb, for twenty-five years the director of the Hampton History Museum, is the coauthor of the *Hampton* volume in the Images of America series and of a history of Fort Wool as well a leader in the effort to preserve and interpret historic Fort Wool in Hampton Roads. In his essay on daily life and emancipation at Fort Monroe, he opens a door on the learning by trial and error that became the roots of future Reconstruction policy in the halting and all-too-ineffective effort to bring former slaves into the mainstream of postwar America.

As before in this series, one Virginian speaks at length of the wartime experience, and that is Judith Brockenbrough McGuire. Her invaluable diary is made the more so by the skillful and illuminating editing and annotation provided by James I. Robertson Jr., Alumni Distinguished Professor of History and director of the Virginia Center for Civil War Studies at Virginia Tech. As in previous volumes, the necessity to maintain balance requires that the McGuire diary be spread across the series less by calendar year than by length. Consequently, this 1864 volume contains the McGuire diary entries from June 1863 to July 1864. It was a momentous period of time. Virginians learned of and coped with the news of Gettysburg, and then the unceasing overland campaign of U. S. Grant as he confronted Lee in the Wilderness, then Spotsylvania, Cold Harbor, and finally the opening days of what would be a ten-month siege around Petersburg and Richmond. The trials of being a civilian—the fear, the rumors, the shortages, and more—are all revealed in McGuire's diary, here edited and annotated for the first time. Her voice, added to those of the distinguished authors of these essays, captures the wartime experience of the Old Dominion as nothing else could.

None of these essays and volumes in this series would be possible without the generous support of the William E. Jamerson family of Appomattox, Virginia, and the editors wish again to extend their gratitude to the Jamersons for their generous and sustained support of this work. We wish to thank, as well, the editors and staff of the University Press of Kentucky, that other commonwealth that was once a part of this one, especially Joyce Harrison, Ila McEntire, and Robin DuBlanc. They have all lent their efforts to making this series better than the sum of its parts.

Virginia at War, 1864

Land Operations in Virginia in 1864

The Tightening Noose

Richard J. Sommers

Strategic stalemate still settled over Virginia as 1864 began. Robert E. Lee's Army of Northern Virginia and George G. Meade's Army of the Potomac glowered across the Rapidan River from their respective winter quarters in Orange and Culpeper counties. All other Virginia fronts continued comparably quiescent.

Two Yankee raids in February achieved nothing. Isaac Wistar's raid from Williamsburg toward Richmond, February 6–8, could not even cross Chickahominy River, and Federal diversions on the Rapidan gained nothing, either. Judson Kilpatrick's strike southward from Culpeper, February 28–March 4, actually reached Richmond's northern defenses. He, however, did not press the attack; his subordinate Ulric Dahlgren was repulsed farther west; and Union troopers deflected eastward to escape pursuit.

Raids and rest gave way to major combat in May. Campaigning that spring was far more intense, sustained, and focused than previously. New Federal general-in-chief Ulysses S. Grant initiated two fundamental changes in grand strategy that decisively affected the war's outcome. He seized and retained the strategic initiative unrelentingly, and he concerted the armed might of the Union. These innovations proved crucial for converting the North's potential advantages of manpower and matériel into strategic success.

Grant transferred forces from backwaters like the Carolinas and Louisiana to reinforce major Federal armies' simultaneous onslaughts in Virginia, Georgia, and later Alabama. Within the Old Dominion, during the first week of May, moreover, he unleashed two divisions against southwestern Virginia, two more to move up the Shenandoah Valley, seven divisions

1

(including three from South Carolina and Florida) to strike westward from Fort Monroe against Richmond, and eighteen to operate directly against the Army of Northern Virginia. To fight Lee himself, Grant established his own headquarters in Virginia, not supplanting Meade but heading a force composed of Meade's army and Ambrose E. Burnside's independent IX Corps. Grant thus served as "army group" commander, eastern theater commander, and general-in-chief. Grant's approach of attacking simultaneously and unrelentingly eventually won the war. Victory, however, came neither easily nor soon—due largely to Lee's skillful generalship and his soldiers' hard fighting.

Such fighting erupted immediately, as the two sides clashed in the tangled Wilderness, May 5–6. Grant risked fighting on such unfavorable terrain because he wanted to free himself from the vulnerable Orange & Alexandria Railroad supply line, where John Pope and Meade had suffered in 1862–1863. He instead moved eastward by his strategic left flank to reach Virginia's great tidal rivers—Potomac, Rappahannock, York-Pamunkey, and James—supply lines virtually invulnerable to disruption. To reach them, the Yankees had to penetrate the Wilderness. They crossed the Rapidan, May 4, and hoped to hurry through those thickets and fight Lee in more open country farther south.

Lee was too good a general to concede that advantage. As he would do all year, he did not supinely stay in his trenches awaiting Grant's onslaughts but instead counterattacked. Lee thereby challenged the Bluecoats for the tactical initiative; he hoped to use his knowledge of local terrain to surprise them and beat them piecemeal. Sometimes his counterattacks succeeded; sometimes they failed. Yet from now to Appomattox, Lee would fight back rather than just fall back. His approach glowingly contrasts with "Retreating Joe" Johnston's operations in Georgia and helps explain why Confederates enjoyed much greater success in Virginia that year.

Rather than remain in his Rapidan–Mine Run fortifications, Lee struck eastward into the Wilderness. This threat caused Meade to stop advancing southeastward and send troops west to confront this danger. Heavy fighting raged all day, May 5. Winfield Scott Hancock's devastating attack, May 6, threatened to shatter the Confederate right. James Longstreet's timely arrival with three fresh divisions hurled the Unionists back. Amazingly, Longstreet was then shot by his own men—on almost the same date and spot where "Stonewall" Jackson was mortally wounded in 1863. Longstreet survived and returned to duty, October 19, but his fall disrupted exploiting this success. When Southerners did resume attacking, Hancock repulsed them. Meanwhile, a belated Butternut effort to roll up the Federal right flank gained only limited success.

The battle of the Wilderness sputtered to a close with light skirmishing, May 7. Casualties amounted to 20,000 Unionists and 11,000 Secessionists.[1] Such a disparity and such a check to Yankee efforts to rush southward unopposed made this opening battle a Confederate victory, tactically. Grant, however, made it a strategic victory for the North. Not only had he absorbed Graycoat counterattacks, but he also saw no need to retreat across the Rappahannock to refit and recuperate, as Burnside and Joseph Hooker did in 1862–1863. Instead, he disengaged from the Wilderness and continued pressing southward. He thereby retained the strategic initiative and would continue dominating operations in Virginia. Except briefly in July, he held that initiative all the way to Appomattox. Fighting resumed at Spotsylvania, May 8. Lee and his subordinates skillfully interposed forces to slow the Yankees' advance. Federal efforts to envelop the Butternuts' left rear and penetrate their left front, May 10, initially achieved limited success, but the Yankees were soon driven out. Meade's greatest gain came May 12, as Hancock stormed the "Muleshoe Salient," virtually annihilating the Stonewall Division. The Unionists, however, could not exploit their breakthrough. Secessionist counterattacks blunted such follow-up and bought time to erect new trenches across the salient's gorge. Union attempts to storm that gorge wall, May 18, were repulsed. However, Richard Ewell's effort to turn Meade's right the following day ended disastrously. The May 19 debacle demonstrated that the Army of Northern Virginia was losing its vaunted ability to counterattack decisively. Fighting May 8–19 produced 18,000 Yankee and 9,500 Southern losses.[2]

By mid-May, Grant's four other Virginia offensives had also provoked considerable fighting but not much gain. Most successful was George Crook's division moving southward from the Kanawha Valley. It defeated (and killed) Albert Jenkins at Cloyd's Mountain, May 9; cut the Virginia & Tennessee Railroad, and destroyed the railroad trestle over New River. Crook, however, felt isolated so deep in southwestern Virginia and withdrew into West Virginia. Farther west, John H. Morgan's and William E. Jones's Graycoats defeated William W. Averell's cavalry division at Crockett's Cove, May 10, before it reached Wytheville's lead mines and Saltville's saltworks.

Even greater disaster befell Franz Sigel's two Union divisions moving up the Shenandoah. With three brigades and the Virginia Military Institute cadets, John C. Breckinridge beat Sigel at New Market, May 15, and compelled him to flee northward. Crook's withdrawal and Averell's and Sigel's defeats freed Breckinridge to join Lee, while Jones assumed responsibility for all Virginia west of the Blue Ridge.

Meanwhile, the largest cooperating column, Benjamin F. Butler's Army of the James, suffered the largest defeat. Its campaign began auspiciously, as it sailed up James River and occupied City Point and Bermuda Hundred, May 5. Hesitancy, overcaution, and controversy with his corps commanders thereafter paralyzed Butler's operations. Two probes against the Richmond & Petersburg Railroad were repulsed, May 6–7. He did cut those tracks, May 9, but then vacillated between advancing on Petersburg or Richmond, did neither, and withdrew into Bermuda Hundred. By the time Butler again moved north through Chesterfield County against the capital, Gen. P. G. T. Beauregard opposed him with a makeshift army of fifteen brigades (drawn from as far away as Florida and east Tennessee).

Beauregard with ten brigades defeated Butler at Second Drewry's Bluff, May 16. The Yankees were lucky to escape into Bermuda Hundred. Behind his trenches across the hundred's western mouth, Butler repulsed Southern assaults, May 20 and June 2. Beauregard built his own line of fortifications across the peninsula's mouth, thus "corking Butler in his bottle." Actually, egress southward, eastward, and northward remained to the Bluecoats, and they eventually used all three routes. Nevertheless, the image of Butler corked in his bottle haunted that quintessential political general ever afterward.[3]

While the Bermuda Hundred campaign still hung in the balance, Philip H. Sheridan's three cavalry divisions from Meade's army reached James River opposite City Point, May 14. They had cut loose from Meade, May 9; struck southward for Richmond; killed Confederate cavalry chieftain "Jeb" Stuart at Yellow Tavern, May 11; yet did not try storming Richmond but escaped down the peninsula to Haxall's Landing, barely avoiding disaster at Meadow Bridges, May 12. Sheridan started overland to rejoin Meade, May 17. When the troopers arrived a week later, the armies were again heavily engaged at North Anna River.

Grant resumed moving south from Spotsylvania, May 20, again by his left. Lee countered by repositioning forces along the North Anna, covering Hanover Junction, where the Virginia Central and Richmond, Fredericksburg & Potomac railroads crossed. On May 23, Hancock on the Federal left fought his way across the river at Chesterfield Bridge. Farther upstream Gouverneur K. Warren's V Corps crossed at Jericho Mills and withstood heavy counterattacks. In the center, however, Burnside could not force passage at Ox Ford, May 23–24. The Graycoats thus held a central position south of the river, between Warren's and Hancock's isolated corps. Lee, though, was too ill and his subordinates were too inexperienced or lethargic to exploit that advantage. By May 27, all Meade's men had withdrawn safely to the left bank. Casualties at the North Anna came to 2,000 on each side.[4]

Already on May 26, the Yankees started shifting downstream (again moving leftward) and began crossing Pamunkey River, May 27. Sheridan's returned cavalry led the way and battled Wade Hampton's troopers at Haw's Shop, May 28. Fighting flared throughout Hanover County into early June at Totopotomoy Creek, Matadequin Creek, and Bethesda Church, as Grant sought openings around the Confederate right and as Lee shifted forces to cover his railroads and to counterattack. Reinforcements reached both sides in late May. Beauregard returned five brigades to Lee before North Anna; he now sent four more. Breckinridge brought two brigades from the Valley. Meantime, William F. Smith's reinforced XVIII Corps (four divisions) left Butler, sailed down the James and up the York-Pamunkey to reinforce Meade. Burnside, too, magnanimously waived rank so his IX Corps could join Meade's army, thus creating unity of command.

Fresh troops and veterans clashed at Cold Harbor, June 1–3. The Secessionists opened that battle with a disastrous, ill-coordinated attack on Sheridan, whose dismounted troopers with repeating carbines actually repulsed infantry. Later on June 1, Smith's and Horatio Wright's VI Corps assaulted Lee's works. They broke through briefly but were soon driven out. June 2 witnessed Burnside repel attacks against Meade's right but Hancock not take Turkey Hill on the left. June 3 proved decisive. Hancock's, Wright's, and Smith's massive frontal assaults bloodily failed. Cold Harbor was Grant's worst defeat of the Overland campaign, among the worst all year. More than that it was not. It is wrong to equate June 3 at Cold Harbor with Grant's conduct of operations all spring or all year. His generalship previously and subsequently proved much more skillful. Cold Harbor no more characterized Grant's generalship than Malvern Hill typified Lee's. Both were far better commanders than they appeared on those two days. Casualties, May 28–June 15, were 15,000 Northerners and 6,000 Butternuts.[5]

As the battered, exhausted armies briefly rested around Cold Harbor until mid-June, dangers and opportunities elsewhere diverted some of their divisions. Warfare again raged in the Shenandoah Valley, as Sigel's successor, David Hunter, struck south, defeating and killing Jones at Piedmont, June 5. Crook and Averell then joined Hunter from West Virginia. Hunter occupied Staunton and Lexington unopposed, burning VMI, and threatened Lynchburg. To save that key industrial city and perhaps catch Hunter, Lee returned Breckinridge and then sent Jubal Early's II Corps. These forces handily repelled Hunter at Lynchburg, June 17–18, but could not overtake his flight down the New-Kanawha Valley to the Ohio River. Meantime, at Trevilian Station, June 11–12, Hampton turned back Sheridan's two divisions, which rode west from Meade's army in hopes of joining Hunter.

Sheridan had moved west from Hanover County. Grant's main body moved southeast, as ever advancing leftward. From May 4 to June 3, Grant carried the war from the Rapidan to the Chickahominy, inflicted—and suffered—heavy losses of leaders and soldiers, and dominated the initiative. He continued controlling the course of events, but he no longer drove straight south for Richmond. The swampy, easily defended Chickahominy and the well-fortified capital proved too formidable. Ever one to learn from experience, Grant now launched bolder strategic maneuvers, reminiscent of his decisive strikes against Vicksburg in May 1863.

First, he sent Smith back to Bermuda Hundred by water. Meade crossed the Chickahominy onto the westerly peninsula. There he directly threatened Richmond, as George McClellan and John Dix did in 1862–1863. To meet that danger, Lee moved troops east of the capital and skirmished with Warren at Second Riddell's Shop, June 13. Warren, however, simply shielded the main army, which continued south to James River at Wilcox's and Wyanoke landings. Hancock sailed from Wilcox's to the right bank, June 14–15. Burnside, Warren, much of Wright, and eventually Sheridan (returning from Trevilian) crossed on a pontoon bridge that engineers laid between Wyanoke and Windmill Point. This 2,100-foot bridge across a broad, deep tidal river ranks as one of the great engineering feats of the Civil War.

Grant sent Smith, Hancock, and Meade to the Southside to capture Petersburg. A large, important city and site of Confederate lead works for making bullets, Petersburg was most strategic as Richmond's rail center. Railroads from Lynchburg and the Great Valley, City Point, southeastern Virginia, and blockade-running ports on the lower Atlantic coast united in

Petersburg. One railroad north through Chesterfield County linked these lines to Richmond. Only one other railroad, running southwest through Danville to the Carolina piedmont, connected the capital to the Confederate interior without passing through Petersburg. Holding Petersburg thus was crucial to holding Richmond. Losing Petersburg would compromise Confederates' control of their capital. Fighting for Petersburg and its supply lines dominated Grant's and Lee's operations for the rest of the war.

Butler sent four brigades against the "Cockade City" (Petersburg's nickname) as early as June 9, to no avail. Now, in mid-month, Grant's two armies struck the city. Smith stormed its outer defenses, June 15, but failed to exploit his advantage. Nor did Meade commit Hancock's exhausted troops that evening. By the time Meade engaged the next day, Beauregard had dug new trenches and stripped his line of fortifications to save Petersburg. The Bluecoats made limited gains, June 16–17, but their grand assault, June 18, was bloodily repulsed. In that charge the First Maine Heavy Artillery lost 632 men (70 percent of its strength): the largest one-day absolute loss for any Union regiment in the war.[6] Abandoning the Howlett Line uncorked Butler. He probed westward tentatively, June 16, and actually cut the Richmond & Petersburg Railroad. By then, however, Lee had not only returned one division to Beauregard but was rushing his own army to the Southside. Richard H. Anderson's Confederate I Corps handily beat Butler at Clay's Farm, June 16–17, and corked him back in his bottle on Bermuda Hundred.

East of Petersburg, Grant immediately cut two railroads. He paused briefly and again struck westward with his left against a third line, the Weldon Railroad, which connected with Wilmington, Charleston, & Savannah. Savage Confederate counterattacks, June 22–23, routed the II Corps (now under David B. Birney) and defeated Wright. Then two raiding Federal cavalry divisions were also thrashed at First Reams's Station, June 29.

With that first battle of the Weldon Railroad, the mobile warfare of spring stagnated into the siege of summer. The siege of Petersburg, as it is properly called, was not primarily a tactical siege, in which attackers attempted to storm, level, or undermine defenders' ramparts. Grant, indeed, had learned the lessons of May 18, June 3, and June 18 and explicitly forbade frontal assaults against defended positions. Rather, Petersburg was a strategic siege. Grant's siege lines east of Petersburg proved a great entrenched camp, from whose security he launched offensives against lightly guarded Richmond and against mostly unfortified country south of Petersburg, through which ran vital supply lines. These offensives provoked a series of field battles north and south of James River. Cumulatively these battles and offensives constitute the siege of Petersburg.

The first two offensives occurred June 15–18 and June 22–29. The third offensive was delayed a month, partly due to both armies' compelling need to rest. Even veteran soldiers and veteran commanders had never before experienced the incessant fighting raging May 5–June 23. They were exhausted; they had lost their fighting edge; and they needed rest.

Another cause of delay was that, for the only time between the Wilderness and Appomattox, Lee regained the strategic initiative in early summer. Hunter's retreat through West Virginia uncovered the Shenandoah Valley. Early's six divisions struck down that historic avenue of war and erupted on the upper Potomac, July 5. They crossed into Maryland, won at Monocacy, and skirmished outside Washington itself, July 11–12. Early then withdrew to Leesburg and eventually Berryville.

Such a strategic surprise caused Grant to cancel an attack at Petersburg and to divert northward Wright's corps and two divisions arriving from Louisiana. Grant intended not merely to defend D.C. but to eliminate Early. That proved no easy task. The Butternuts beat Wright at Cool Spring, July 18, and routed Crook (who had succeeded Hunter) at Second Kernstown, July 24. Early returned to the Potomac; two of his cavalry brigades actually burned Chambersburg, Pennsylvania, July 30. Grant then sent one and later another cavalry division from Meade to confront Early. On August 7, he united all Federal forces on that front into the new Army of the Shenandoah under Sheridan.

One reason Grant launched his third offensive was to cut railroads to Early. Hancock, advancing across Bermuda Hundred onto the peninsula via the Deep Bottom bridgehead, July 27, overran outer lines but got nowhere near those tracks. He had to repulse counterattacks, July 28, and returned to the Southside, July 29. On July 30, Burnside detonated a mine beneath Pegram's Salient east of Petersburg. This dazzling deed degenerated into depressing defeat, as Secessionists counterattacked the bewildered and leaderless Unionists. This Crater debacle is mistakenly equated with the siege of Petersburg. Really, it is utterly uncharacteristic of the siege.

More typical were the fourth offensive's battles, beginning August 14. Hancock and Birney (now leading the X Corps) again sallied out of Deep

Bottom. Again their initial gains produced no breakthrough. Again Hancock withdrew from the bridgehead, August 19–20. The previous day Warren struck west to cut the Weldon Railroad at Globe Tavern, four miles below Petersburg. He reeled under vicious counterattacks by first Beauregard and then Lee, August 18–21, but retained his clutch on the railroad. As Hancock tore up those tracks southward, however, A. P. Hill and Hampton routed him at Second Reams's Station, August 25. Denied uninterrupted use of the Weldon Railroad, Confederates still ran trains to Stony Creek Depot, and then transshipped supplies via Dinwiddie County's backroads into the Boydton Plank Road, thence to Petersburg. Defending and cutting the plank road and the last railroad (the Southside) now became Lee's and Grant's respective goals. These routes were targets of Grant's fifth offensive. So was Richmond. Butler's whole army crossed the James at Deep Bottom via a new pontoon bridge to Varina, September 29, stormed outer defenses at Fort Harrison, and exposed Richmond to greatest danger of capture any time before April 1865. Ewell's skillful leadership, heroic defense of Forts Johnson and Gilmer, and blundering by Butler and his subordinates cost the Yankees that prize. Yet Lee himself failed to recapture Fort Harrison, September 30, nor could he dislodge Birney at First Darbytown Road, October 7. This time the Northerners did not withdraw but kept an army on the peninsula until the siege's final week. Lee had to content himself with sealing the breach and foiling efforts to disrupt the new lines at Second Darbytown Road, October 13. He had to leave a corps to hold those peninsula lines, forces he could ill afford diverting from the Southside.

To save Richmond, Lee actually considered abandoning Petersburg, September 29–30. Yet he did not yield to such fears but fought back and retained both cities. After Warren punched through Confederate trenches west of Globe Tavern, September 30, Hill's and Hampton's counterattacks stopped the IX Corps short of the plank road. The Southerners, however, could not recapture Peebles's Farm, October 1. This battle of Poplar Spring Church extended Union fortifications westward but left the supply lines in Secessionist hands. The sixth offensive, October 27, reached the plank road at Burgess's Mill, south of Hatcher's Run. This threat provoked massive counterattacks by Hampton and Hill. In his final Civil War battle, Hancock displayed his mastery of minor tactics in repulsing attacks from four directions and successfully extricating his isolated force overnight. His skill cannot mask what a strategic Union defeat First Hatcher's Run was. Even more decisive was Longstreet's repulse of Butler's simultaneous attack at Second Fair Oaks, a failed effort to get around the Butternut left into Richmond.

Despite limited gains in the fifth offensive and complete failure in the sixth, September and October saw Federal efforts in Virginia fare well, thanks to Sheridan. After sparring with Early for six weeks, Sheridan beat him at Third Winchester, September 19, and Fisher's Hill, September 22. Early retreated southward, and Bluecoats again occupied Staunton. On withdrawing northward, they devastated this granary of the Confederacy. Reinforced by five brigades, Early followed and delivered a surprise attack at Cedar Creek, October 19. Initial Southern success proved fleeting, as the returning Sheridan rallied his men to win one of the great Federal victories of the war.

Cedar Creek decided the Valley campaign and contributed to President Lincoln's reelection, which he won overwhelmingly. Armies remained in the Shenandoah country until Appomattox but at much reduced strength. Early returned fifteen brigades to Lee in November–December, and Sheridan sent fourteen brigades to Grant in December and transferred three more to Savannah in January. These reinforcements helped replace four brigades Lee sent to Wilmington in December to counter six brigades that Butler led against that port.

These Valley veterans began reaching Petersburg as final fighting flared there for 1864. No longer conducting two-pronged attacks on both sides of James River, Grant unleashed the first of three massive first strikes by his left. Warren led five divisions south, December 7, to destroy the Weldon Railroad. He skirmished at Belfield, then eluded Hill's pursuit and rejoined Meade, December 12.

The last significant operations of the year occurred at the opposite end of the Commonwealth, where Northerners continued threatening lead mines and saltworks. Stephen Burbridge's strike from Kentucky was repulsed at Saltville, October 2. December 16–21, however, George Stoneman's column from East Tennessee seriously damaged both that site and Wytheville.

Casualties at Petersburg in the June 9 attack, the first six offensives, the Belfield Raid, and the incessant shelling and sharpshooting east of town came to around 48,000 Northerners and 20,000 Secessionists.[7] Another 24,000 Bluecoats and 15,000 Confederates fell west of the Blue Ridge from before Cloyd's Mountain to Second Saltville.[8] Overall losses in the Old Dominion in 1864 approximate 134,000 Yankees and 70,000 Southerners, almost equal to the 206,000 losses in the ten largest eastern battles, 1861–1863, combined, including Antietam and Gettysburg.[9]

Such staggering casualties were not only numerical but qualitative. Many of the most senior leaders on both sides were gone. Among corps commanders, "Jeb" Stuart and John Sedgwick were killed; Birney died of disease; Beauregard and Hancock were transferred to other fronts; Sigel, Hunter, Burnside, Smith, Quincy Adam Gillmore, and William Brooks were shelved. Six Union and four Confederate division commanders were killed; another such Graycoat was captured.[10] For battle-leading brigadiers and brevet brigadiers, the dead, appallingly, totaled sixty.[11]

What did such losses gain the two sides? Against overwhelming odds, Lee successfully defended his capital and its rail center and prolonged the life of his nation another year. Yet the war was not going Lee's way. Except for those few weeks in early summer, he no longer controlled the strategic initiative and was reduced to contesting the tactical initiative. Denied his preferred course of keeping Yankees far from Richmond, he was confined to the constricting strategic imperative of the close and immediate defense of his capital. It was Grant who forced that necessity on the Southerners; who controlled the course of operations virtually all year; who drove the military frontier from Culpeper to Dinwiddie. It was Grant's strategic siege at Petersburg that pinned the Graycoats on the Appomattox while other Northern armies devoured the rest of Virginia and the rest of the Confederacy.

None could foretell what 1865 would bring. But as military operations in the Old Dominion closed in 1864, Federal prospects proved promising, and the outlook for the South was ominous.

Notes

1. Gordon Rhea, *The Battle of the Wilderness* (Baton Rouge: Louisiana State University Press, 1994), 34, 435–40.

2. William D. Matter, *If It Takes All Summer: The Battle of Spotsylvania* (Chapel Hill: University of North Carolina Press, 1988), 348.

3. Casualties in the Bermuda Hundred Campaign, May 4–June 2, were approximately 6,100 Bluecoats and 4,800 Secessionists. U.S. War Department, *War of the Rebellion: A Compilation of the Official Records of the Union and Confederate Armies* (Washington, D.C.: Government Printing Office, 1880–1901), series 1, vol. 36, pt. 2, 13–18, 57, 262, 266 (hereafter cited as *OR*, with all refer-

ences to series 1); Herbert M. Schiller, *The Bermuda Hundred Campaign* (Dayton, Ohio: Morningside, 1988), 81, 94–95, 160, 285–87, 306.

4. J. Michael Miller, *The North Anna Campaign: "Even to Hell Itself," May 21–26, 1864* (Lynchburg, Va.: H. E. Howard, 1989), 138.

5. *OR,* vol. 36, pt. 1, 164, 180; Gordon Rhea, *Cold Harbor: Grant and Lee, May 26–June 3, 1863* (Baton Rouge: Louisiana State University Press, 2002), 392.

6. William F. Fox, *Regimental Losses in the American Civil War* (Albany: Albany Publishing, 1889), 5–6, 36.

7. These statistics are based on this author's research for his article "Petersburg Campaign, 15 June 1864–3 April 1865," in David S. Heidler and Jeanne T. Heidler, eds., *Encyclopedia of the American Civil War* (Santa Barbara, Calif.: ABC-CLIO, 2000), 3:1494–1504.

8. Frederick Dyer, *A Compendium of the War of the Rebellion* (New York: Thomas Yoseloff, 1959), 2:929–59; William C. Davis, *The Battle of New Market* (Garden City, N.Y.: Doubleday, 1975), 201; Marshall M. Brice, *Conquest of a Valley* (Charlottesville: University of Virginia Press, 1965), 78–79; Peter Meaney, *The Civil War Engagement at Cool Spring* (Berryville, Va.: Clarke County Historical Association, 1980), 54; Edward J. Stackpole, *Sheridan in the Shenandoah* (Harrisburg, Pa.: Stackpole, 1961), 404–8; Frederick Phisterer, *Statistical Record of the Armies of the United States* (New York: Blue and Gray, 1963), 216–18.

9. Dyer, *Compendium,* 2:929–59; Phisterer, *Statistical Record,* 216–18. The 206,000 total loss figure is derived from Phisterer, *Statistical Record;* Heidler and Heidler, *Encyclopedia;* Mark Boatner, *Civil War Dictionary* (New York: David McKay, 1959); Brian K. Burton, *Extraordinary Circumstances: The Seven Days Battle* (Bloomington: Indiana University Press, 2001); Edward J. Stackpole, *From Cedar Mountain to Antietam* (Harrisburg, Pa.: Stackpole, 1959); Stephen W. Sears, *Landscape Turned Red* (New York: Houghton Mifflin, 1983).

10. The fallen division commanders, along with dates when they were killed or mortally wounded, are: Federals James S. Wadsworth, May 6; Thomas G. Stevenson, May 10; James A. Mulligan, July 24; David A. Russell, September 19; and Joseph Thoburn and J. Howard Kitching, October 19. The Confederates are: William E. Jones, June 5; Robert E. Rodes, September 19; John Hunt Morgan, September 4; and Stephen D. Ramseur, October 19. Nine of these officers fell in Virginia. Morgan spent most of the year in the southwestern part of the Old Dominion but had advanced west from there just eleven days before he was killed at Greenville in east Tennessee. The captured general was Edward Johnson at Spotsylvania, May 12.

11. Fallen Butternut brigadiers and the dates when they were killed or mortally wounded are: John M. Jones and Leroy A. Stafford, May 5; Micah Jenkins,

May 6; Albert G. Jenkins, May 9; James B. Gordon, Junius Daniel, Abner M. Perrin, and Jesse M. Williams, May 12; James B. Terrill and Edward S. Willis, May 30; Laurence M. Keitt, June 1; George P. Doles, June 2; William H. Browne, June 5; John S. Fulton and Richard H. Keeble, June 30; Victor J. Girardey and John R. Chambliss, August 16; John C. C. Sanders, August 21; Archibald C. Godwin and George S. Patton, September 19; John Dunovant, October 1; John Gregg, October 7; and Archibald Gracie, December 2. James J. Archer died of illness, October 24. John W. Henagan was captured, September 13, and died at Johnson's Island prison the following April 26.

Even more Northern brigadiers were killed or mortally wounded: Alexander Hays, May 5; James C. Rice, May 10; Arthur H. Dutton, May 26; Jeremiah C. Drake, June 1; Richard Byrnes, Frank A. Haskell, Henry B. McKeen, Oliver H. Morris, and Peter Porter, June 3; Lewis O. Morris, June 4; Simon H. Mix, June 15; Patrick Kelly, June 16; William Blaisdell, June 23; Griffin A. Stedman, August 5; Calvin A. Craig and Freeman McGilvery, August 16; Daniel Chaplin, August 17; Nathan T. Dushane, August 21; Hiram Burnham, September 29; George D. Wells, October 13; and Daniel D. Bidwell and Charles Russell Lowell, October 19. Former brigadier general James St. Clair Morton was killed, June 17. Joshua B. Howell died in an accident, September 12. Cleaveland J. Campbell's death, June 13, 1865, is definitely attributable to illness incurred in 1864. Similar sickness and debility from 1864's rigorous campaigning may also account for the deaths of Charles Wheelock, January 21, and David Shunk, February 21, 1865. The following eight Union officers did not command brigades but were brevetted brigadier general posthumously to rank from or near their dates of death or mortal wounding: Henry L. Abbott, May 6; John McConihe, June 1; William Sackett, June 11; George Prescott, June 18; Henry L. Patten, August 14; and Willoughby Babcock, Alexander Gardiner, and Frank H. Peck, September 19. These totals come to twenty-five Secessionists and thirty-five Bluecoats. Of them, fifty-four died due to combat; two perished of illness or injury in 1864; and at least one, perhaps as many as four, passed away early in 1865 from the effects of the 1864 campaign.

Politics in Civil War Virginia

A Democracy on Trial

Aaron Sheehan-Dean

If war is really "the continuation of politics by another means," as Carl von Clausewitz said, then Virginia found war and politics so intertwined by 1864 that one could hardly be distinguished from the other. "We appeal to the voters to give their support to . . . good men and patriots . . . [who are] best suited to the respective stations required to be filled," declared a Richmond editor the year before.[1] At first blush, such an appeal sounds like standard fare for mid-nineteenth-century America. Readers could be expected to know whom the paper meant by "good men" because papers existed to advance partisan interests. The curious thing about the above quote, which pertained to the 1863 Virginia state elections, was that it was intended to be read straight, not with a wink and a nod. Among the most important changes made by the Confederate States of America, when it organized in February 1861, was the informal abolition of political parties. This necessitated a major shift in thinking in Virginia, where the second party system remained vital through the secession crisis.[2] Virginians did adapt, though not without difficulty. The same may be said of the other wartime challenges faced within the state. Politicians and voters had to reckon with new issues and a new context that defied traditional ideological divisions. The partition of the state, the disintegration of slavery, the crisis of food and housing, and the increasingly centralized nature of Confederate political authority all required new responses. Through it all, Virginians struggled to fit the new demands of war into their old conceptions of politics; by war's end, both concepts and even politics itself seemed insufficient.[3] The result was a new political landscape, one with substantially broader vistas than the prewar era. The enfranchisement of black men was the most obvious change, but

15

within Virginia the war also destabilized the prewar elite in fundamental ways. As a result of the loss of economic power and simple attrition, the state's traditional ruling coalition shrank. The contested politics produced by the war invited poorer men to participate more actively, and this habit continued after the war.

Prior to the war, propertied white men controlled politics.[4] Virginia grew slowly out of the system of Tidewater planter rule established in the colonial era, mostly as a result of environmental change and demographic pressure. By the early nineteenth century, the Tidewater region had been intensively farmed for well over a century, and as the soil thinned out and lost nutrients farmers began pushing farther into the Piedmont and Shenandoah Valley and started diversifying their crops. The result was a population shift that unsettled the previously stable politics of the state. The northwest—primarily modern West Virginia—outpaced the rest of the state in terms of population growth by a factor of three during the 1830s and 1840s, and slaveholders from the eastern side of the state viewed this trend with alarm because the regions west of the Appalachian Mountains had fewer slaves than regions to the east. The new western men, though certainly not abolitionists, protested the state's unequal apportionment and tax structure, built as it was on slaveholder advantage.

Responding to these pressures, Virginians assembled special conventions to modify the state political system twice in the antebellum era. The remarkable session of 1831–1832 was held just after Nat Turner's bloody slave revolt in Southampton County claimed fifty-five white lives and shattered the myth of the contented slave. The convention included luminaries from the constitutional era but, after seriously considering the abolition of slavery in the state, backed away and made only modest changes to the state's governmental structure. The ensuing decades saw white Virginians redouble their commitment to slavery, developing new uses for slaves in industrial enterprises and a vibrant market in slave rentals. This process belied how closely the state had come to a truly momentous shift. In late 1831, governor and future Confederate general John B. Floyd confided to his diary, "I will not rest until slavery is abolished." Though he failed to articulate such a policy publicly, Floyd might have drawn support. At the time, the *Norfolk and Portsmouth Herald* bemoaned that "there is nothing more sickening to us as a native Virginian, that the idea that our noble state is forever to be saddled within the incubus of slavery."[5] Such expressions became rare and then impossible to voice as the economic advantages of slavery and the necessity of defending the institution against the charges of abolitionists together inspired a "pro-slavery" defense within Virginia and across the South.

But if slavery remained beyond reproach, the unequal distribution of power within the state did not. Westerners and yeomen around the state pushed for changes, and in 1851–1852 another state convention yielded to these demands and instituted a slate of democratic reforms, including the abolition of property requirements for voting and officeholding, the direct election of most local offices, and a reapportionment of seats in the state legislature with greater weight given to free population rather than property. The result was a political system in which most white men had a vested interest and which seemed, to them, to prove the compatibility of an expanding democracy and slave-based economy. The development of the second party system—that is, political competition between Democrats and Whigs—accelerated the process of democratic reform and stimulated popular interest in politics with parades, newspapers, and patronage.[6] Party leaders sought to naturalize this system by demonstrating that party ties could bridge the dangerous regional divide within the state. Using appeals to religion, ethnicity, and kin ties, they built alliances across space, wealth lines, and ideology.[7] Then, as now, some critics bemoaned the influence of parties and politics more generally, seeing it as a malignant rather than benign force. But enthusiasm for party politics was too great and by the 1850s too central to the operation of American life.[8] Nonetheless, Virginia's antebellum political system was a curious affair. Its origins in a colonial-era notion of hierarchy grew more irrelevant each year as yeomen pressed the state to democratize and expand access to politics (though only so far). The war arrived in the midst of these changes and reshaped Virginia politics in fundamental ways—shattering the old partisan alignments and fostering new alignments along the lines of region and experience.

Virginia's secession effectively came on April 17, 1861, after the firing on Fort Sumter and Lincoln's militia call, when the state's Secession Convention voted 88–55 to secede.[9] Pressed between their slaveholding peers in the lower South and the increasingly antislavery North, Virginia's once-staunch Unionists chose secession as the only viable way to preserve their society and its institutions.[10] At the head of the state was Democrat John Letcher, a Shenandoah Valley man who had inclined toward the Union but dedicated his term to serving the Confederacy. With little experience in military affairs, Letcher was assisted in this early period by an Advisory Council composed of the "best men" of the state, drawn without regard to party or region, which helped him through the complex business of organizing an army and a defense of the state.[11] Letcher's decision to ignore party labels mirrored the preferences of Confederate leaders who imposed an unofficial ban on political parties in the new nation, hoping that by eliminating the infrastructure that sustained competition under the U.S. system they would eliminate competition in politics itself.[12] Letcher's task was complicated by the fact that the Confederate capital was moved to Richmond from Montgomery, Alabama, immediately after Virginia's secession. The move consolidated the political and industrial headquarters of the Confederacy and ensured a vigorous defense of the Old Dominion, but also complicated politics in the state because of the active nature of the Confederate government.[13]

The state's newspapers, long an integral part of the party system in Virginia, mostly complied with the no-party policy as well. When printing records from the General Assembly debates or reporting on election returns, papers listed speakers and candidates by geography but not party. The state election in May 1863, which selected a new governor and general assembly, generated from papers of all stripes professions of partisan disinterest.[14] The *Richmond Sentinel* was typical at the time in proclaiming that the candidates "are before us simply on their personal merits, and the capacity for the positions sought."[15] Nonetheless, at least one paper seemed to sanction an intervention that would ensure party preference played no role. The *Richmond Whig* printed a proposal from a letter writer named "Virginian" that called for the names of two prominent Democrats and two prominent Whigs to be placed in a hat and the governor and other high state offices chosen randomly, suggesting that the paper believed people had to be protected from their old habits.[16]

The conduct of the election drove to the foreground lingering suspicions that party sentiment had not died, at least among some. The *Richmond Examiner,* while flatly asserting that Democrats would be casting their ballots "for sound and reliable men, without any regard to their ancient partisan affiliations," lamented, "Party is not dead in Virginia." Blaming the Whigs, whom the paper accused of continuing to vote in blocs, the *Examiner* explained to readers that the loss of northwestern Virginia lay at the Whigs' feet because they had dithered in debate inside the secession convention in 1861 instead of girding the state for war.[17] For its part, the *Richmond Whig*, the party's leading organ in the prewar period, sounded a conciliatory theme by declaring two days after the election that the returns thus far "incline us to think that Gen. Smith is the successful man. If so, nobody will feel much hurt. He is a game old fellow, a true patriot, and has mind and experience."[18]

Smith had served as governor before the war and was a brigadier general in the Confederate army, so perhaps the Whigs settled for him as a known quantity. The newspapers dutifully chronicled election returns into the summer, but offered almost no commentary on the nature of the state-level changes.[19] None of the most well-known diarists of the war in Virginia expended much ink on the subject either. Federal-level posts, in contrast, attracted more attention, reflecting Virginians' awareness of the growing influence of the Confederate government. As in the Confederacy as a whole, the results revealed a divided electorate. Voters in one-half of Virginia's sixteen congressional districts replaced incumbents, but they mostly replaced them with members of the same party.[20] The returns suggest a fairly high degree of dissatisfaction with the state of Virginia and Confederate politics in 1863, but not a uniform response. Whether it was continued partisanship or varied responses to the contingencies of war, Virginians remained engaged with and divided by politics throughout the conflict.

If Virginians tried to reorganize their political institutions to reduce ideological friction, they also sought ways to stave off whatever class conflict might arise during the war and so retained the democratic system they instituted in the 1851 Constitution.[21] White men formed the core of the system and by 1863, with the war's conclusion apparently many years off, the state made provisions for soldiers to be able to vote in the field.[22] This practice was adopted in the North as well, where the 1864 presidential election, which Lincoln won with the substantial support of soldiers in the field, is regarded as a signal accomplishment for a democracy in the midst of war. Because of the presence of slavery, Southern states are generally regarded as only partly democratic, despite the fact that most observers at the time regarded them as fully so. Nonetheless, Virginia, like other Southern states, held regular elections during the war. The mass of personal correspondence between soldiers and their families indicates that volunteers remained members of their home communities even while in the army and retained an active interest in local and state politics. Because most Virginia soldiers served in the state, they had ample access to the newspapers that flowed through the camps. Nor could they be ignored by candidates. In 1863, Smith himself won the gubernatorial election largely on the strength of his support among soldiers.[23]

In addition to the new wartime issues that demanded the attention of the state's legislators, they had to maintain the routine management of state institutions like colleges, hospitals, and asylums as well as manage the budget and trade. The difficulty for legislators was that even routine issues demanded new attention in the context of war. For instance, in the first wartime session of the legislature, the House of Delegates addressed banking-related matters in over sixty different pieces of legislation during the short term. Some of these measures—establishing new banks, amending rules on credit, distribution of specie, and the role of the public auditor in administration of banks—would have happened regardless of the war, but the necessity of maintaining the state's economic system added an urgency to the process. Perhaps as a reflection of the wartime spirit of cooperation, banking measures elicited little partisan fighting (as they had often done in the prewar years) in the state's General Assembly.[24]

State leaders offered competent if uninspired leadership during the war (much like the lackadaisical direction coming from the Confederate Congress). The *Lynchburg Daily Virginian* offered a blunt assessment, but one with which many would have agreed: "[I]t is a real misfortune to us that, if Virginia has the men capable of guiding a great revolution—such men as graced her legislative halls when she tried conclusions with George the Third—they are not in civil employment."[25] Instead, many of the state's prewar political leaders pursued military fame rather than staying behind the scenes in civilian administration. John B. Floyd and Henry Wise, both former governors, were given commissions as generals and subsequently gained notoriety for their incompetence on the battlefield. Other Virginians—some from old and distinguished lineages in the state and others rising from obscurity—provided effective leadership at all levels of the army and enough wherewithal to direct the state through a maze of dangers during four years of war, but no Jefferson, no Madison, no Marshall emerged during the Civil War.

The first and, in some ways, most lasting challenge for the state was assembling the manpower needed to defend the borders and ensure that the state stayed seceded. Although legislators spoke with unanimity on the necessity of a strong defense, in policy terms that unity proved elusive. Legislators debated the wisdom of offering exemptions based on age, occupation, nationality, residence, and physical condition. In many respects, these debates mirrored those of the Confederate Congress on the same topic, but as the Confederate military increased its call for men to join the national armies, the state had to work harder to ensure the presence of active home defense forces.[26] Although the legislature amended the state's militia call repeatedly during the war, the problem remained. In mid-1863, the *Lynchburg Daily Virginian* expressed dissatisfaction with what the legislature had accomplished thus far. It echoed the sentiments of several state papers in calling for an expanded militia act that would make all men aged sixteen to sixty eligible for militia duty.[27]

While manpower problems proved divisive, maintaining the state's territorial integrity did not. On May 23, 1861, the state had subjected the convention's secession ordinance to the voters for ratification, a step that was intended to demonstrate solidarity but that, like the convention vote, revealed a divided state. Counties in the extreme northwest of the state voted down the resolution. A Lexington native sent to the state's northern border with Maryland to guard against incursions reflected the biases of many when he blamed opposition to the ordinance on class and ethnicity. "The better class of people here are for secession, but the other class (who outnumber them) are the other way," he explained to his wife.[28] After Berkeley County voted against ratification of the move to secede by a 700-vote margin, he blamed local workers of German origins who "are very excitable on the subject."[29] Only three days after the vote, Gen. George B. McClellan entered the northwest corner of the state and quickly drove Confederate forces back into the middle of the state. Residents of the northwest used the presence of the Union army, which controlled the region for the remainder of the war, to begin their own process of separation from the Old Dominion. In May 1861, political leaders from the region met in Wheeling, organized a "loyal" government of Virginia (the regular state legislature referred to it as the "usurped government"), and received quick recognition from the United States. Local leaders managed the political side of this process ably, but the final establishment of the state of West Virginia in 1863 patched together a northern tier of mostly Unionist counties with a southern tier of pro-Confederate ones.[30] Even after the political settlement in 1863 (which Confederate leaders regarded as illegal), conflict manifested itself in guerrilla warfare between civilians and soldiers from both armies throughout the remainder of the conflict.

Governor Letcher addressed the problem, what he called the "unpatriotic spirit" expressed by "a portion of our people in Northwestern Virginia" during his annual address to the legislature in December 1861. The "unnatural, disgraceful and treasonable" actions of those Virginians aiding the Union occupiers would be repaid with "retribution," he promised. In fact, despite his condemnation, the exit of many northwestern representatives from the Virginia legislature eased the internal pressure to find common ground. As a result, both the Senate and the House of Delegates adopted a firm policy with regard to the region that changed little over the course of the war. In his December speech, the governor laid out what became not the party but the state line regarding the issue for the remainder of the war: "The Northwestern portion of Virginia must not be abandoned and surrendered to the traitor residents and mercenary soldiers who now occupy it. . . . The commonwealth must not be dismembered."[31] The Senate, late by perhaps a decade, briefly discussed building a railroad "which shall connect [the northwestern section of the state] with the interior and seaboard."[32] If this project had been undertaken when westerners were clamoring for an equal share of the state's resources, the wartime dismemberment of the state may well have not occurred. As it stood, the proposal and sentiment behind it both disappeared in the fighting of 1862. State leaders rallied behind Letcher's opinion—the northwest could not secede from the state—even as the forty-five counties that would comprise West Virginia were organized into formal statehood in the Union. In his January 1863 address, Letcher again repeated the dogma: "It is better that this war should continue for an indefinite period of time, than that Virginia, shall be even partially dismembered. Let every Virginian, then, kneeling at the altar, swear that the commonwealth shall remain one and indivisible, and that he will never assent to an adjustment which will take from her one square foot of her territory."[33]

Few other wartime issues provided the same opportunities to build Confederate solidarity. The problem of food scarcity and cost hit Virginia civilians especially hard and proved difficult for the legislature to address without creating new problems. The situation came to a head on the morning of April 2, 1863, when Richmond residents were startled by the presence of a large crowd, mostly women, streaming through the city streets in search of bread. Wives of workers at the local Tredegar Iron Works, or workers themselves in various city enterprises, the women ransacked stores and warehouses in search of flour and meal for their families. The protesters were confronted by the mayor and eventually the president of the Confederacy himself, who dispersed the crowd by assembling soldiers around the main square and promising to open fire on those who remained. Public actions like the Richmond Bread Riot were rare but not unheard of in antebellum Virginia cities, where a nascent practice of worker organization was developing in the years before the war.[34] But for women to protest and attack private businesses signaled a dramatic change in the nature of gender roles and in the question of who possessed public authority. Virginia politics was changing.

The authorities in Richmond realized this and immediately set about discrediting the rioters. The *Richmond Examiner* described them as "a handful of prostitutes, professional thieves, Irish and Yankee hags, gallows-birds from all lands but our own, congregated in Richmond, with a woman huckster at their head."[35] The *Whig* called the assembled women "a throng of courtezans and thieves."[36] But the strenuous efforts to deny both hardship and dissatisfaction concealed a growing awareness that the war was placing new strains on the relationship between citizens and their government. Only the day before the riot, Confederate government clerk Robert Garlick Hill Kean, no bleeding heart, noted ominously in his diary that "indications of famine thicken."[37] Kean identified a problem that others had observed, even as the leading newspapers excoriated the protesters. The papers had, in fact, recognized the importance of provisions and, implicitly, the unequal distribution of existing resources earlier in the year. The *Richmond Sentinel*, in March 1863, called for a greater emphasis on food production and condemned those who were planting tobacco. "He who plants tobacco now, plants for the enemy!" the paper charged, calling on citizens to make these profit seekers feel "shunned as a leper."[38] The *Sentinel* stopped short of calling for government regulation of the crops, but the threat was clear—the war was imposing unprecedented burdens on the home front and, in the process, transforming the nature of the state.

State leaders had trouble shrugging off the Bread Riot because it was not only poor women who were objecting to Confederate policies. In the fall of 1863, with prices still high and goods still scarce, mechanics and working men in Richmond held public meetings and called for mandatory price controls. Local elites were alarmed by these assemblies and condemned the proposed solution in newspapers and from the city council. The mechanics proclaimed themselves loyal Confederates and turned their ire on "extortion-ists" and "speculators" who overcharged the common people on daily neces-sities. But it was clear to Richmond's leaders that the language and goals of the mechanics went beyond bread. One of the widely circulated resolutions produced by the mechanics explained that "as freemen we abhor and detest the idea that the rich must take care of the poor."[39] The city council failed to adopt price controls and public enthusiasm for the measures ebbed, but the episode revealed the corrosive nature of the war in Virginia.

Other towns showed the accumulated hardships of the winter as well. An Albemarle soldier recuperating in a Petersburg hospital in March 1863 observed, "You may know it is dear living in toun [town] I cant see what Poor people will do thet Live in town."[40] But not just the poor suffered. One wealthy slave owner who lived just outside Richmond wrote to a friend with a plea for help. "We are on the eve of starvation," he begged, "and unless the ways are opened up very shortly we will all be laid low. I write to ask if you can't buy for me fifty bushels of wheat and have it ground for me . . . on which I may feed my servants."[41] In prewar Virginia, there were few provisions for public charity. Charitable aid flowed through the same personal channels as power and influence generally. Wealthy citizens, the Commonwealth's self-styled "first families," took it upon themselves to assist the less fortunate during hard times.[42] But the war's demands overwhelmed the private system and state and local governments stepped in, requisitioning foodstuffs and redistributing them to needy families, particularly those with men in the armies.[43] State leaders increased their efforts in the spring of 1863 and, while hardship continued through the war, the new programs staved off any more large-scale protests. The Richmond Bread Riot revealed a crisis of politics that war forced upon the state.

As a response to the Bread Riot and the general public anxiety regard-ing food the 1863 General Assembly adopted several new policies on relief. The most direct route required that county courts make lists of the families of injured or deceased servicemen and "make an allowance, in money or supplies, to the persons and families . . . of such liberal amount and in such proportion as they may think just and sufficient for their maintenance."[44] The General Assembly also demonstrated its willingness to conscript pri-vate business into the business of relief as well, by requiring that "it shall be the duty of every such company [railroads], during the present war, under regulations to be prescribed or approved by the board of public works, to give priority of transportation to articles intended for food, in the hands of, or purchased by consumers, or in the hands of, or purchased by cities, counties and corporations, and designed for gratuitous distribution, or for sale at prices not exceeding the cost and charges."[45] These efforts were supplemented by actions taken at the local level. The closest student of this process in Virginia concludes that after the Bread Riot, "an increase in charitable measures on the part of counties and towns became the immediate, widespread by-product of the agitation" and that "the campaign appeared to stave off the worst cases of starving."[46] But while these measures may have helped stem hardship among civilians, they generated political controversy and conflict. Before the riots, the press had condemned legislative efforts to address issues of price and access. Although it recognized the problems of scarcity and inflation, the paper supported only voluntary efforts to address the issue, and its position changed little after the riots.

Equally thorny from a policy perspective and equally embarrassing for the propertied white men who comprised the state's official political actors was the deterioration of slavery and related problem of free blacks within the state. Virginia, like other upper South states, listed a considerable number of free blacks as residents in 1860. Almost 60,000 free black men and women—most living in the cities of Richmond, Petersburg, and Norfolk—resided in the Commonwealth, and despite Virginians' protests that the war was not about slavery and that slaves would stay loyal, the General Assembly began addressing this population even before the state seceded. On January 19, 1861, a resolution was introduced to facilitate the "voluntary enslavement" of the state's free blacks.[47] The measure streamlining this process was passed on March 12, still before the state's secession, but this hardly solved the problem. Each subsequent legislature during the war spent time administering the state's free black population. For those who did not avail themselves of voluntary enslavement, the legislators argued over how much they should be paid, what occupations they could hold, where they could live, and under what terms and for what purposes their labor could be impressed by the state. Unlike issues of banking and state administration, the discussions of free blacks were rarely harmonious.[48]

A large body of historical literature now reveals that slaves manifested widespread opposition throughout the war and that their actions frequently brought whites themselves into conflict.[49] Even while individual slaves and their families fled to freedom from Virginia, the more general attack on slavery as an institution (symbolized by Lincoln's Emancipation Proclamation) helped bind white Virginians and increase political support for both the Confederacy generally and the policies it imposed in order to ensure separation from the North. The erosion of the institution corresponded to the movement of Union forces into the state. An 1862 *Richmond Dispatch* editorial lamented that "the Federal invasion, especially in its relations to negroes, has thus far been a John Brown raid on a grand scale. Wherever the Federal armies have advanced the negroes have been swept off as clean as the Eastern locusts sweep a field of grain. Not one green or black thing is left in the line of the Yankee march, nor in the whole country for many miles around."[50]

Faced with this problem, the *Dispatch* made the extraordinary recommendation that the state legislature remove "negroes from all threatened districts to the interior," a policy never implemented by the private-property-friendly General Assembly.[51] The Emancipation Proclamation increased both the scale of slave flight and white solidarity over the issue. As a Confederate soldier observed of his peers in a letter written just after Lincoln announced the preliminary proclamation: "[T]he[y] will all die before they can submit to that—at first there was not real hatred against the northern people; in the masses of our army—but now I cannot describe it—nothing can make these people one again, many many generations will have to pass ere there will be any change—and every day it grows worse."[52] Then governor Letcher issued a public response to Lincoln's edict and to its encouragement by Union general Robert H. Milroy, in control of a Federal garrison at Winchester. He began by condemning Lincoln's policy as "in violation of all the principles of humanity, and of the nobler and more generous impulses of our nature, in disregard of all the social, moral, and political obligations which should influence a wise and just ruler . . . and in wanton heedlessness of the peace, the happiness, and even the lives of thousands of innocent and unoffending women and children." Like many, he read the proclamation as a call for servile insurrection by the South's slaves, something he was proud to report did not happen. "The institution of slavery which he [Lincoln] considered an element of weakness, has in fact proved the bulwark of the south," Letcher asserted.[53]

This proved to be wrong; over half a million enslaved African Americans fled bondage during the war, and this process caused chaos in many parts of the South. Virginia's wartime newspapers were filled with advertisements for escaping slaves and reports of captured runaways.[54] Even as slavery's collapse created enormous legal and administrative problems within the state—from the violence that sometimes accompanied flight to the loss of labor to produce crops, build fortifications, staff hospitals, and generally do the work of the white men who were in the armies—white Virginians refused to abandon the institution. The slave trade remained surprisingly robust during the war itself, with prices and demand both rising, until by August 1863, the *Richmond Sentinel* could report "all kinds of slaves commanding higher prices than ever before."[55] Slaveholders had struggled for decades to convince nonslaveholders that supporting the institution was in their interest—its violent collapse during the war gave an urgency and force to their arguments that all the rhetoric of the prewar period had failed to impart.

While civilians generally accepted the necessity for greater authority to hold slavery in place during war, other centralizing measures generated outright opposition. Relief efforts may have helped hungry people, but they added to the centralization of power by Virginia's state and local government, broadening the powers previously attributed to the state. Worse still, they represented only one of a host of such centralizing moves enacted during the war years. The most invasive and hated of these policies—conscription, the tax in kind, and impressment—were enacted by the Confederate government, but they were partly managed by the states and localities. Local draft boards, state officers monitoring price levels for goods, and field agents collecting taxes all made plain to Virginians that the war had changed their relationship to the government. Conscription proved a particularly useful tool because the state could use exemptions to control the labor supply, ensuring that militarily necessary industries retained enough workers to function but rarely allowing men to remain out of the armies for other reasons. The governor and the General Assembly facilitated the work of conscription both through the enactment of laws to organize the process and through frequent public pronouncements on the virtues and necessity of military service by all white men.[56]

Virginians suffered the additional burden of the suspension of the privilege of the writ of habeas corpus on several occasions. Accompanying the March 1862 suspension for Richmond and surrounding areas was an extraordinary call for all private firearms to be turned in to the Ordnance Department or face seizure by the provost marshal.[57] Civilians were subject to more routine interference by the state as well, including the humiliating requirement that white citizens carry passes, something previously required only of slaves. Under the headline "Show Your Passes," the *Richmond Dispatch* warned citizens to carry passes with them "if they wish to avoid getting into trouble." The paper noted summarily that, in their efforts to ensure full compliance with conscription laws, "parties who cannot show cause why they are not in the army, or with their regiments, will be arrested and put in prison."[58] Even this feature of wartime life seems to have been accepted by Virginians.[59] Within the Confederacy as a whole, the areas hardest hit by the invasion and occupation of Northern soldiers tended to support more aggressive policies, and this was true of Virginia as well.[60] On the question of Jefferson Davis's suspension of habeas corpus, a pivotal issue for civil libertarians within the Virginia delegation, only the congressman representing the middle of the state opposed suspension.[61] For westerners exposed to the brutal guerrilla war and easterners exposed to the invasion by Federal troops, a temporary suspension of habeas corpus apparently seemed a price worth paying.

Ample evidence—in the form of letters and appeals to the governor, the General Assembly, and Confederate officials of all ranks—suggests that women on the Virginia home front, and their male relatives both in and out of the armies, opposed national, state, and local governmental policies enacted in response to the war. Impressment and the tax in kind were particularly galling to a people reared to believe devoutly in the sanctity of private property, to say nothing of a people starving. The difficulty for historians has been translating that into the terms of the debate about whether Virginians stayed "loyal" to the Confederacy through the conflict. Research on North Carolina suggests some residents of that state may well have reached a point in early 1864 when they were willing to accede to a return to the Union if it brought peace.[62] The evidence for Virginia does not support such a conclusion. Virginians' anger over food scarcity, inflation, impressment, and the numerous other effects of the conflict blended together into a hatred of the war but not into a willingness to suspend fighting and return to the Union.[63] As one recent scholarly assessment concludes, "[O]ver the course of the war, soldiers' families and government leaders actually appear to have grown closer to an agreement about how to reconcile the interests of families and the greater nation."[64] This is not to deny the obvious anger of Confederate civilians at their government but to suggest that the willingness of individuals to blame the government indicates their faith that the government could and would respond to their complaints.[65]

Assessing the role of Virginia within the Confederacy answers an important question about the relationship between Virginia politics and the Civil War, but wartime events generated even more profound changes within the state itself. The key elements included the blurring of prewar ideological and party lines, the introduction of new issues, and the imposition of new actors, at least along the margins of the official political system. As the Richmond Bread Riots and the escalating number of slave escapes suggest, in some cases nontraditional actors imposed changes that left legislators struggling to keep up. After the Civil War, women did not play the role in spurring policies that they did during the conflict, but because of the contested nature of Reconstruction, African American men came to assume key roles in postwar politics. The most unusual episode in Virginia's postwar political history, and perhaps within the whole nineteenth century, was the Readjuster Movement of the 1870s, when a biracial coalition briefly ruled the statehouse on a platform of debt relief for small farmers. From one perspective, this unlikely outcome owed little to the nature of wartime politics, but from another perspective it is clear that the dramatic challenges of the war had already cracked open the state's rigid and hierarchical political system.

Notes

1. *Richmond Sentinel,* May 8, 1863.
2. Daniel Crofts, *Reluctant Confederates: Upper South Unionists in the Secession Crisis* (Chapel Hill: University of North Carolina Press, 1989).
3. "Politics" is a protean concept in American history. The focus of this essay is on changes in what might be called "formal politics"—the actions of elected leaders, institutions, and voters—while paying attention to the challenges to this system that come from actors and spheres typically regarded as outside official channels.
4. That this was not always the case did not obstruct elite views of themselves as possessing the sole power for administering the state. For an important example of how other groups shaped politics, see William A. Link, *Roots of Secession: Slavery and Politics in Antebellum Virginia* (Chapel Hill: University of North Carolina Press, 2003).

5. Both Floyd and the *Norfolk and Portsmouth Herald* are quoted in Alison Goodyear Freehling, *Drift toward Dissolution: The Virginia Slavery Debate of 1831–1832* (Baton Rouge: Louisiana State University Press, 1982), 124–25, which remains the best study of the topic.

6. William G. Shade, *Democratizing the Old Dominion: Virginia and the Second Party System, 1824–1861* (Charlottesville: University of Virginia Press, 1996).

7. For the country, see Michael F. Holt, *The Political Crisis of the 1850s* (New York: Norton, 1978); for Virginia, see Shade, *Democratizing the Old Dominion.*

8. For the opposite view—that most people maintained only cursory connections with party politics—see Glenn C. Altschuler and Stuart M. Blumin, *Rude Republic: Americans and Their Politics in the Nineteenth Century* (Princeton, N.J.: Princeton University Press, 2001).

9. Two earlier efforts to pass a secession ordinance failed by large majorities.

10. The literature on Virginia's decision to secede is extensive. See Henry T. Shanks, *The Secession Movement in Virginia, 1847–1861* (Richmond: Garrett and Massie, 1934); Crofts, *Reluctant Confederates;* Daniel Crofts, "Late Antebellum Virginia Reconsidered," *Virginia Magazine of History and Biography* 107 (Summer 1999): 253–86; James I. Robertson Jr., "The Virginia State Convention of 1861," in William C. Davis and James I. Robertson, eds., *Virginia at War, 1861* (Lexington: University Press of Kentucky, 2005), 1–26.

11. James I. Robertson Jr., ed., *Proceedings of the Advisory Council of the State of Virginia, April 21–June 19, 1861* (Richmond: Virginia State Library, 1977).

12. The best analysis of this process at the national level is George C. Rable, *The Confederate Republic: A Revolution against Politics* (Chapel Hill: University of North Carolina Press, 1994).

13. For a fuller discussion of the capital's move, see William C. Davis, "Richmond Becomes the Capital," in Davis and Robertson, eds., *Virginia at War, 1861,* 113–29.

14. The irregular nineteenth-century election cycle, which included staggered local and state races, continued during the war, but the 1863 election was the major one of the period.

15. *Richmond Sentinel,* May 8, 1863.

16. *Richmond Whig,* January 6, 1863.

17. *Richmond Examiner,* April 9, 1863. A similar lament about the state of party spirit still alive in 1863 can be found in a June 1, 1863, *Richmond Sentinel* editorial regarding the gubernatorial election, in which "the vote had been nearer a party one than was expected."

18. *Richmond Whig,* May 30, 1863.

19. The election was held in May 1863, but the new members took their seats only at the start of 1864.

20. Of the eleven seats for which I could make positive party identifications, five remained in Democratic control, three in Whig control; the Democrats lost two, and the Whigs lost one. Within the Confederacy, voters replaced 54 out of 107 incumbents.

21. But note that after passing the secession ordinance, the convention did attempt to repeal several of the most democratic of the 1851 provisions. See Henry T. Shanks, "Conservative Constitutional Tendencies of the Virginia Secessionist Convention," in Fletcher Green, ed., *Essays in Southern History Presented to Joseph Gregoire de Roulhac Hamilton, PH.D., LL.D., by His Former Students at the University of North Carolina* (Chapel Hill: University of North Carolina Press, 1949).

22. *Acts of the General Assembly of the State of Virginia, Passed at Called Session, 1863, in the Eighty-eighth Year of the Commonwealth* (Richmond: William F. Ritchie, 1863), 71–75. Newspapers recorded these votes separately, based on their polling stations. See, for example, the returns printed in the May 30, 1863, *Richmond Whig,* which list "The Military Vote" broken down by regiments within the state.

23. Emory M. Thomas, *The Confederate State of Richmond: A Biography of the Capital* (Austin: University of Texas Press, 1971), 136.

24. This conclusion comes from a survey of banking-related measures for the 1862, 1863, and 1864 sessions of the state legislature. Most bills passed without votes, and even those that required recorded votes usually passed by very large margins.

25. *Lynchburg Daily Virginian,* November 4, 1863.

26. The initial Draft Act of April 1862 called for men aged eighteen to thirty-five; this was subsequently broadened to seventeen to forty-five and eventually seventeen to fifty-five.

27. *Lynchburg Daily Virginian,* August 10, 1863.

28. James K. Edmondson to Emma Edmondson, May 22, 1861, in Charles W. Turner, ed., *My Dear Emma (War Letters of Col. James K. Edmondson, 1861–1865)* (Verona, Va.: McClure, 1978), 14.

29. Ibid., 25.

30. See Richard L. Curry, *A House Divided: A Study of Statehood Politics and the Copperhead Movement in West Virginia* (Pittsburgh: University of Pittsburgh Press, 1964); George Ellis Moore, *Banner in the Hills: West Virginia's Statehood* (New York: Appleton-Century-Crofts, 1963).

31. John Letcher, "Governor's Address to the Virginia Legislature," in *Jour-*

nal of the Senate of the Commonwealth of Virginia, 1861 (Richmond: James E. Goode, 1861), 16–17.

32. *Journal of the Senate of the Commonwealth of Virginia, Extra Session of 1862* (Richmond: James E. Goode, 1862), 106–7.

33. John Letcher, "Governor's Message," January 7, 1863, in *Journal of the Senate of the Commonwealth of Virginia, 1862* (Richmond: James E. Goode, 1862), 161.

34. Werner H. Steger, "'United to Support, but Not Combined to Injure': Free Workers and Immigrants in Richmond, Virginia, during the Era of Sectionalism, 1847–1865" (Ph.D. diss., George Washington University, 1999); L. Diane Barnes, "Southern Artisans, Organization, and the Rise of a Market Economy in Antebellum Petersburg," *Virginia Magazine of History and Biography* 107 (Spring 1999): 159–88.

35. *Richmond Examiner,* April 4, 1863.

36. *Richmond Whig,* April 6, 1863.

37. Diary entry, April 1, 1863, in Robert Garlick Hill Kean, *Inside the Confederate Government: The Diary of Robert Garlick Hill Kean,* ed. Edward Younger (1957; repr., Baton Rouge: Louisiana State University Press, 1993), 47.

38. *Richmond Sentinel,* March 13, 1863.

39. Quoted in William A. Blair, *Virginia's Private War: Feeding Body and Soul in the Confederacy* (New York: Oxford University Press, 1998), 98.

40. William H. Jones to Eliza L. Jones, March 21, 1863, in Rick Britton, ed., "Letters Home from Private William H. Jones of the 'Albemarle Rifles,'" *Magazine of Albemarle County History* 57 (1999): 65–70.

41. T. Bassett French to James Dorman Davidson, March 31, 1863, in Bruce Greenwalt, ed., "Life Behind Confederate Lines: The Correspondence of James D. Davidson," *Civil War History* 16 (September 1970): 220.

42. Suzanne Lebsock, *The Free Women of Petersburg: Status and Culture in a Southern Town, 1784–1860* (New York: Norton, 1984).

43. Blair, *Virginia's Private War,* 75–76.

44. "An Act for the Relief of the Indigent Soldiers and Sailors of the State of Virginia Who Have Been or May Be Disabled in the Military Service, and the Widows and Minor Children of Soldiers and Sailors Who Have Died or May Hereafter Die in Said Service, and of the Indigent Families of Those Now in the Service," in *Acts of the General Assembly of the State of Virginia, 1863,* 21–23.

45. "An Act to Amend and Re-enact the 17th Section of the 61st Chapter of the Code of Virginia, Giving Priority of Transportation for Food to Consumers," in *Acts of the General Assembly of the State of Virginia, 1863,* 14.

46. Blair, *Virginia's Private War,* 75.

47. Virginia General Assembly, *Journal of the House of Delegates of the*

State of Virginia, for the Extra Session, 1861 (Richmond: William F. Ritchie, 1861), 70.

48. See, for example, the divisive voting on a measure to allow localities to "furnish" free blacks as part of their quotas toward public defense. *Journal of the House of Delegates of the State of Virginia, for the Called Session of 1862* (Richmond: William F. Ritchie, 1862), 68–69.

49. Most of the primary source material on this topic may be found in the papers of the Freedmen and Southern Society Project. For a general survey, see Ira Berlin et al., eds., *Free at Last: A Documentary History of Slavery, Freedom, and the Civil War* (Edison, N.J.: Blue and Gray, 1997).

50. *Richmond Dispatch,* September 27, 1862.

51. Ibid.

52. Randolph Stiles to Clifford Stiles, September 30, 1862, Robert Alonzo Brock Collection, box 106, Henry E. Huntington Library, San Marino, Calif.

53. John Letcher, January 20, 1863, "Document No. X: Communication from the Governor relative to Abraham Lincoln's Proclamation of Emancipation," *Confederate Imprints* (Farmington Hill, Mich.: Primary Source Microfilm, n.d.), reel 69.

54. See, for example, the *Staunton Spectator,* July 14, 1863, notice offering $400 for four slaves presumably "making their way to the Yankees."

55. *Richmond Sentinel,* August 12, 1863.

56. For an early example, see John Letcher, "By the Governor, a Proclamation," *Staunton Republican Vindicator,* June 7, 1861.

57. John H. Winder, "General Orders No. 1," March 2, 1862, printed in *Richmond Whig,* March 3, 1862.

58. *Richmond Dispatch,* July 17, 1862.

59. Mark E. Neely, *Southern Rights: Political Prisoners and the Myth of Confederate Constitutionalism* (Charlottesville: University of Virginia Press, 1999), 6.

60. Richard Bensel, *Yankee Leviathan: The Origins of Central State Authority in America, 1859–1877* (Cambridge: Cambridge University Press, 1990), 221–25.

61. For the vote authorizing suspension, see the February 5, 1864, vote in U.S. Congress, *Journals of the Congress of the Confederate States of America* (Washington: Government Printing Office, 1904), 6:764.

62. See Paul D. Escott, *After Secession: Jefferson Davis and the Failure of Confederate Nationalism* (Baton Rouge: Louisiana State University Press, 1978).

63. Most of the recent studies of Civil War Virginia recognize that class conflict occurred during the war, but stress the cohesive power of Confederate identity within the state. See Daniel E. Sutherland, *Seasons of War: The Ordeal*

of a Confederate Community, 1861–1865 (Baton Rouge: Louisiana State University Press, 1995); Stephen V. Ash, *When the Yankees Came: Conflict and Chaos in the Occupied South, 1861–1865* (Chapel Hill: University of North Carolina Press, 1995); Steven Elliott Tripp, *Yankee Town, Southern City: Race and Class Relations in Civil War Lynchburg* (New York: New York University Press, 1997); Aaron Sheehan-Dean, *Why Confederates Fought: Family and Nation in Civil War Virginia* (Chapel Hill: University of North Carolina Press, 2007); Blair, *Virginia's Private War.*

64. Amy E. Murrell, "'Of Necessity and Public Benefit': Southern Families and Their Appeals for Protection," in Catherine Clinton, ed., *Southern Families at War: Loyalty and Conflict in the Civil War South* (New York: Oxford University Press, 2000), 79.

65. The debate over Southerners' responses to Confederate nationalism and centralization is large and complex. These issues will be dealt with more fully in a separate essay on the Virginia home front in the last volume in this series.

A "Patriotic Press"

Virginia's Confederate Newspapers, 1861–1865
Ted Tunnell

Neither war nor politics in Virginia—or anywhere else in the divided nation—could escape being inextricably intertwined with the banner of any free society, the press. At the time of the Civil War newspapers were vital to the American way of life, and by 1864, late in the war, Virginians turned to them for signs of hope even as the press was itself the principal conduit of the unrelentingly bad news from the war fronts.

In Virginia, as in the nation, almost every small town had at least a weekly newspaper. Richmond, a city of nearly 39,000 in 1860, boasted four daily papers. New Orleans, the South's only metropolis, had six.[1] It was an era of intensely personal journalism in which editors freely blurred the distinction between news and opinion, making no effort to report the news impartially. To modern readers, the acerbic tone of the era's reporting seems more akin to partisan propaganda than objective journalism. Nonetheless, editors had profound influence. They "served as the eyes and ears of their communities," writes historian Edward L. Ayers. They "knew everyone in town and wanted their patronage, but they also spoke for specific political, business, family, and even religious interests. They had to be neutral and partisan at the same time, cheerful boosters of the community at large and vigilant advocates of particular people within that community."[2] Editors were "custodians" of the white South's "symbolic polity," and exerted a profound influence on the political and intellectual life of the region.[3]

The outbreak of war in April 1861 had the paradoxical effect of greatly increasing public demand for news while, at the same time, closing newspaper offices all over the state. At the time of Lincoln's election some 120 newspapers were published in Virginia; two years later only 17 remained (and the attrition was not over). By mid-1864, outside Richmond and Petersburg, the number of pro-Confederate presses in the state could be counted on one hand.[4] The reasons for this decline were numerous. Like men in other occupations, editors, printers, and their employees joined the army, creating a severe labor shortage. Then, as the conflict lengthened, the cost of newsprint, lead typeface, glue, and other supplies spiraled out of control, making it harder to stay in business. Yankee occupation of northern Virginia, Norfolk, and other places closed still more papers or converted them into Yankee organs. Recovery was slow. Five years after Appomattox, Virginia still had only half the newspapers it had had in 1860.[5]

The state's most influential newspapers embraced secession prior to Virginia's actually leaving the Union. The formerly Unionist *Petersburg Daily Express* announced in early 1861 that "Black Republican impertinence, insolence," and other abuses "had pretty essentially and effectually cured us of *unionism.*"[6] Robert Ridgeway, editor of the *Richmond Daily Whig* and the only editor in the city to oppose secession after Lincoln's election, had been forced to resign in March 1861. "Lincoln gives us no alternative," his successor declared, "but to fight or run."[7] In the Shenandoah Valley, the *Staunton Vindicator* had been as pro-secession as any paper in the state. The *Staunton Spectator,* on the other hand, remained strongly Unionist right up to the moment that Lincoln called for 75,000 state militia to quash the rebellion in South Carolina. A day after the president's proclamation, the *Spectator* declared angrily: "War has actually commenced. After all his declarations in favor of peace, President Lincoln has taken a course calculated inevitably to provoke a *collision,* and to unite the whole South in armed resistance"; there was no alternative but to fight.[8]

In late May 1861 the capital of the Confederacy moved to Richmond, and the city became the hub of the Confederate newspaper world, its hotels home to correspondents from the far corners of the South. The fall of New Orleans to the Federals in May 1862 only enhanced the city's status as the lodestar of Confederate journalism. Its four daily newspapers, the *Enquirer,* the *Examiner,* the *Dispatch,* and the *Whig,* were all fervent supporters of the Confederate cause, if not of President Jefferson Davis and his administration. In 1863 a fifth Richmond daily (the *Sentinel*) began publication.[9]

The *Enquirer,* the *Whig,* and the *Examiner* ranked among the best newspapers in the South. Before the war the *Enquirer* had earned a reputation as the "Democratic Bible."[10] When the fighting began its chief editor, O. Jennings Wise (son of former governor Henry A. Wise), entered the army and lost his life defending Roanoke Island. As a rule, Wise and his successors objectively reported the news rather than venting their dissatisfaction with Confederate conduct of the war. According to historian Harrison A. Trexler, "The *Enquirer's* editorials were restrained and balanced and had real literary merit."[11] The *Whig* had long been the only Whig paper in the capital, and it retained its partisan identity during the war. Early on it evinced distrust of Davis's administration, one reason being the president's perceived bias against former Whigs. "Of hundreds of Brigadiers," the paper observed, "less than a half-dozen Whigs, who happened to be West Pointers, were deemed fit for public duty and the rule was even more stringent in the civil service."[12] The *Examiner's* chief editor, John Moncure Daniel, was known for his mordant, combative personality and rapierlike pen. Diminutive in size but big in talent, Daniel gathered around him a talented editorial staff that included Edward A. Pollard and H. Rives Pollard. The former would become the first Confederate historian of the war and would coin the term "Lost Cause"; the latter, his younger brother, was a considerable journalistic talent in his own right. Along with the *Whig,* the *Examiner* would become one of the Confederacy's most influential critics of the Davis administration.[13]

The *Dispatch* had the largest circulation in Richmond and, unlike the *Whig* and the *Examiner,* was more concerned with reporting the news than in airing editorial commentary. This was perhaps just as well. According to Trexler: "Its editorials, juvenile if not sophomoric, were devoid of critical content and were flamboyantly patriotic." The *Sentinel* moved from Alexandria to Richmond in March 1863, where it became a staunch defender of the government.[14]

Despite differences of style and policy, the Richmond papers set the tone of unflagging patriotism that characterized Virginia's Confederate press throughout the war. The city's journals, writes historian Amy R. Minton, "relentlessly promoted a spirit of nationalism and commonality among the members of the fledgling Confederate nation."[15] Tirelessly, they depicted loyal Confederates as virtuous, moral, and respectable people. Indeed, according to the newspapers, virtue, patriotism, and respectability were inseparable. Thus, in March 1862 the *Dispatch* urged its readers to "ask why it is that, with scarcely an exception, the best members of society are the most loyal in their devotion to the South; whilst those who are doubtful are, with scarcely an exception, men who are doubtful in the relations of social life, who are dissolute, or dishonest, or false in their private character, or, if not absolutely vicious, who are weak minded, eccentric, and unstable?" The emphasis on morality and respectability as key elements of patriotism had the vital effect of uniting people of different social classes in the ranks of patriotic Southerners; included among the "best people" were plain farmers as well as great planters, common laborers and mechanics as well as wealthy merchants and bankers. In other words, being a good Southerner was a matter of character, not wealth or station. Men of good character were patriots; on the other hand, shirkers and fair-weather patriots were by definition men of bad character. The emphasis on character cut across gender lines, too, including women as well as men in patriot ranks. In short, in the great crisis of Southern nationality, newsmen promoted the broadest possible definition of patriotism, enabling all classes of society to join the struggle against the Yankees.[16]

The fusion of morality, respectability, and patriotism conditioned the press's interpretation of the dark underside of life in wartime Richmond—the crime, drunkenness, and prostitution—and the suffering of the city's people caused by inflation and food shortages. The newspapers, Minton argues, harmonized "the deplorable state of affairs in the city with the idea of a virtuous and moral Confederacy" by depicting "all disruptive elements in the city as disreputable people . . . excluded . . . on the basis of their immorality and lack of patriotism, from the ranks of true Confederates."[17]

Consider, for example, press accounts of the famous Richmond Bread Riot. In early April 1863, a band of hungry women from Oregon Hill, unable to buy food at inflated wartime prices, complained to Governor John Letcher about their plight. Unsatisfied with the governor's response to their pleas, the women headed for Main Street, a mob of men and women forming about them as they marched. At their head was Mary Jackson, described by Varina Davis, wife of the president, as "a tall, daring, Amazonian-looking woman, who had a white feather standing erect from her hat."[18] When the mob reached Main Street a riot commenced. Crying for "bread," women brandishing axes, kitchen knives, and six-shooters broke into stores and confiscated some $13,000 worth of food, clothing, and other items. A column of soldiers appeared; then President Davis arrived on the scene. In Emory Thomas's account, "Davis informed the crowd that such lawlessness must cease immediately." When the mob did not respond, "the president took out his watch, glanced at the troops, and gave the rioters five minutes in which to disperse." When the mob still did not break up, the troop commander, according to Thomas, ordered "his soldiers to load and to shoot to kill when the five minutes elapsed." Another five minutes passed and still the mob remained defiant. As Davis pondered his next move, the crowd finally began to disperse.[19]

The scene of hungry women rioting for food was deeply embarrassing to Confederate authorities, and the War Department urged the city's newspapers to ignore it. Newsmen were as chagrined by the riot as the government, but the story was too big to cover up. Refuting the notion that the fray was a "hunger riot," the *Sentinel* depicted the protesters as thieves and plunderers.[20] The *Examiner*, typically caustic in its criticism of Confederate officialdom, ignored the chance to blame the government for hunger in the city and blamed the victims instead. The leaders of the "so-called riot," it alleged, were "a handful of prostitutes, professional thieves, Irish and Yankee hags, gallows-birds from all lands but our own . . . with a woman huckster at their head."[21] The *Whig* denied the existence of hunger in the capital, describing the riot as "daylight burglaries" perpetrated by a "throng of courtezans and thieves." The paper's chief complaint against Confederate authorities was that they tolerated such lowlifes in the city and foolishly attempted to cover up news of the "ridiculous affair."[22] In the Valley, Staunton's newspapers shared the Richmond papers' view of the lawlessness. "It was not a food riot as pretended," the *Vindicator* informed its readers, "but simply a villainous, wholesale robbery." The *Spectator* agreed: "[I]t did not proceed from want, but crime." The latter even implied that Yankee agents were behind the rampage, "with the view of encouraging the North to prosecute the war by making the impression that the South is approaching a starving condition."[23]

The first obligation of the wartime press was to report the war, which was no easy task given the era's transportation and communications. Then, too, beginning in 1861 and continuing for the duration of the war, Confederate military and civilian officials censored war news, mainly through their monopoly of the telegraph.[24] Richmond and other Virginia papers often supplemented the lack of news from Confederate authorities with reports from Northern papers or with reports from sources that reported as facts what in reality were only rumors. For over a week after Pickett's charge at Gettysburg on July 3, 1863—a disaster from which the Army of Northern Virginia and the Confederate cause never fully recovered—Richmond newspapers were totally reliant on Northern papers and rumors for news of the battle. On July 7, at a time when Robert E. Lee's army was in retreat from the Pennsylvania battlefield, the *Examiner* reported: "LATEST NEWS FROM THE NORTH. THE BATTLE RENEWED AT GETTYSBURG—THREE DAYS FIGHTING—THE BATTLE STILL RAGING—DESPERATE FIGHTING." The next day, relying on erroneous reports from Martinsburg, West Virginia, the *Examiner* claimed: "OUR ARMY AGAIN VICTORIOUS—MEADE'S ARMY AN-NIHILATED—FORTY THOUSAND PRISONERS TAKEN."[25] The *Dispatch* was more skeptical of the Martinsburg news: "We have no means of testing the accuracy of the dispatch from Martinsburg. Correspondents—especially telegraphic correspondents—with the best intentions, are often led astray." Still, the *Dispatch* remained "confident that Gen. Lee has struck some great blow. . . . He would never have ventured upon a march, apparently so hazardous as that into Pennsylvania, had he not well calculated all the chances beforehand."[26]

It was mid-July before the Richmond papers conceded that Gettysburg was no great victory. How, though, did a "patriotic press" report defeat, much less military disaster? It was a dilemma the state's newspapers never resolved. "The Confederates did not gain a victory" in Pennsylvania, the *Examiner* wrote, but "neither did the enemy. He succeeded in defending himself, and we failed in some portions of an attack.—But the failure was very different from that of the enemy at Chancellorsville and Fredericksburg. We killed more of the enemy than we lost; we took very many more prisoners than [we] lost."[27] With great reluctance the *Dispatch* also retreated from the notion that Gettysburg was "a triumphant success." General Lee, the paper claimed, abandoned the battle only after the Yankees fled to the high ground behind the town, occupying impregnable positions. That Lee "was repulsed in his attack on the entrenchments—that he fled in disorder—that his army was demoralized—are Yankee lies of the first magnitude." A few days later, the *Dispatch* opined "that, like most other events in this world," Gettysburg "has been productive both of good and evil, though we are disposed to think that the good more than balances the evil."[28]

The loss of Vicksburg with its 27,000 defenders on July 4 was harder to extenuate or exculpate. Taken by surprise, the *Examiner* allowed that the news from Vicksburg "is not less astonishing than unpleasant. It is the most unexpected announcement which has been made in this war. So astoundingly contradictory is it to every particle of intelligence lately received from that quarter, either from our own people or through the enemy, that there is a strong disposition to doubt the authenticity of the dispatch s⸱ ⸱t to the Secretary of War over the signature of General Joseph E. J⸱ ⸱⸱ ⸱n." The defeat was all the more shocking because Vicksburg "was impregnable by assault," rued the *Examiner.* Indeed, the city's "sudden surrender cannot be explained at present, without resort to theories, all unpleasant, and none justified by known facts." John M. Daniel's paper, however, quickly slipped into propaganda mode: "We do not hesitate to repeat what we have said before, that the public of the North and the South both rate the importance of Vicksburg far too highly."[29] After first calling the news from Mississippi "a heavy blow," the *Dispatch,* like its rival, resorted to propaganda: "We tell our countrymen that they have no reason for despair, or even for despondency at the loss of Vicksburg. The pertinacious gallantry with which it has been defended has made our people place too high an estimate upon its importance."[30]

A year later the Richmond papers struggled to explain the loss of Atlanta to Gen. William T. Sherman's army. On August 26, just a week before Confederate general John Hood abandoned the Georgia city, the *Examiner* and the *Sentinel* believed—or pretended to believe—that the Federal siege was no closer to success than it had been the month before. Three days later the *Examiner* printed this remarkable rumor: "It was reported yesterday that official intelligence had been received that Sherman was retreating from Atlanta, and that Hood was pressing him heavily. We are much disposed to believe this report, though no information on the subject has been given the press."[31] Rumor notwithstanding, Sherman captured the city on September 2. The *Whig* and the *Examiner* promptly labeled the loss a "disaster" and blamed the defeat on General Hood, who both papers claimed was unfit for high command.[32] A week later, however, the *Examiner* assured its readers that Atlanta's fall was a "trifling affair"; its only real importance being that it "would be puffed and swelled out of all proportion by that party in the enemy's country which hopes to re-elect Abraham Lincoln."[33] The *Whig,* too, retreated from its initial gloom and joined the *Sentinel* in assuring the public that the morale of Hood's veterans remained undaunted in the face of Sherman's host. It is not in the nature of Hood's Army of Tennessee "to grow dispirited and despondent," the *Whig* wrote. "Every disaster that has fallen to its lot has but served to stimulate it to renewed deeds of valor and daring."[34] The *Dispatch,* too, discovered a silver lining: "[T]he evacuation of

Atlanta by our troops is a misfortune only in so far as it will have the effect of consolidating all parties in the North in favor of a continued prosecution of the war."[35]

Editors doubtless struggled with the burden of reporting bad news. Having adopted the posture of a "patriotic press," they felt duty bound to sustain public morale and minimize setbacks. Admitting defeat, moreover, meant admitting that Billy Yanks made good soldiers. It suggested, too, that Confederate generals had been outmaneuvered and outfought by Yankee generals. Above all, the logic of defeats such as Gettysburg, Vicksburg, and Atlanta meant thinking the unthinkable: that the South might lose the war. Honest, objective reporting thus became tantamount to sedition, to being a "croaker," to loss of faith in the cause. It meant loss of honor, too, and diminished respectability. It meant joining those unpatriotic, disreputable elements of society who avoided the draft, stole bacon and flour, and staged bread riots. Editors were caught in a trap of their own making. Notwithstanding the ever-lengthening casualty lists, the $125-a-barrel flour, and the suffering of tens of thousands, defeat became that which could not be mentioned.

Defeat trapped editors in yet another dilemma, this one vis-à-vis President Jefferson Davis and the Confederate government: how did a "patriotic press" report what it perceived as government mistakes damaging to the war effort? The *Whig* grappled with the dilemma in the wake of the Atlanta defeat. Like the *Examiner,* the *Whig* believed that President Davis had committed an egregious error when he relieved Joseph E. Johnston as commander of the Army of Tennessee in July 1864 and replaced him with John Bell Hood. The change of command, the paper concluded, had led directly to the loss of the Georgia city. A few days after Atlanta's fall, the *Whig* reflected philosophically on the problem:

> Whenever a manifestly injudicious appointment is made, the exclamation is made, "Do not destroy confidence in the new commander and in the Government by objections which come too late to do any good. Since the appointment is made, the plain duty of every patriot is to uphold the Government, give the officer a fair trial, and await the result." Nor is this reasoning without force. Whenever the legitimate consequences of an injudicious appointment ensue in the shape of a disaster, such as the fall of Atlanta, the cry is raised, "Beware how you make bad worse. At a time like this, when the sky

is dark, the plain duty of every patriot is to put on a smiling face, cheer up the people and sustain the government," etc. This reasoning also has its force; and thus the Administration is secure in its appointments, however unwise they may be. The most temperate and sensible opposition to such appointments is promptly silenced by the clamor "faction," "faction"; at all events, it is unavailing; compulsory acquiescence is claimed as popular approbation, and so the chain of causes and consequences (bad appointments and disasters) extends, link by link, its dangerous length, until, at last, the cause itself may be imperiled.[36]

Richmond's newspapers never resolved the dilemma. At the positive end of the spectrum, the *Enquirer* generally supported the Davis administration, and earned the reputation of being an administration organ.[37] In May and June 1862, when the Army of the Potomac hammered at the gates of Richmond, it sustained public faith in the government, cautioning against know-it-all newspaper editors who wrote as if they could order victories with their meals. The president and his generals, the journal observed, bore the responsibility for tens of thousands of lives and the fate of the Confederacy itself; they had to "weigh the results of actions" as "newspaper generals" did not. Moreover, the *Enquirer* charged, the very editors who urged decisive action on the government would be quick to condemn it if such action led to disaster.[38]

In the years that followed, the *Enquirer* often chided its journalistic peers for what it deemed unwarranted attacks on the government. After Vicksburg fell, almost alone it defended Gen. John C. Pemberton and his nominal superior, Joseph E. Johnston, against "people in civilian life who scarcely know what a siege is." Both officers, it argued, had done their best to save the beleaguered city.[39] The journal's patience with the administration's conduct of the war, though, was neither uncritical nor inexhaustible; and Davis's dogged support of Gen. Braxton Bragg taxed it beyond the limit of its endurance. Even before the hapless commander of the Army of Tennessee suffered a humiliating defeat at Chattanooga in November 1863, the *Enquirer* had joined the legion of Confederate editors urging the president to replace him.[40] In the larger picture, though, however much Davis and his lieutenants may have disappointed, Trexler writes, the *Enquirer*'s editors "always kept before their eyes the supreme objective, southern independence."[41]

Established in spring 1863, the *Sentinel,* too, was a firm backer of the government, at times even more than the *Enquirer.* It continued to defend Secretary of State Judah P. Benjamin, for example, even after the *Enquirer* had lost faith in him.[42] The *Dispatch* occupied a middle ground, often critical of the administration without joining the president-can-do-no-right naysayers. At the other end of the spectrum from the *Enquirer* and the *Sentinel* were the *Whig* and the *Examiner.* Even in the first months of the war, neither was more than lukewarm in support of Davis's administration. In early 1862 both abandoned any semblance of neutrality. A month after the fall of Fort Henry and Fort Donelson, the *Whig* declared: "The Knowledge of a disease is necessary to a cure.—Our President has lost the confidence of the country."[43] The *Examiner* struck a similar note after the Henry and Donelson defeats: "If any candid observer is asked for the cause of our present tide of misfortune, he will be compelled to give the mortifying answer: that the Yankees have outwitted us; that they have managed their power with much more judgment; and that on just the point where the South was supposed superior to the North—that is to say, in the art of government—the Yankees have beaten us."[44] Two weeks after Antietam, the *Examiner* declared: "In military genius the South is far more rich than the North. Its fighting capacity is still more disproportionately great. But in civil talent and in the Executive management it must be confessed that the Confederacy is far inferior to her adversary. The political machinery of the Southern Confederacy has really not done one single thing to help it."[45] Two years later, with defeat looming on the horizon, the *Examiner* charged that "every military misfortune of this country is palpably and confessedly due to the personal interference of Mr. Davis."[46]

The antiadministration papers believed that the president showed poor judgment and favoritism in his appointments to high command. After the fall of Vicksburg, for example, the *Examiner* attacked Davis's appointment of "second-rate," "obscure" General Pemberton to defend the city. Some of the reasons for the disaster remained in dispute, the newspaper conceded. "But on one thing it is not necessary to suspend judgment. It is the policy of appointing unknown, inexperienced men, whose services give them no title, to the highest positions, to the most important trusts, to the command of the greatest armies, solely because the opinion, prejudice; or fancy of the President is favourable to them."[47] As Confederate defeats mounted, the *Examiner* grew even more exasperated. The president seemed determined, the journal complained, to deny field command to the nation's ablest soldiers: "he has made up his mind upon that; we shall be saved from subjugation by his favourite minions, whose fame and fortune he has sworn to make—or we shall not be saved at all."[48] The *Whig,* too, complained that, with exception of General Lee, Davis refused commands to the Confederacy's ablest soldiers.[49]

The *Examiner* and the *Whig* became the journalistic voices of the political faction in the Confederate Congress backing Gen. Joseph E. Johnson in his long-running quarrel with President Davis. Three days after Atlanta fell to the Federals, the *Examiner* lamented: "So much for the third removal of General Johnston. First, he was virtually removed, by being deprived of power to direct his lieutenant, Pemberton; and the cost of that gratification to the feelings of Mr. Davis was the army of Vicksburg. Next he was superseded by Bragg; and the organization of the second army was destroyed at Missionary Ridge.—Thirdly, after restoring it, he was removed at the very moment when his knowledge, skill and energy was indispensable to the success and even the safety of the campaign." Worse, the newspaper charged, in Johnston's place the president chose John Bell Hood, an officer "notoriously incapable of managing anything larger than a division. The result is disaster at Atlanta, in the very nick of time when such a victory alone could save the party of Lincoln from irretrievable ruin."[50] The *Whig* was equally bitter about the removal of Johnston: he was "a Lieutenant General of large experience, and of capacity proved on many a hard-fought field," while General Hood, on the other hand, was "an inexperienced officer." Like the *Examiner,* the *Whig* blamed Davis as the real author of the Atlanta disaster.[51]

It is a fair conclusion that the *Whig* and the *Examiner* came to see Jefferson Davis as no less a threat to the Confederacy than Abraham Lincoln. Indeed, the *Examiner* said as much in the last winter of the war: "[W]e are not afraid of being conquered by the enemy, so much as of being defeated by Mr. Davis." It was the South's hard luck that Mr. Davis thinks "himself to be, a military man," the *Examiner* opined in another scathing editorial that winter:

If he had been some worthy planter, who never was either at West Point or Mexico, and had no special qualification save a manly, straightforward Southern spirit, then he would never have thought himself competent to plan distant campaigns and interfere with

Generals in the field. . . . But Mr. Davis unluckily studied at West Point: still more unfortunately, in Mexico, he one day formed his regiment of two hundred and fifty Mississippi volunteers into the shape of a V, and received a charge of Mexicans *a la fourchette*. By reason of that tiresome *fourchette*, the Colonel conceived him indeed a military genius: we feel its evil effects to this day; and if we are to perish, the verdict of posterity will be, Died of a V.[52]

To be sure, Jefferson Davis was a flawed leader who made serious mistakes, and given the Confederacy's record of defeat from mid-1863 on, it is hardly surprising that the press became increasingly critical of the official who bore ultimate responsibility for success or failure of the Southern cause. Long before the war was lost, however, the *Whig* and the *Examiner* targeted the Confederate president for unrelenting attacks, attacks that became increasingly personal and questioned not merely the president's direction of the war but his character and intelligence, as well as that of his cabinet officers, especially Judah P. Benjamin of the War and State departments, Christopher G. Memminger of the Treasury, and Stephen Mallory of the navy.[53] In June 1864, for example, a bill increasing the president's $25,000-a-year salary, to be paid partly in gold, was before Congress. Mr. Davis, the argument went, needed to entertain dignitaries and to maintain a household befitting a head of state. While none of Davis's modern biographers has accused him of graft or greed, nevertheless John Moncure Daniel's newspaper seized on the salary issue for a vicious attack on Davis's character, accusing him of craving "the luxuries and gewgaws of Europe": "The persistent selfishness—rapacity—covetousness—which characterizes the effort to increase the pay of the highest paid functionary of the land is both surprising and disgusting." Confederate money, the *Examiner* remarked, "can no longer satisfy the President's wants; he must have two thousand dollars of his salary in Federal gold. It has been hitherto considered unpatriotic and disgraceful for any man to refuse Confederate notes. But what words could justly qualify such a refusal by the man whose signature created that currency, and whose instrument—Memminger—reduced them to their present value?"[54]

Less vituperative than its rival, the *Whig*'s sardonic prose could be equally corrosive. "The stationing of 30,000 men at Vicksburg," it commented, "where they could neither get away nor be reinforced, and where they became, of course, a prey to the enemy, was, we presume, more in the nature of a sacrifice to friendship, on the part of the sublime military genius by whom it was conceived, than the result of a systematic plan."[55] The *Whig* focused much of its ire against Davis indirectly on the Cabinet, constantly reminding its readers that the president's ministers were incompetents: "We have a Department of State, that has not been able in nearly three years to establish relations with any other State—a Treasury Department, that has failed to keep its finances from running to ruin . . . a Navy Department without a navy . . . a Department of Justice vacant." These attacks were invariably coupled with urgings for the president to reorganize his government, appointing abler and wiser men.[56]

Such censorious writing doubtless influenced the public mood in Virginia and in the South as a whole. Harrison Trexler concludes that editors' constant attacks on President Davis "injured the cause they all asserted that they loved." Without exception, he writes, "Richmond editors declared— some of them blatantly—that they were loyal to the cause of southern independence. But in their efforts to belittle, even besmirch, the administration and its head, they unquestionably exercised a baleful influence. In view of the wide southern circulation of the Richmond press this attitude of their editorials must have affected southern morale."[57] Trexler is doubtless right about the impact of Richmond's antiadministration press on the Southern cause. The deeper question that still remains to be explored, though, concerns editors' motivations. What motivated newsmen dedicated to the cause of Southern independence to systematically undermine the head of state and his ministers responsible for achieving that independence?

Notes

1. Emory M. Thomas, *The Confederate State of Richmond: A Biography of the Capital* (Austin: University of Texas Press, 1971), 17–18; J. Cutler Andrews, *The South Reports the Civil War* (Princeton, N.J.: Princeton University Press, 1970), 34.

2. Edward L. Ayers, *In the Presence of Mine Enemies: War in the Heart of America, 1859–1863* (New York: Norton, 2003), 44–45.

3. Ted Tunnell, "Creating 'the Propaganda of History': Southern Editors and the Origins of *Carpetbagger* and *Scalawag*," *Journal of Southern History* 72 (November 2006): 796, 821–22.

4. This essay examines only Virginia's Confederate press. It excludes West

Virginia and newspapers taken over by Federal occupation and converted into Union organs.

5. Lester J. Cappon, *Virginia Newspapers, 1821–1935: A Bibliography with Historical Introduction and Notes* (New York: Appleton-Century, 1936), 17–18, and passim.

6. Quoted in Harry T. Shanks, *The Secession Movement in Virginia, 1847–1861* (1934; repr., New York: AMS, 1971), 173.

7. Ibid., 184; Marvin Davis Evans, "The Richmond Press on the Eve of the Civil War," *John P. Branch Historical Papers of Randolph-Macon College*, n.s., 1 (January 1951): 21; *Richmond Whig*, April 18, 1861. The full title of the *Whig* was the *Richmond Whig and Advertiser*. The author has followed the general practice of contemporaries and historians and referred to it simply as the *Whig*.

8. Ayers, *In the Presence of Mine Enemies*, 135.

9. Andrews, *The South Reports the Civil War*, 26; see also J. Cutler Andrews, "The Confederate Press and Public Morale," *Journal of Southern History* 32 (November 1966): 445–65.

10. Evans, "Richmond Press on the Eve of the Civil War," 17.

11. Harrison A. Trexler, "Davis Administration and the Richmond Press, 1861–1865," *Journal of Southern History* 16 (May 1950): 178.

12. Ibid., 185–86.

13. Ibid., 181–85; on John Moncure Daniel, see Peter Bridges, *Pen of Fire: John Moncure Daniel* (Kent, Ohio: Kent State University Press, 2002), and Frederick S. Daniel, *The Richmond Examiner during the War; or, The Writings of John M. Daniel, with a Memoir of His Life* (New York: Arno, 1970); on Edward A. Pollard, see Jack P. Maddex Jr., *The Reconstruction of Edward A. Pollard: A Rebel's Conversion to Postbellum Unionism* (Chapel Hill: University of North Carolina Press, 1974).

14. Trexler, "Davis Administration and the Richmond Press," 191–92.

15. Amy R. Minton, "Defining Confederate Respectability: Morality, Patriotism, and Confederate Identity in Richmond's Civil War Public Press," in Edward L. Ayers, Gary W. Gallagher, and Andrew J. Torget, eds., *Crucible of the Civil War: Virginia from Secession to Commemoration* (Charlottesville: University of Virginia Press, 2006), 80–81.

16. *Dispatch,* quoted in ibid., 80–82.

17. Ibid., 86.

18. Varina Davis, quoted in Thomas, *Confederate State of Richmond*, 119.

19. Ibid., 119–21.

20. Minton, "Defining Confederate Respectability," 88–89.

21. *Richmond Daily Examiner*, April 4, 1863.

22. *Richmond Whig*, April 6, 1863.

23. Ayers, *In the Presence of Mine Enemies,* 375.

24. Andrews, *The South Reports the Civil War,* 63–64, 79, 103, 149–50, and passim.

25. *Richmond Daily Examiner,* July 7, 8, 1863.

26. *Richmond Daily Dispatch,* July 8, 1863.

27. *Richmond Daily Examiner,* July 13, 1863

28. *Richmond Daily Dispatch,* July 13, 18, 1863.

29. *Richmond Daily Examiner,* July 9, 1863.

30. *Richmond Daily Dispatch,* July 10, 1863.

31. *Richmond Daily Examiner,* August 26 (*Sentinel* cited), 29, 1864.

32. Ibid., September 5, 1864; *Richmond Whig,* September 5, 1864.

33. *Richmond Daily Examiner,* September 12, 1864.

34. *Richmond Whig,* September 5 (*Sentinel* cited), 7, 1864.

35. *Richmond Daily Dispatch,* September 5, 1864.

36. *Richmond Whig,* September 5, 1864.

37. Trexler, "Davis Administration and the Richmond Press," 178–80. Careful analysis of the stance of Virginia's Confederate newspapers outside of Richmond toward Davis's administration has yet to be done. None of the following works, for example, addresses the issue: Ayers, *In the Presence of Mine Enemies;* Steven Elliott Tripp, *Yankee Town, Southern City: Race and Class Relations in Civil War Lynchburg* (New York: New York University Press, 1997); A. Wilson Greene, *Civil War Petersburg: Confederate City in the Crucible of War* (Charlottesville: University of Virginia Press, 2006); Noah Trudeau, *The Last Citadel: Petersburg, Virginia, June 1864–April 1865* (Boston: Little, Brown, 1991). In the main, the farther from Richmond newspapers were published, the more supportive of the administration they seem to have been.

38. *Richmond Daily Enquirer,* May 7, June 26, 1862.

39. *Richmond Semi-weekly Enquirer,* July 9, 21, 1863.

40. Ibid., September 18, October 30, November 12, 1863.

41. Trexler, "Davis Administration and the Richmond Press," 179.

42. *Sentinel,* discussed and quoted in *Richmond Semi-weekly Enquirer,* September 17, 1863. The assessment here of the *Sentinel*'s attitude toward the government is based less on what historians have written about the paper (which is very little) and more on the columns of the *Enquirer,* cited here, and those of the *Whig,* April 30, June 17, 1863, and January 27, 1865.

43. *Richmond Whig,* March 18, 1862.

44. *Richmond Daily Examiner,* February 24, 1862.

45. Ibid., October 2, 1862.

46. Ibid., December 21, 1864.

47. Ibid., July 10, 1864.

48. Ibid., January 19, 1865.

49. *Richmond Whig,* December 20, 1864.

50. *Richmond Daily Examiner,* September 5, 1864.

51. *Richmond Whig,* December 20, 1864.

52. *Richmond Daily Examiner,* January 9, 1865. A "fourchette" is a gloved hand with the forefinger and middle finger held in the shape of a "V," as in a "V for victory" sign.

53. Examples of attacks on Benjamin and Memminger are in ibid., June 17, August 26, 1864; the *Examiner* attack on Mallory is cited in Thomas, *Confederate State of Richmond,* 80.

54. *Richmond Daily Examiner,* June 13, 1864. See William C. Davis, *Jefferson Davis: The Man and His Hour* (New York: HarperCollins, 1991); William J. Cooper Jr., *Jefferson Davis: American* (New York: Knopf, 2000); Felicity Allen, *Jefferson Davis: Unconquerable Heart* (Columbia: University of Missouri Press, 1999); for an excellent account of Davis's presidency, see Herman Hattaway and Richard E. Beringer, *Jefferson Davis: Confederate President* (Lawrence: University of Kansas Press, 2002).

55. *Richmond Whig,* December 29, 1864.

56. Ibid., December 1, 1863; other *Whig* attacks on the Cabinet are in issues of April 23, August 13, September 5, December 5, December 15, 1863.

57. Trexler, "Davis Administration and the Richmond Press," 195.

Clinging to Patriotism

The Fourth of July in Civil War Virginia
Jared Bond

It is ironic that the press unwittingly did so much to discourage confidence in the Confederate government, while all the time protesting its patriotic motives. Confederates wanted to be patriotic over their new nation, as they demonstrated from the outset, and as they would continue to do even as the darkening days of 1864 made it increasingly difficult to stave off gloom. Perhaps the greatest irony of all is that in doing so, Virginians and their fellow Confederates clung to the most iconic of all of the old Union's patriotic symbols, the Fourth of July.

The nineteenth-century celebration of the Fourth of July depicted the embodiment of national identity in citizens across the country. The annual commemoration of the "Glorious Fourth" linked the past ideals and aspirations of the Founding Fathers to the present through editorials, orations, and public gatherings that unified communities. However, the coming of the Civil War brought about a perplexing dilemma for the South. Virginians, along with other members of the Confederate states, had to decide how they should celebrate the founding of the nation with which they had just severed ties.

Being the heart of the new Confederacy, Virginia played a key role in defining the identity of an America that was no longer united. Newspaper editorials and numerous orations delivered on the Fourth of July during the Civil War debated the merits of the holiday and its role in Southern society. These writings acknowledged that with secession, changes lay in store for the South. Among the changes occurring during this Confederate nation-building period were opinions on the commemoration of the Fourth of July. While it still was a noteworthy and distinguished day, the veneration it once held had diminished. However, the South remained unwilling to relinquish the day.[1]

Virginians felt that the South had not yet secured the vision and ideals set down by the Founding Fathers. Among these were notions of independence, liberty, human rights, and the right to rebel to secure these values. Many of these ideas were inspired and promoted by the efforts of Founding Fathers who were also Virginians, including Patrick Henry, Thomas Jefferson, Richard Henry Lee, James Madison, George Mason, James Monroe, Edmund Randolph, and George Washington. Therefore, the philosophy of the Founding Fathers was in a sense the attitudes and beliefs of Virginians. The Fourth of July, which celebrated not only the Declaration of Independence but also the success of the American Revolution, honored these ideas. The achievements of 1776 were seen as a stepping-stone for finally securing the vision of the Founding Fathers in the nineteenth century.

With the start of the War between the States, Virginians decided that with the changing times their focus should be on present efforts rather than past commemorations. To that end, some advocated moving their celebrations to December 20, the anniversary of the first ordinance of secession. However, while Virginians recognized that war would bring imminent changes, many felt that abandoning this holiday was not a necessary adjustment. The move to celebrate independence on December 20 failed to take hold; instead, Virginians used the Fourth of July to discuss, debate, and question the achievements of the Founding Fathers in light of the current struggle.

That being said, other Southerners questioned the right of the South even to recognize the Fourth of July. From the war's beginning, and on each Fourth of July until the war's end, through newspaper editorials Virginians continued to address the question of the proper ownership of the holiday. It was a day that awakened, the *Lynchburg Virginian* declared, "mingled emotions of pleasure and pain" in the Confederacy.[2] Newspapers stressed the parallels between December 1860 and July 4, 1776. The first revolution was but the start, and the Revolution of 1861 would complete what their ancestors had begun. "It is for this Virginia bleeds," wrote the *Richmond Dispatch*.[3]

Focusing on the glory of their ancestors and the role that Virginians played in the struggle for independence against Britain proved to be a key reason for Virginia's unwillingness to abandon the holiday. To ignore the military victories and the principles created and embodied in the Declaration of Independence would be to ignore the strongest aspects of Southern glory. The day embodied their inheritance, and Virginians felt it was their right to honor the achievements of their ancestors in the successful fight against tyrannical rule.

This is an important delineation. Virginians did not view the holiday as commemorating the founding of America, but as commemorating the founding of the American idea of independence. This concept focused on the right to rebel and the right to proclaim independence from tyranny. This strong belief supported the Confederacy's justification for secession when it perceived that the Union threatened its liberty.

The *Lynchburg Virginian* insisted: "Shall we then abandon the celebration of the 4th of July to them? Never! It is ours to keep alive forever the memory of the men whose principles we were indoctrinated in," and for Virginians to pass down to their children and their children's children.[4] The *Richmond Dispatch* declared that the day was "memorable for the assertion of principles we revere, and mean to defend with our lives and the last drop of our blood." And it was these same principles that the North had lost, "probably forever, in order to force the yoke of tyranny upon the South."[5] In fact, rather than abandoning it, Virginians declared that the day should be embraced.

After asserting the right to celebrate the Fourth of July, writers quickly invalidated the Northern claim to the holiday. The actions of the North went against the ideals and principles of the Founding Fathers; thus Northerners had no right to the day. Because of this, Virginians felt the Fourth of July should be celebrated in the South, and it should be a solely Southern institution. Citing inheritance not only through Washington and Jefferson but also through loyalty to the doctrines set down on that day, Virginians felt that they had a right to the patriotic pride that surrounded the holiday.[6]

However, the Fourth of July did not represent the memory of a complete victory for the South. Their struggle for independence only began in 1776, and had to be taken up again in 1861. In the midst of this renewed struggle, the Fourth of July would be different from those of past years, the *Richmond Dispatch* noted. Regardless of how it would be commemorated, "it is a sufficient tribute to it that we are engaged in the maintenance of the principles of human rights and liberty it announced, and that we are ready to sacrifice our lives and all we have in the effort."[7] While the war would change how the South celebrated the day, concerns over the legitimacy of the commemoration would remain.

The following year, in 1862, the *Lynchburg Virginian* again questioned the ownership of the holiday. "To whom does the 4th of July, with all of its hallowed associations, belong? To the people who have repudiated the doctrines for which Jefferson and Washington fought? Or to us who this day reiterate all that may be fairly and legitimately inferred from the Declaration of Independence?"[8] Not only did Virginians feel the South had a right to the day, but they also asserted ownership by default, for the North had abandoned its claim by failing to uphold the principles of the Founding Fathers.

The *Lynchburg Virginian* further claimed that while Southerners had a right to the day, they had conceded the loss of the national flag to the North: "Let it go, for it has been sadly prostituted and dishonored."[9] Instead, the newspaper suggested the South preserve the principles and memories once symbolized by the flag. It was acceptable to abandon certain aspects of the Fourth of July as long as the South remained true to its original premise.

While in past years the Fourth of July had become so firmly tied to honoring the old Union, many Virginians recognized that the day was as much a national anniversary for the South as it was for the North. They felt that the South's claim to the holiday was even truer because the North had desecrated the day by ignoring the principles of the Founding Fathers. In 1862 the *Richmond Dispatch* again questioned the Northern celebration of the Fourth of July. It wondered what reason the North would have to honor the day, after trampling upon all the principles it represented.[10]

Other 1862 editorials, however, were hopeful that this Fourth of July would bring a change in the war. "To-morrow, July the 4th, is the anniversary of American Independence, declared in 1776, and of which the Northern half of the late Union are trying their best to rob us of. Perhaps, like their brother Hessians of a by-gone era, they may be on that day fleeing before the avenging arm of a roused and insulted people."[11] This again expressed the spirit that the efforts in 1776 were just the beginning, and the war begun in 1861 might finally secure the July 4 principles.

Still, the question of ownership of the holiday would continually resurface. Even in 1863, the *Lynchburg Virginian* had to bluntly state that the holiday "is our's and not their's, and we hope that our people will no more yield it to the Yankees, than they would the graves of Washington and Jefferson."[12] The South would fight to retain the holiday, as it had fought the North for the two previous years.

The war, however, had changed the holiday for the South. The intent of the Civil War was to finally secure the principles of self-government set forth during the American Revolution. Naturally, then, rather than continuing to celebrate the Union on the Fourth of July, as had been done in previous years, during the war the emphasis was on securing victory. Civic parades and ceremonies often had to be shelved in order to fulfill the duties and obligations of war.

While Southerners in 1863 were less inclined to commemorate the Fourth of July actively, the *Richmond Dispatch* wrote that the holiday was "still dear to the Southern people, and they prove their devotion to it by maintaining with their blood and their lives the rights and principles asserted by our fathers in '76. The Yankees . . . have desecrated both the day and the principles which it commemorates, and the very best way in which we can celebrate it is by whipping them."[13]

Even in the midst of war, though, Virginian newspapers still held onto hope of a resurgence of the holiday in the South. The *Lynchburg Virginian* declared: "The liberties for which so many of our noble heroes have sacrificed their lives in the last two years, shall be firmly established, the memories of 'Independence Day,' will be all the more dearer, and its re-baptism of blood will consecrate it anew in the hearts of the true countrymen of Washington and Jefferson."[14] This rhetoric suggested that jubilant Fourth of July celebrations would resume once the South finally secured its independence.

Debate over the ownership of the holiday continued to recur each year in Virginia around the Fourth of July. By 1863, newspapers still felt they had to address the issue of whether or not the South had a right to celebrate the holiday. Since the Confederacy remained committed to the principles behind the Declaration of Independence, which the Fourth of July commemorates, Virginian editors believed the South still had a claim to the day: "If the battle has to be fought over again, because the faithless people of the North themselves ignore the doctrines of the Declaration, there is no obligation devolved upon us, and no propriety in our abandoning the anniversary with all the glorious memories of Independence Day, to the people who occupy towards us the very position which the British nation held towards the colonies."[15]

Newspaper editorials continued to assert Virginia's right to the principles set forth in the Declaration of Independence and to the celebration of the Fourth of July, and generally questioned how the Fourth of July could ever cease to excite the emotions of patriotism and pride in the hearts of Americans.[16] The Fourth of July was an inherent part of Southern culture, which they would not abandon during the Civil War. Virginians did not reach this conclusion lightly. Writers continued to debate the finer points of what the holiday represented to Virginia and to the South as a whole.

The conflicting views over whether or not the South had a right to celebrate the Fourth of July were not confined to editorial rhetoric; they also were present in domestic celebrations of the Fourth of July in 1861. This being the first Independence Day of the Civil War, consensus over how to regard the holiday had not yet been reached. Consequently, many communities across Virginia held subdued celebrations or none at all.

Seeing the confusion among its readers, the *Richmond Dispatch* suggested to Virginians to "let everyone celebrate the day as may seem best to himself or herself, but let no one indulge too frequently in 'bumpers,' even though they be drank to the memory of the Departed Union."[17] Regardless of how the rest of the community celebrated the day, though, newspapers still recognized the holiday, banks closed, and there was a traditional suspension of regular business across Virginia.[18]

Some Virginian communities saw the war as a reason to show strong Confederate support for the holiday. Traditional picnics, bands, boat excursions, and an outpouring of Confederate flags were still common. In Halifax County, citizens arranged a grand Fourth of July picnic in a grove outside town. A group of uniformed soldiers arrived with a band and flags proclaiming: "Our Fourth of July, in memory of '76" and "*Sic Semper Tyrannis,* Liberty or Blood!" After drilling and a picnic dinner, a local orator gave a speech and a group of veterans presented the young soldiers with a new cannon.[19] Citizens of nearby Amelia Springs described a procession of Confederate banners, flowers, and wreaths, followed by a night display of fireworks.[20]

However, traditional military displays were often missing from these Southern celebrations. While less than half of men in the North served in the army, four out of five white men of military age served in Confederate armies. This significantly changed the atmosphere of celebrations on the home front. At a Fourth of July celebration in Halifax, crowds consisted almost entirely of "the fair sex."[21] However, some celebrations still managed to retain their military displays, and in Richmond in 1861 a few hundred men paraded in clean gray uniforms.[22]

Coupled with the lack of men, an air of sadness and regret often sur-

rounded the Fourth of July. Some Virginians foresaw the lasting implications of the war, lamenting that while the Americans were eventually able to
become friends with the British after the Revolution, "hatred of the North
will be a legacy of future generations of the South."[23]

The war had changed society in other ways as well. The gravity of the
conflict replaced the former lightheartedness. The Civil War was a tragic
time for the country; many people felt that it was out of place for them to
celebrate when sons and fathers were dying in battle. This was an issue
that would surround the Fourth of July commemorations on both sides of
the war. The *Richmond Dispatch* noted that the holiday would pass "under
circumstances novel and strange. It cannot be celebrated in the usual style.
The condition of the country does not admit that."[24]

This viewpoint coincided with the opinion that while now was not the
time for celebration, once victory was at hand and the fighting was done,
the South could resume celebrating the Fourth as a holiday. From a Virginia
plantation, Maria Louisa Fleet described "the most dreary '4th of July' I ever
saw," vowing that "we Southerners will not celebrate it any more but will
celebrate the day forever afterward when we whip the Yankees."[25]

As the war continued, celebrations in the South shrank in size, from
either a shift in mood or a shift in resources. Nevertheless, Virginians expressed a desire to continue commemorating the Fourth of July, both during
and after the war. Capt. Charles Blackford, Second Virginia Cavalry, noted in
1863, "I hope we shall continue to celebrate the day for all time. It is a day of
Virginia's making," even though the only observance he witnessed in town
was the firing of a salute at the raising of the Confederate flag.[26] Regardless
of whether Virginians were in the mood to celebrate the day or not, almost
all agreed that it was inappropriate for the North to do so.

This transition in the mood of Southern home front celebrations—from
prewar gaiety to wartime solemnity—was likewise present in the war front
celebrations. In army camps and on the battlefield, the Fourth of July had
special significance for Virginians away from home. In 1861, the young
women of Hanover turned out to shower soldiers en route to Camp Ashland
with bouquets of flowers on the Fourth of July.[27] At Fort Powhatan, Fourth
of July ceremonies began with the reading of the Declaration of Independence (a practice that reflected the South's perspective on what the holiday
represented). A reading of the secession ordinance and other addresses and
orations often followed this.[28]

Meanwhile, at Camp Pickens, near Manassas Junction, while the typical holiday festivities were absent, the soldiers individually honored the day. "Many a silent vow went up to Heaven that the remembrance of the 'glorious Fourth' should not be lost to us."[29] In the spirit of the day, soldiers at Camp Pickens refused to drill, instead insisting on a full-dress parade around the encampment. Officers later arranged a dinner catered by one of the corporals.[30] Outside of Fairfax Church House, the echoes of celebratory cannons in Washington were not well received by Southern soldiers, who thought it was inappropriate for Northerners to celebrate their independence while trying to deprive Southerners of theirs.[31] Feeling likewise, many Virginian soldiers looked forward to the Fourth of July as a day when fighting might be more intensified, in order to dynamically preserve the values represented by the day. However, the war had altered the mood and the content of celebrations within the army. As the war progressed, dress parades became less common, and rare was the Fourth of July feast. However, with the unpredictable nature of war, some impromptu Fourth of July celebrations did occur among Virginia's soldiers.

In 1864, Ellen Renshaw House recorded she heard on July 3 that Confederate lieutenant general Jubal Early had surprised the enemy at Martinsburg, captured a number of soldiers, and procured a Fourth of July dinner.[32] Similarly, near Harpers Ferry that year, Henry Beck of the Fifth Alabama reported driving the enemy from Bolivar Heights. Upon entering the town the soldiers learned that the Northerners had made preparations for a large Fourth of July celebration; "Our boys destroyed their fun however by giving them a little skirmish." The Confederate troops then proceeded to gorge themselves on candy, ice cream, cakes, and whiskey, after being "invited" by the town citizens to join the festivities.[33] However, this was a rare example of a late-war celebration, as Southerners' commemoration of the Fourth of July changed dramatically after 1863.

On July 4, 1863, the *Richmond Dispatch* reminisced that in past celebrations, alcohol fueled the patriotic sentiments of Southerners, and everyone happily honored the nation. However, "the day is now changed. We have no holiday. The ruthless enemy who has trampled upon every principle and right commemorated by the day itself, given no intermission for festive enjoyments, were we so inclined." The newspaper did, however, assert that Southerners still sustained with their lives the principles set forth by their ancestors. While the continued fight against the Yankees prevented traditional celebrations, the *Dispatch* thought that the best way to honor the day would be to strike a victory against the North in memory of the Founding Fathers.[34] This was not to be the case. Even as the editors were composing these ideas, the city of Vicksburg surrendered after a six-week besiegement. That Fourth of July also marked the beginning of Robert E. Lee's retreat from defeat at Gettysburg and the Union victory at the battle of Helena, Arkansas, which provided the Yankees with an important access to the Mississippi River.

After the military losses of Vicksburg, Gettysburg, Helena, and even Port Hudson, Louisiana, which were all centered around the Fourth of July in 1863, the optimism that had fueled the Confederacy and its commemoration of Independence Day began to wane. On July 2, 1864, the *Richmond Dispatch* observed that the Confederacy had lost Vicksburg the previous year, and currently Richmond itself was threatened. "With the capture of Richmond, the war is to end, the principal rebels be executed, the plantations and negroes of the South pass to Northern proprietors, its mighty States dwindle into subjugated territories."[35] It was not a time for celebration. The Fourth of July was a reminder of crushing 1863 defeats.

Regardless of the mood of Virginians, they felt the parallels between the tyrannies of the past three years and those of the Revolution should have been obvious to Northern orators. The *Richmond Dispatch* even suggested that Northerners should be allowed to read the Declaration of Independence only in the winter, when temperatures dipped below freezing.[36] As the spirit of the Confederacy deteriorated, Virginians could not understand how the North could continue to lay claim to the holiday. Nor could Virginians abandon their own entitlement to the Fourth of July. The Fourth of July had originated in Virginia, inspired by the actions of Virginians such as Richard Henry Lee, Thomas Jefferson, and George Washington—"to add new glories to the 4th of July by crushing Virginia forever to the dust is a conception which could enter none but the brains of a 'peculiar people.'"[37] Recognizing that the Confederacy might actually lose the war only made celebrating the Fourth of July, and the principles upon which it was founded, more tragic.

Still, the South recognized the day, just in a more muted and somber way than prior commemorations. The *Richmond Examiner* declared that the holiday of 1864 was "more honoured in the breach than in observance." The firecrackers, the orators, the bunting, and the drinking were all absent. Rather than being the Glorious Fourth, it was simply the fourth day in July.

Richmond's courts, though, were still closed "out of respect for the memory of the day and the deceased eagle."[38] Though Virginians did not know it at the time, the day was to be the last Fourth of July of the war.

The Southern vision of America focused on the idea of continuing the work of the Founding Fathers. Virginians felt like they were still fighting for their independence in this, the direct sequel to the American Revolution. They sought to protect a vision of the American idea of independence. Yet as the war shifted and the losses mounted after July 1863, this vision and the hope for freedom began to fade. While the South may have asserted its right to celebrate the Fourth of July, the defeat of the Confederacy was also a defeat of its will to honor the founding of America.

Memories of the success of the first revolution were much more upsetting considering the loss of the Confederacy in this second revolution. By the war's end, Virginia had basically abandoned the commemoration of the Fourth. Every community had suffered great losses in men, property, and capital. Exhausted and impoverished, Virginia was in mourning. The Virginian spirit in the Fourth of July had died. The *Lynchburg Daily Virginian* lamented on the day, "Alas for Virginia that has lost all but her honor!"[39] It was no time for festivities. For most white Virginians, the desire to commemorate the Fourth of July faded away with the end of the Confederacy.

Postwar celebrations were virtually nonexistent for Virginians of Southern descent. On the Fourth of July in 1865, the *Lynchburg Daily Virginian* even ran an article by Henry Lee (brother of Robert E. Lee), which scathingly criticized the writing contained within the Declaration of Independence. Faulting everything from redundant word use to the misuse of the article "a," Lee revealed how disillusioned Virginians had become with the once-sacred document.[40]

The *Richmond Dispatch* wrote in 1866 how times had changed for citizens in the South. "The Southern people, feeling that they have no part in the government of the country, have little disposition to participate in the national jubilees."[41] That same year, The *Abingdon Virginian* recognized that "the truth is, 'Hail Columby,' 'Yankee Doodle' and the 'Fourth of July,' have 'done gone up' in these diggins."[42]

The *Lynchburg Virginian* declared that Virginia had lost its freedom as a result of the war. "We are again united, but when shall we be the free and happy people that once we were?"[43] During the war, Virginia's soldiers often wished to commemorate the day with a sound victory. Victory, however, had escaped the Confederacy. The Southern vision of America could not survive the death of the Confederate states. Yet even as white Virginia's views and hopes of freedom were fading, the black population in Virginia began to celebrate its new independence. If Virginia's ex-Confederates chose not to embrace the Fourth of July, her newly freed black population would. Beginning with the Union occupation of Southern cities during the Civil War, blacks began to identify strongly with the holiday. By July 1865, this freed black presence made itself known in Virginia.

Except for transplanted Northerners, Richmond's white population no longer celebrated the Fourth of July. In 1865 there was just "a slight sprinkling" of citizens and soldiers out to celebrate the day, while "every describable species of the African was present."[44] Virginians, however, did not take this change lightly. If Virginians were appalled at the Northern claim to the Fourth of July, they were horror-struck at the freed black appropriation of the day. The *Richmond Examiner* declared that Virginians did not like to see the Fourth of July "desecrated by negroes. We almost lost our faith in the day as we saw the blacks parading in grand procession—claiming the day as theirs."[45] In fact, Virginians did not even understand this adoption of the holiday by the freed population. In Petersburg, a commentator acknowledged the validity of the freedmen's desire to celebrate their emancipation, but could not understand how this became linked to the Fourth of July, as the population had no connection to the holiday itself. In fact, this confusion over the proper ownership of the holiday led to a minor disturbance in 1866, when a procession of celebrating blacks ran into a gathering of the old Twelfth Virginia Infantry on the Poplar Lawn in Petersburg.[46]

By the Fourth of July in 1866, Virginians saw that the freedmen and freedwomen of Richmond "took complete possession of the day and of the city; the highways, the byways, and Capitol Square, were black with moving masses of darkeys."[47] The *Richmond Dispatch* questioned whether a white Virginian might believe he was not in America but in some far-off African nation, and pointed out that the only whites around the Capitol Square were the statues of Washington, Jefferson, Madison, Mason, and Clay.[48] In Abingdon, the day was silent except for "two wagon loads of freedmen on their way to a picnic, and a greasy looking black boy with a bunch of ribbons on the lapel of his coat."[49] Apart from the Federal troops, the commemoration of the Fourth of July in Virginia lay solely in the hands of the black population. By 1867, enough Virginians had abstained from commemorating the day that Joseph Mayo, the mayor of Richmond, issued a proclamation imploring Richmond's citizens to unite together to show to rest of America that Virginia was a loyal state of the Union that did not require further legislation to ensure its obedience.[50] But even with the mayor's exhortations, save for the soldiers, Richmond's whites did not participate in the public celebrations.[51]

The end of the Civil War emancipated almost 4 million slaves throughout America. The contrast between the situation of blacks in Virginia during the first Fourth of July of the Civil War and the last sparked a new, hopeful vision of America in the black population. Stressing the ideas of liberty and freedom, this view of America would build momentum in the years after the Civil War, and the freed black population would take up the buoyant celebration once shared only by white Virginians.

For Confederate Virginia, however, America was about liberty and independence. Virginians sought to protect this through secession. With the defeat of the Confederacy, there was no way to maintain this view of America. After the number of painful Confederate losses around the Fourth of July in 1863, the holiday took on an even more dismal tone. White Virginians were in no mood to celebrate. As the Civil War ended, so, too, did the Southern commemoration of the Fourth of July for more than a generation.

Notes

1. Few historians have written about the Fourth of July, especially in relation to its celebration during the sectional discord of the nineteenth century. In *Celebrating the Fourth: Independence Day and the Rites of Nationalism in the Early Republic* (Amherst: University of Massachusetts Press, 1997), Len Travers argued that as the sectional crisis approached, individualized interpretations of the Fourth of July actually worked against national unity. However, this is where his analysis ended, as the book does not venture into the Civil War years. In *The Glorious Fourth: An American Holiday, an American History* (New York: Facts on File, 1989), Diana Applebaum devoted an entire chapter to the commemoration of the holiday in the Civil War. However, her focus was primarily on the Northern celebration. She then erroneously stated that the Fourth of July was not celebrated by the Confederacy after 1861. Matthew Dennis devoted a chapter of *Red, White, and Blue Letter Days: An American Calendar* (Ithaca, N.Y.: Cornell University Press, 2002) to the Fourth of July, but again, limited

discussion of the Civil War to only a paragraph. Dennis stated that as the Civil War approached, Southerners questioned the observance of Independence Day, but in the end had to abandon the holiday with their eventual defeat.

Scholars often sidestep the fact that the Confederacy actively celebrated the holiday during the first years of the war, though they do often mention two points in referring to the Fourth of July and the Civil War. The first is that after the losses in 1863, the South stopped celebrating the holiday. The second point is that when Southerners abandoned the holiday, freed African Americans and victorious Republicans claimed the holiday as their own and celebrated it with enthusiasm. However, without the proper context and understanding of how and why Americans celebrated the Fourth of July during the Civil War, the two facts cannot be fully understood.

2. *Lynchburg Virginian,* July 4, 1862.
3. *Richmond Dispatch,* July 10, 1861.
4. *Lynchburg Virginian,* July 4, 1862.
5. *Richmond Dispatch,* July 4, 1861.
6. *Lynchburg Virginian,* July 3, 1863.
7. *Richmond Dispatch,* July 4, 1861.
8. *Lynchburg Virginian,* July 4, 1862.
9. Ibid.
10. *Richmond Dispatch,* July 4, 1862.
11. Ibid., July 3, 1862.
12. *Lynchburg Virginian,* July 4, 1863.
13. *Richmond Dispatch,* July 4, 1863.
14. *Lynchburg Virginian,* July 3, 1863.
15. Ibid.
16. Ibid., July 5, 1864.
17. *Richmond Dispatch,* July 4, 1861.
18. Charles Minor Blackford and Susan Leigh Blackford, eds., *Letters from Lee's Army; or, Memoirs of Life in and out of the Army in Virginia during the War between the States* (Lincoln, Neb.: Bison, 1998), 155.
19. *Richmond Dispatch,* July 10, 1861.
20. Ibid., July 12, 1861.
21. Ibid., July 10, 1861.
22. *Charleston (S.C.) Mercury,* July 8, 1861.
23. *Richmond Dispatch,* July 4, 1863.
24. Ibid., July 4, 1861.
25. Betsy Fleet and John D. P. Fuller, eds., *Green Mount: A Virginia Plantation Family during the Civil War; Being the Journal of Benjamin Robert Fleet and Letters of His Family* (Lexington: University Press of Kentucky, 1962), 63–64.

26. Blackford, *Letters from Lee's Army,* 2:59.

27. *Richmond Dispatch,* July 8, 1861.

28. Ibid.

29. Ibid.

30. Ibid.

31. Guy R. Everson and Edward H. Simpson Jr., eds., *"Far, Far from Home":* *The Wartime Letters of Dick and Tally Simpson, Third South Carolina Volunteers* (New York: Oxford University Press, 1994), 23.

32. Ellen R. House, *"A Very Violent Rebel": The Civil War Diary of Ellen Renshaw House* (Knoxville: University of Tennessee Press, 1996), 136.

33. G. Ward Hubbs, ed., *Voices from Company D: Diaries by the Greensboro Guards, Fifth Alabama Infantry Regiment, Army of Northern Virginia* (Athens: University of Georgia Press, 2003), 297.

34. *Richmond Dispatch,* July 4, 1863.

35. Ibid., July 2, 1864.

36. Ibid.

37. Ibid.

38. *Daily Richmond Examiner,* July 5, 1864.

39. *Lynchburg Daily Virginian,* July 4, 1865.

40. Ibid.

41. *Richmond Dispatch,* July 6, 1866.

42. *Abingdon Virginian,* July 6, 1866.

43. *Lynchburg Virginian,* July 4, 1865.

44. Ibid., July 10, 1865.

45. *Richmond Examiner,* July 6, 1866.

46. *Richmond Dispatch,* July 6, 1866.

47. Ibid.

48. Ibid.

49. *Abingdon Virginian,* July 6, 1866.

50. *Richmond Dispatch,* July 4, 1867.

51. Ibid., July 5, 1867.

Trains, Canals, and Turnpikes

Transportation in Civil War Virginia, 1861–1865
Bradford A. Wineman

By 1864 a passenger fare on a Virginia railroad cost as much as twenty-five times what it had in 1861. The state's canal system was in a fatal downward spiral, and even the roads had been reduced to rutted wastes by the armies' traffic. Transportation had become almost a nightmare, crippling military and civilian movement alike. Yet Virginia's storied role as the central battlefield in the American Civil War has obscured how its transportation system played a critical part in the conduct of military operations, the welfare of the Confederacy's most populous state, and even in the politics of forging a new Confederate nation.

The development of Virginia's transportation network, however, began early, albeit innocuously, with the construction of the Little River Turnpike in 1785 connecting Alexandria to Aldie. Yet by the early nineteenth century, as populations spread westward beyond the Blue Ridge, creating means to move people and goods across the state became one of the Commonwealth's key political, economic, and social issues. Virginia formalized its movement for internal improvements with the establishment of the Board of Public Works in 1816. The board's mandate of providing better methods of transportation between the east and west became a constant yet volatile theme for the remainder of the antebellum period.[1]

All of Virginia's turnpikes began as toll roads that were built, operated, and maintained by corporations approved by the General Assembly and Board of Public Works. Although the state imposed no standards regarding amounts for tolls, types of surfaces, or dimensions on any of these roads, the board typically contributed nearly half of the funding for these companies as stockholders. As settlements in Virginia expanded westward, the turnpike movement became especially active in the Shenandoah Valley, with over a dozen roads constructed between 1830 and 1840. The most traveled of these was the famous Valley Turnpike that, after its completion in 1834, extended from Winchester to Staunton on an old Indian trail and would be the state's only macadamized road at the outset of the Civil War.[2]

From the days of its early settlement, eastern Virginia had benefited geographically from the numerous east-west-running rivers such as the Potomac, Rappahannock, York, and James, which provided farmers access to deepwater ports in the Tidewater such as Norfolk, Hampton Roads, and West Point. However, as crop production grew, these rivers became inadequate and occasionally hazardous for transporting larger cargoes eastward, as most were not deep enough for steamboats. In order to facilitate transportation around dangerous waterfalls and other obstacles in these rivers, as early as 1785 enterprising Virginians such as George Washington proposed a canal to connect Richmond to the region beyond the Blue Ridge Mountains. By the nineteenth century, the canal had become the pet project of the Board of Public Works as well as eastern politicians, who saw it as a means to appease the growing discontent in the west. The company constructed the canal alongside the James from the capital westward since the river was not continuously navigable above the falls to anything but rowboats and other small craft. The canal finally connected Richmond to Lynchburg in 1840 and extended to Buchanan by 1851, moving both passengers and goods from the capital to the west. While the James & Kanawha River Canal was the largest in the state, it was by no means the only one. Several smaller canals scattered throughout Virginia reflected the broader changes toward more efficient and available transportation designed to keep up with the rapidly developing market economy.[3]

As the prosperity of the western counties become increasingly intertwined with state-supported internal improvement funding, transportation projects factored more prominently into Virginia politics. With over $50 million appropriated during the antebellum period to develop interstate transportation, communities scrambled for funds and fostered intense local political rivalries. A large number of Virginians beyond the Blue Ridge perceived that state appropriations disproportionately benefited the east at the expense of the west. Many identified the James River Canal as a fitting example of a project that wasted state funds while producing little result. Political parties in the state drew more distinct lines in their platforms regarding internal improvements, as most Democrats complained bitterly about the burden of state debt, wishing to dismantle the public works and limit the legislature's power to borrow money for development projects. By 1861, the Board of Public Works had become focused more on politics than on promoting economic prosperity for the Commonwealth.[4]

In spite of the breakthrough initiated by canals and roads, neither would be nearly as significant to the development of the Old Dominion as the coming of the railroad. Virginia's first rail line, the Chesterfield Railroad, began operations just outside of Richmond in 1831 to transport coal excavated from the Midlothian Mines. The Commonwealth would never be the same after this momentous event. By 1861, seventeen railroads stretched throughout the Old Dominion, covering nearly 1,800 miles. Virginia ranked seventh among states in the Union in railroad mileage and first among the slaveholding states.[5] And until the war's outbreak, there was no end in sight for the development of railroads within the Commonwealth. The length of tracks had more than quadrupled in the 1850s alone. The railroad's expansion accelerated the momentum in the agricultural market economy started originally by turnpikes and canals just decades before. This new access gave small towns contact to markets while making the larger cities, particularly Richmond, into centers of trade, finance, and transportation. It became increasingly apparent to many Virginians that by the 1860s the future of the state's prosperity would be dependent upon the rate of its railroad construction and development. It also gave individual travelers a new freedom of movement not experienced in the days of roads and canals. The geographically remote southwestern counties of Virginia were now connected with eastern markets, bolstering their once-isolated economy. This social and fiscal integration with the rest of the Commonwealth, according to historian Kenneth Noe, also allowed slavery to thrive in this part of the state for the first time.[6]

When Virginia seceded from the Union on April 17, 1861, its railroads were in full operating condition and ready to perform. Four years later, the state's entire network would lie in near ruin. The railroads' ultimate failure by 1865 came not from their initial poor condition or operation but rather from the length of the war itself. The longer the war lasted, the more apparent became their fragility and the inability to sustain their success over a long, attritional war.

The greatest disadvantage endured by Virginia's railroads actually devel-

oped before the war. None of the state's railroad companies had the resources
to execute its own repairs and had grown dependent on the Northern states
and Europe for its supply of repair materials, particularly new rails. With
open access to these markets before the war, companies had little incentive to
stockpile crucial commodities, or the foresight to anticipate its necessity. The
lone exception came in 1863 when Richmond, Fredericksburg & Potomac
Railroad president Moncure Robinson traveled secretly to London and procured a supply of iron from English merchants.[7] Moreover, the handful of
facilities (rolling mills, foundries, repair shops, and so on) in Virginia used
before the war to provide support for the railroads were converted early in
the war to produce goods for the military. The Tredegar Iron Works, for
example, manufactured its last railroad engine in 1858 and focused exclusively on munitions and artillery pieces after 1861. Of the 113 engines that
comprised the five largest Virginia rail lines, 80 were manufactured in the
North.[8] Nor did these railroads have any way to replace engines through
either construction or purchase. With such few resources at their disposal,
the high wartime demand for railroad service forced the government to
authorize the cannibalization of lesser-used lines and send their tracks and
rails to those of more crucial importance, such as the Richmond & York
River, Manassas Gap, and Roanoke & Seaboard lines.[9]

In addition to deficiencies in material, Virginia's railroads suffered
from shortages in labor. Before the war, the railroad companies employed
hundreds of workers of all kinds: laborers, technicians, clerks, and administrators. But the call for volunteers for the army in 1861 and eventually
the conscription in 1862 depleted the personnel of every railroad in the
Commonwealth. Draft laws technically exempted railroad workers, but the
manpower-starved government did little to enforce this clause. While the
absence of laborers hindered operations, the loss of skilled personnel, such
as engineers, maintenance workers, and bookkeepers, devastated several
companies since such employees could not easily be replaced. Railroad
presidents protested vehemently to the state and Confederate governments
with little result until Congress eventually issued an amended conscription
policy in 1864, but this came too late in the war to have any effect.[10] But
even then railroad employees could not always avoid the call to the ranks,
such as occurred in the spring of 1864 when Grant's army closed down
on the Confederate capital, and the railroad and Tredegar Iron Works
workers were called to help man Richmond's defenses. Virginia railroads

also endured the same challenges maintaining its unskilled labor force, which consisted almost exclusively of slaves. Once the war began, neither the railroad companies nor the government could procure the number of slaves needed to keep proper maintenance on the rapidly degrading lines. Owners rarely hired away their bondsmen as they habitually ran away by the hundreds to nearby Union armies or were confiscated by enemy cavalry raids along the rail lines. Eventually, commanders pulled weary troops from the trenches around Richmond in late 1864 to repair the rail lines coming into the capital.[11]

Oftentimes the most dangerous obstacle that confronted the Virginia railroads was their own ownership. Individual companies vehemently refused to cooperate with other railroads, which they regarded as competition first and partners in a war effort a distant second. Owners almost never shared resources with fellow railroads for fear of giving their competitors an advantage. Railroad companies continued to eye each other with suspicion, to loan the rolling stock to one another with greatest reluctance. Presidents and superintendents leveled numerous complaints lamenting the abuse of cars borrowed by other railroads and citing difficulties retrieving equipment loaned to rival companies. Others refused to let any competitor utilize their lines under any circumstances. The Confederate government urged the companies to consolidate their efforts and resources to both compensate for shortages and to promote the good of the Confederacy. These requests typically went unheeded, causing delays, confusion, and logistical inefficiency throughout the war.[12]

The railroad lines that led into Richmond exemplified the ultimate absurdity of this collective lack of cooperation. Six separate lines funneled into the capital, more than any other city in Virginia, which made it the state's largest market. However, not one of these lines connected with any another. Their termini lay scattered throughout the city. The failure to join these lines forced passengers to wait in the city for up to an entire day in order to depart with a different company if traveling beyond Richmond. Freight had to be unloaded at one depot, hauled across town, and reloaded on cars at another, often at exorbitant cost. Freight still had to be unloaded and reloaded on other cars, as no company would willingly entrust its cars to another line. The high volume of troops and supplies being transported into the war capital made Richmond's lack of rail linkages a logistical nightmare. Frequently soldiers and cargoes were compelled to wait for days and even weeks before they could move to the next terminus. These stations became congested with troops, ordinance, quartermasters, and commissary stores, which accumulated into an organizational mess, causing even greater confusion and further delay.[13]

Proposals made by military logisticians and politicians to construct connecting lines in the capital raised the ire of not only the hypercompetitive railroad owners but also of many local citizens as well. Several Richmond entrepreneurs, particularly owners of hotels and transfer companies, made a lucrative business providing services for those individuals trapped in the city's gridlock and opposed every effort to provide connections for through traffic. In January 1862, a special committee convened to examine the option of the military controlling the railroads terminating in or passing through Richmond but soon dissolved with no results. Even the appeals of the respected Gen. Robert E. Lee, who was desperate for supplies tied up in the capital for his army in Petersburg, fell on deaf ears in the government.[14] Railroad executives argued that they could not proceed with such construction without a government loan. Eventually, they did construct a temporary line linking two of the termini, but the haste and indifference with which it was constructed did not make it a safe line for heavy freight. The citizens of both Richmond and Petersburg continued to oppose a permanent connection, so no further action was taken and the congestion persisted.[15]

In crises such as this, the Confederate politicians could do little to influence the decision making of the railroad companies. The government, however, could only blame itself for this dilemma as it made a conscious commitment not to interfere in the business of the railroad's management, even in time of war. This hands-off approach to Virginia railroads reflected the broader laissez-faire philosophy of Confederate political ideology. The Virginia state government did have board members on every major railroad in the state and required the companies to file annual reports with the state auditor. However, as a whole, both the Confederate Congress and the state legislature remained reluctant to use coercive measures to control the railroads. The Confederate government relied on persuasive language, urging the companies to consolidate resources both to offset shortages and in the name of patriotism, but to no avail. Even the frustrated Richmond newspapers lamented the self-interest of the railroads.[16] As a compromise, the Confederate government organized several conventions for all the railroad companies to meet with the government in order to discuss greater cooperation for the war effort. These meetings, both on the state and national level, did result in a limited amount of coordination and fare standardization but ultimately failed to meet the intended purpose of harmonizing all the separate companies in synchronization with the army's needs.

Fearing the specter of complete politico-military domination of the railroads, the Confederate government gave the responsibility of coordinating the railroads to underqualified and lower-ranking officers (a lieutenant colonel or colonel) with little military or political clout. The railroad presidents and government fought most often over the issue of fare prices. Several politicians expected gratis transportation of personnel and goods for the Confederate army. Railroad administrators, however, offered the government a reduced rate, typically half the full fare, at the war's outset as a token of good faith and patriotism. But since civilian passengers and cargo paid more money, military transport became a low priority. Plus, the railroads received no compensation from the government to repair damage inflicted on their tracks and facilities by the Union army. As these conditions made railroads less cooperative, the government looked for more control as the war wore on but only met with greater resistance. Individual companies continually acted as independent entities and articulated an increasing sensitivity to paternalistic interference. The Confederate government eventually acquired full control of the railroad system by early 1865 but not in time to save the collapsing rail networks or the war effort.[17]

The construction of the Piedmont Railroad typifies the Virginia railroad experience and all of its major problems during the Civil War. In spite of protests from President Davis, the Confederate Congress passed a bill in February 1862 appropriating $1 million for the construction of the Piedmont Railroad. The line would cover only the less than fifty miles between Danville, Virginia, and Greensboro, North Carolina, but would provide a vital connection between the Old Dominion and the various lines stretching southward into the heart of the Confederacy. Problems, however, plagued the road from the beginning. First, since the line crossed the state border, engineers had to rectify the differences in gauge width (the space between the rails) as North Carolina railroads utilized a 4 feet, 8½ inches gauge and most Virginia roads used 5 feet (since nearly all of the line traveled through North Carolina, they chose the former gauge as the standard). Procuring the rails themselves, however, was a separate dilemma. With Northern and European sources now inaccessible and local rolling mills defunct, the government resorted to cannibalizing smaller lines, particularly the Roanoke & Seaboard Railroad, as well as small North Carolina lines, but only after lengthy political consternation.

Once engineers acquired these already-worn-down tracks, they had to contend with a critical shortage of labor. Local landowners refused to hire out their slaves, forcing the government to pull soldiers from the winter quarters to complete the road's construction. Then, facing a critical shortage in supply, the administrators had to find rolling stock for the line. The track was finally completed on May 22, 1864, and did provide some temporary relief for Lee's army and Richmond during the remainder of the campaigns that year. However, the poor quality of the hastily constructed track, the decrepit state of the rolling stock, and the harsh winter weather led to numerous delays and wrecks. In the winter of 1864, the shortage of cars forced railroad officials reluctantly to dump off the side of the track much-needed supplies of food intended for Lee's starving troops. The railroad fell into Federal hands in April 1865, having accomplished little due to political stagnation, logistical inefficiency, and the overall dysfunctional relationship of the railroad companies and the Southern government.[18]

Despite all of the seismic changes brought on by the war and the needs of the government, the railroads endeavored to preserve prewar levels of services to the civilian population and businesses. Most of the Old Dominion's railroad lines maintained prices of passenger tickets at a steady rate for as long as they could given the conditions of the unstable economy, holding them at a fixed price until 1864. The Virginia Central attempted to keep passenger fares reasonable but progressively increased the cost of freight. The line succeeded in carrying 166,000 passengers in 1861, keeping pace with its prewar numbers. Passenger rates at the beginning of the war ranged from about 1¢ to 3¢ per mile, with the choice of traveling in either first- or second-class cars (a difference of 1¢ per mile in 1861).[19] The cars typically accommodated thirty to forty passengers, depending on the design and the railroad company. Some railroads, such as the Richmond & York River line, charged as much as 5¢ per mile, the highest fare in state. Most trains before the war offered few luxuries such as dining or sleeping cars, as interstate travel remained rare and travelers could reach any point within Virginia during daylight hours.[20] But travel became more limited during the war, as high rates for cargo transportation made passenger movement less of a priority for the railroads. All railroads made their best effort to keep passenger rates as affordable as possible but found themselves having to increase fares in order to keep up with the Confederacy's rapid currency inflation by 1863–1864. By late 1864, passengers on the Richmond, Fredericksburg & Potomac line paid as much as 25¢ per mile.[21]

Transporting commodities, however, presented a far more daunting challenge for the Old Dominion's railroads during the war. Even amenities as innocuous as firewood created a near crisis between the people, the government, and the railroad companies. By the winter of 1862, the major cities in Virginia suffered from a growing wood shortage. In November, the Confederate and state government put pressure on Virginia's railroads to transport more wood into the population centers, particularly Richmond. The railroad presidents, however, reacted strongly against this demand and chided the government for not acknowledging the fundamental realities of the railroads' decrepit condition. Some, such as Virginia Central president Edmund Fontaine, complained that his line did not have the cars available to get even a fraction of the wood demanded, even in peacetime. Others lamented the crisis in labor, citing the absence of native white workers and plantation owners' refusal to rent out their slaves at any price. Even if wood were available and loaded, the presidents argued, the labor shortage had caused the track condition to deteriorate so badly that the already-complicated process of transporting cargo to Richmond moved closer to impossible. The broken rails leading into the capital had already caused an increased number of derailments that the companies could ill afford given their inability to replace cars damaged in accidents. The railroads did what they could for the city, but these grim realities were a harbinger of things to come for Richmond's citizens.[22]

The growing demand for food in Virginia's cities placed a similar burden on the railroads, forcing both railroad companies and politicians to take desperate measures. When a late-season snowstorm prevented trains from entering Richmond with much-needed foodstuffs in late March 1863, it helped to precipitate the notorious Bread Riots.[23] Just one year later, critically low supplies forced all passenger trains from North Carolina to stop for several days in order to permit passage of corn to Richmond.[24] By the winter of 1864, the food shortage had reached a critical state for both army and civilians. Worn-out and destroyed track, lack of rolling stock, poor coordination, raids, and bad weather all contributed to the meager times on the front lines and in Virginia towns still in Confederate control. Food supplies waited for delivery in the Virginia countryside and neighboring states but often could not get into the cities because of the condition of the railroads. Out of desperation, Governor William "Extra Billy" Smith actually commandeered a train from the Richmond & York Railroad and sent it to the Deep South states in order to procure corn supplies for Virginia's starving citizens.[25]

Along with their responsibilities to serve as the lifeline for both the army and civilian populace by transporting much-needed supplies, the railroads also shouldered the responsibility to transport mail throughout the Commonwealth. Companies such as the Virginia Central accepted a contract from the Confederate government to transport mail, among its other commitments. However, in 1864, when the government fell behind in its payments to the railroad, Virginia Central Railroad superintendent Henry Whitcomb temporarily suspended postal service, resulting in a heated exchange between the two parties that lasted over a month.[26] Additionally, the postal service found plenty to complain about with the railroads, as delays, derailments, and the higher priority for military supplies frequently delayed the delivery of mail throughout the war for days and often weeks. The Confederate postal service, reflective of the government's general attitude, never established a truly amenable relationship with the railroads in Virginia, often failing to agree on rates, priority, and overall cooperation.

Still, the Virginia railroads maintained a surprising amount of success in spite of shortages and political problems, primarily due to the skill and dedication of the railroad owners themselves. The administrations of these companies found ways to make the best of the situations presented them in order to get people and cargo moved and, above all, to keep trains running.[27]

The Civil War also proved catastrophic for the state's canal transportation, particularly the James River Canal Company overseeing Virginia's largest man-made waterway. The company opened the canal's use to the Confederate government and gave priority to the transportation of troops and military cargo. However, the Confederate Congress only offered rates one-half of those paid to the railroad companies for the same service. Meanwhile, the blockade of Virginia's ports also drastically reduced the supply and demand for the movement of goods. These two factors crippled the company's revenues from the war's outset, and income continued to decline through the rest of the conflict. With revenue disappearing, the funds no longer existed to execute much-needed maintenance along the canal. Making matters worse, attempts at repairs suffered the same fate as the railroads experienced: severe shortages in labor—nearly all workers and mechanics were called to service by 1864—supplies, and funding. Then in 1864 the legislature of the newly formed state of West Virginia confiscated all portions of the canal west of the Allegheny Mountains. Finally, in the final months of the war, Gen. Philip Sheridan's cavalry destroyed major portions of the company's works at Scottsville and continued on to inflict damage all along the canal route.[28] When the Confederate capital of Richmond burned in April 1865, the fire destroyed both the company's general and toll offices, burning most of the contents. The damage inflicted on the canal system, along with the increasing functionality and spread of the railroad, rendered the canal obsolete shortly after the war ended.[29]

Just like their counterparts in the railroad and canal businesses, Virginia stagecoach companies struggled with the changing economic realities of the war. The larger towns throughout the state maintained their stagecoach lines to connect citizens with other locations not reachable by train. Nearly every sizable town still had coach lines providing much-needed transportation to neighboring communities more accessibly than the railroad, albeit over shorter distances. For those population centers close to the war front, civilian travel became increasingly difficult with the continual disruptions of combat operations. All stagecoach companies contended with the same financial burdens as other transportation industries; rapid inflation, scarce commodities, and shortages of horses, feed, repair parts, and labor caused several enterprises to close down altogether.[30]

Virginia's road network was as unprepared as the railroads to deal with the increased traffic of wartime. While antebellum roads and turnpikes may have been satisfactory for moving agricultural goods to market for civilians during peacetime, they proved woefully inadequate for the maneuvering of modern mass armies. Few roads other than the main turnpikes had ever been adequately mapped, often confusing commanders on both sides. Troops marching in the summer endured the choking dust only to contend with red clay paths that turned into quagmirelike mud during the winter months.[31]

The Old Dominion's railroad system proved vital to the success or defeat of the armies that campaigned there throughout the war. Many historians identify the Civil War as the first "modern war" wherein generals factored in railroad logistics as a key element of their operational and strategic plans.

With Virginia the primary theater of the war, the state's railroads were crucially important to both armies. Towns that had developed into railheads during the 1850s, such as Winchester, Manassas, Orange, and Lynchburg, now became locations of vital military importance and exchanged hands numerous times throughout the war. Meanwhile, cavalry and guerrillas invented and crafted methods of railroad destruction in an attempt to disable their enemy's capabilities by dismantling miles of track, destroying repair facilities, and cutting telegraph cables, particularly by 1864–1865.[32]

This new military reality of the strategic railroad became apparent in the first major engagement of the war during the Manassas campaign in July 1861. Confederate troops that arrived by train on the Manassas Gap line from Winchester helped turn the tide of the battle and routed Union forces. Ironically, a year later, at the second battle of Manassas, Federal troops, lethargically disembarking from their trains, did not arrive on the field in time to save the beleaguered army under Gen. John Pope. In September 1863, the daring relocation of Longstreet's 12,000-man corps from Virginia to Gen. Braxton Bragg's army in northern Georgia began at Orange Courthouse Depot on the Virginia & Tennessee line.

Railroads figured prominently in the operations of both armies during the 1864 Overland campaign, with both Lee and Gen. Ulysses S. Grant scrambling to either protect or capture key railheads sustaining the Army of Northern Virginia. The Confederate armies never lost a fight on the battlefield because of lack of rail support.[33] However, the deteriorating condition of Virginia's railroads both physically and administratively did have a gradual attritional effect on the logistical sustainment abilities of the Southern army, particularly by the 1864–1865 campaigns. Many historians identify the Federal capture of the Southside Railroad in March 1865 as the final death knell for Lee's army, as it cut off his last line of supply to Richmond and Petersburg.[34]

A great deal of the success enjoyed by Union armies operating in Virginia can be traced to their organization and application of their own rail system in the Old Dominion. Unlike the Confederates, the Federal army placed all of its railroads in the theater under control of the War Department with the creation of the United States Military Rail Road (USMRR). During Federal campaigns in Northern Virginia, the USMRR took advantage of national lines such as the Baltimore & Ohio as well as two main roads captured from the Confederates, the Orange & Alexandria and the Richmond, Fredericksburg & Potomac lines. Control of these roads, particularly the Richmond, Fredericksburg & Potomac, allowed the Army of the Potomac to establish a logistic base at Falmouth from which it supported nearly all of its operations against the Army of Northern Virginia. The port at Aquia Creek received barges loaded with railroad cars shipped from Washington via Alexandria. Federal railroaders then pulled them onshore to Falmouth on a new rail line constructed shortly after the port's capture.[35] Although it had its problems, the USMRR ironically made better use of the rail system in Virginia than did the Confederacy, demonstrating a level of precision, coordination, and efficiency that those lines lacked under Southern control.

In the weeks and months following the surrender at Appomattox, the Federal government worked to resurrect Virginia's railroads, canals, and roads, either by direct control or by providing them with much-needed supplies and maintenance equipment. Most were restored to full operation by the summer of 1865. Whereas before the war, these railroads were largely owned by indigenous stockholders, they now became completely reliant on Northern capital in order to survive. All too often, they devolved into pawns in the machinations of Northern financiers. Over time, these Old Dominion lines simply became elements of larger regional rail networks. Just as the war ended the controversy over the place of state rights in politics, it also marked the passing of state-managed transportation. The idea of the "Virginia" road, canal, and railroad died with the Confederacy.

Notes

1. William A. Link, *Roots of Secession: Slavery and Politics in Antebellum Virginia* (Chapel Hill: University of North Carolina Press, 2003), 20, 29, 132; William G. Shade, *Democratizing the Old Dominion: Virginia and the Second Party System, 1824–1861* (Charlottesville: University of Virginia Press, 1996), 43–44, 181–90; Carter Goodrich, "The Virginia System of Mixed Enterprise," *Political Science Quarterly* 64 (September 1949): 355–87.

2. Robert F. Hunter, "The Turnpike Movement in Virginia, 1816–1860" (Ph.D. diss., Columbia University, 1957).

3. Wayland Fuller Dunaway, *The History of the James River and the Kanawha Company* (New York: Longmans, Greens, 1922), 9–205. See also George William Bagby, *Canal Reminiscences: Recollections of Travel in the Old Days on the James River & Kanawha Canal* (Richmond: West, Johnston, 1879).

4. Philip M. Rice, "Internal Improvements in Virginia, 1775–1860" (Ph.D. diss., University of North Carolina, 1948); Link, *Roots of Secession,* 35.

5. *American Railroad Journal,* January 5, 1861.

6. Kenneth W. Noe, *Southwest Virginia's Railroad: Modernization and the Sectional Crisis* (Urbana: University of Illinois Press, 1994), 67–84.

7. Virginia Central Railroad Company, *Twenty-eighth Annual Report of the President and Directors of the Virginia Central Railroad Company, to the Stockholders, at Their Annual Meeting, November, 1863* (Richmond: M. Ellyson, 1863), 10–11.

8. Angus Johnston, "Virginia Railroads in April 1861," *Journal of Southern History* 23 (August 1957): 319.

9. U.S. War Department, *War of the Rebellion: A Compilation of Official Records of the Union and Confederate Armies* (Washington, D.C.: Government Printing Office, 1880–1901), series 1, vol. 18, 766–70, 951–52 (hereafter cited as *OR*); Johnston, "Virginia Railroads," 318; Michael B. Chesson, "Harlots or Heroines? A New Look at the Richmond Bread Riot," *Virginia Magazine of History and Biography* 92 (April 1984): 131–75.

10. Virginia Central Railroad Company, *Twenty-ninth Annual Report of the President and Directors of the Virginia Central Railroad Company, to the Stockholders, at Their Annual Meeting, November, 1864* (Richmond: M. Ellyson, 1864), 6–14.

11. *OR,* series 1, vol. 25, pt. 2, 683, 704–5.

12. Johnston, "Virginia Railroads," 314.

13. *Fourteenth Annual Report of the Richmond & Danville Railroad Company, Embracing the Reports of the President, Treasurer & Superintendant, Together with the Proceedings of the Stockholders* (Richmond: H. K. Ellyson, 1861), 200–205.

14. *OR,* series 4, vol. 1, 394–95.

15. Ibid., 485–86.

16. *Richmond Daily Enquirer,* September 16, 1864.

17. Charles W. Turner, "The Virginia Central Railroad at War, 1861–1865," *Journal of Southern History* 12 (November 1946): 511, 516.

18. *OR,* series 1, vol. 46, pt. 2, 1085–87, 1166–70.

19. *Annual Reports of the Rail Road Companies of the State of Virginia, Made to the Board of Public Works* (Richmond: Board of Public Works, 1861), 103–7.

20. Ibid., 74–75, 163, 243–44.

21. *Richmond Sentinel,* December 19, 1864.

22. Henry D. Whitcomb to Edmund Fontaine, November 7, 1862, Virginia

Central Railroad Company Records, 1837–69, Library of Virginia, Richmond; Turner, "The Virginia Central Railroad," 522–23.

23. *Richmond Dispatch,* April 3, 1863; *Richmond Enquirer,* April 3, 1863.

24. Charles W. Ramsdell, "The Confederate Government and the Railroads," *American Historical Review* 22 (July 1917): 801.

25. John W. Bell, ed., *Memoirs of Governor William Smith of Virginia: His Political, Military, and Personal History* (New York: Moss Engraving, 1891), 57–60.

26. Virginia Central Railroad Company, *Correspondence between the President of the Virginia Central Railroad Company and the Postmaster General, in Relation to Postal Service* (Richmond: Ritchie and Dunnavant, 1864), 3–25.

27. Angus J. Johnston, "Disloyalty on Confederate Railroads in Virginia," *Virginia Magazine of History and Biography* 63 (October 1955): 410–26. Ironically, a good number of these administrators were Northerners who had migrated to Virginia during the antebellum era but remained in the Old Dominion after secession. Suspicions of their disloyalty spread throughout Virginia and the South, particularly when despair and dissolution flourished during the later years of the war. Allegedly, a handful of railroad men in Richmond furnished besieging Federals in 1864–1865 with valuable information concerning the condition of General Lee's army and his transportation system, although the evidence is still unclear. Most railroad men, however, considered their first duty to be to the railroad, regardless of their state of birth. Betraying the railroad and the Confederate war effort did not make practical sense for these men, as any information afforded to the enemy could have led to the disabling of the railroad and therefore cost them their livelihood. While a handful of the company executives hailed from Northern states, nearly all of the workers and laborers were local Southerners, making any potential espionage or the accusation of doing such a dangerous proposition. Those who did allegedly demonstrate disloyalty appear to have done so out of greedy self-interest rather than dedicated patriotism to the Union cause.

28. *New York Times,* March 18, 1865.

29. Dunaway, *History of the James River and the Kanawha Company,* 205–9.

30. Charles Henry Ambler, *West Virginia: The Mountain State* (New York: Prentice Hall, 1940), 254–58; Douglas Southall Freeman, *Lee's Lieutenants: A Study in Command* (New York: C. Scribner's Sons, 1942), 1:684–85.

31. Freeman, *Lee's Lieutenants,* 1:684–85.

32. *OR,* series 1, vol. 46, pt. 1, 479–85.

33. Christopher R. Gabel, *Rails to Oblivion: The Decline of Confederate*

Railroads in the Civil War (Fort Leavenworth, Kan.: Combat Studies Institute, U.S. Army Command and General Staff College, 2002), 9.

34. Robert C. Black, *The Railroads of the Confederacy* (Chapel Hill: University of North Carolina Press, 1998), 282–87; Charles W. Turner, "The Virginia Southwestern Railroad System at War, 1861–1865," *North Carolina Historical Review* 24 (October 1947): 481. For further reading on the role of railroads in Civil War strategy, see George Edgar Turner, *Victory Rode the Rails: The Strategic Place of Railroads in the Civil War* (Lincoln: University of Nebraska Press, 1992); John E. Clark Jr., *Railroads in the Civil War: The Impact of Management on Victory and Defeat* (Baton Rouge: Louisiana State University Press, 2001).

35. Herman Haupt, *Reminiscences of General Herman Haupt* (Milwaukee: Wright and Joys, 1901), 165–71.

"We are all good scavengers now"

The Crisis in Virginia Agriculture during the Civil War
Ginette Aley

As 1864 approached, a poor woman in Richmond applied to a Carey Street merchant to buy a barrel of flour. He demanded $70. "My God!" she exclaimed, "how can I pay such prices? I have seven children; what shall I do?" "I don't know, madam," he coolly replied, "unless you eat your children."[1] At the same time, a waggish city newspaperman suggested that the poor be fed with worthless Confederate paper money, and that certain classes of merchants and society should subsist by eating each other.[2] Three years of war, with no end in sight, had turned a state that once had been a granary of the South into a scene of hardship and near starvation.

In agriculture, an old, sensible adage cautions farm people against grinding the seed corn; that is, grinding next year's seed corn in trying to meet the food needs of the present. To do so would put one's family at great risk with regard to long-term independence and survival. More broadly, a regional agricultural-based economy that emphasizes and protects highly profitable staple cash crops at the obvious expense of food crops and sustenance creates a serious, if not fatal, disadvantage and vulnerability for itself and its people in meeting an exigent crisis such as war. The Confederacy faced the consequences of its agricultural history from the early days of the secession crisis.[3]

The new Confederate nation comprised a region with a long economic history of being dominated by the major plantation cash crops of tobacco, cotton, sugarcane, and rice, while yet being significantly dependent upon what is now the Midwest for essential foodstuffs, including pork, bacon, beef, livestock, flour, wheat, barley, corn, and oats to supplement its own harvests. Along with a considerable range of manufactured goods, Southerners also

81

sought agricultural products like coffee, butter, cheese, Irish potatoes, and fruits as well as hay, horses, and mules from outside the region. Recognizing the problem but apparently not the dire magnitude of it, the Confederate Provisional Congress in February 1861 immediately moved to pass an act that would allow the continued procuring of foodstuffs from the Midwest (formerly called the Old Northwest states). However, the act was, like this early Confederate Congress, provisional in that a move from secession to war would dramatically alter what the largely pro-Union Midwest states would or could do with regard to supplying foodstuffs to the Confederacy. Indeed, by July the U.S. Congress halted this commerce, some of which continued through the border states, especially Kentucky. Even if generally comprehended at the time, the insurmountable problem facing the Confederate South was, as noted agricultural historian Paul W. Gates explained, that it simply "was not accustomed to feeding itself."[4]

In the decades preceding secession, especially during the 1840s and 1850s, agrarian reformers had in fact advocated a series of important fundamental changes to Southern agriculture that they hoped would put the region on a more secure footing as compared to the rapidly developing North and the emerging agriculturally productive Midwest. They urged better, more progressive farming methods, expanding railroad lines to improve market connections and distribution, and a readjustment of the regional economy that would, among other things, fill the manufacturing gap. Certainly, reformers contended, talk of independence necessitated these changes. Apparently they were correct. As the prosecution of the Civil War soon made painfully clear, particularly to Virginians, sustenance was an elusive resource that was variously in agonizingly short supply, threatened by an out-of-control Confederate currency, made unobtainable because of extraordinary market prices, hoarded and speculated on, stolen by the hungry, taken by impressments officers, woefully mismanaged by officials, and foraged or destroyed by Union soldiers. In Virginia by 1864, but certainly evident in 1863, it all boiled down to food.[5]

"Virginians," as historian William Blair aptly observes, "fought no abstraction." War was brought to their outskirts and barnyards time and time again because of the state's strategic proximity to the North and its housing of the Confederacy's capital, Richmond. Their lives were threatened, their property destroyed, their crops and livestock confiscated by Union troops or Confederate impressments officials, depending on the situation. The year

1864 witnessed Union campaigns that exacerbated an already tenuous food supply and distribution dilemma concerning the feeding of troops and civilians: battles at the Wilderness, Spotsylvania, Cold Harbor, repeated threats of assault on Richmond, the siege of Petersburg, and the inauguration of a deliberately destructive Union raiding strategy in the Shenandoah Valley throughout the summer and fall. Union raiding at this stage of the war was devastatingly effective and ruinous to hungry Virginians, reflecting what historian Mark Grimsley notes as the Union's new "hard war" program. In it, the Confederacy's economic infrastructure, including its food, mills, and rail lines along with civilians' barns and fields, were all targeted for destruction, foraging, or, as in the case of horses, cattle, mules, and food at hand, confiscation.[6]

The repeated raids in northern Virginia are also noteworthy in that the area happened to be one of the vital general farming regions of the South. There, the strategy of raiding in 1864 worked to diminish the supply and distribution of food crops even further, to a famine level in many parts of the state, but perhaps most notoriously in Richmond. Unfortunately for the Confederate cause, raiding and wartime circumstances also dramatically exposed the risks that the South as a region, and many planters and farmers in general, had been long willing to take: privileging the cultivation of commercial cash crops over foodstuffs on the assumption that it was cheaper to buy food elsewhere (both intra- and extraregionally) than to give up acreage devoted to market crop production. The end result was ironic and contradictory. As geographer Sam Bowers Hilliard describes, overall, the antebellum South produced impressive quantities of food products; yet, "abundant evidence" shows that it nonetheless encountered food shortages even prior to secession. Plantation or mono-crop agriculture left numerous crippling legacies in its wake, the foremost of which was slavery. But with regard to the South's food economy, it ultimately imposed a serious disadvantage upon the Confederacy in having directed attention and interest away from the development of sustained, organized agricultural diversification, interior food markets, and essential transportation links as the East had accomplished and the emerging Midwest was accomplishing. These are important fundamental elements of a growing complex diversified agricultural system and food economy.[7]

The South's food economy, then, was uneven at best and required considerable and awkward movement of foodstuffs into and throughout the region.

Tennessee, Kentucky, and the Midwest comprised the major food surplus areas from which the South was fed, but, as noted above, the Midwest and to some extent Kentucky were removed from this equation with the formal outbreak of hostilities. This alteration in circumstances, compounded by wartime requirements, resulted in increasingly desperate food shortages, forcing Virginia soldiers and civilians to scramble for substitutes or, by 1863 and 1864, nearly anything at all to eat. It is interesting to consider what was commonly eaten, with variation, prior to the shortages. Southern foodways chiefly centered upon pork (and bacon) and corn, supplemented with sweet and Irish (white) potatoes, peas, turnips, cabbage, and okra. Fruit and gathered food included peaches, apples, plums, persimmons, nuts, and berries. Catfish, sucker, and shad provided some diversity in meat, as did chickens and hunted game; however, for several reasons neither the beef cattle nor dairy industries were well developed in the South by the Civil War.[8]

Despite the South's troubled food economy, Virginia's agriculture by 1860 had attained a level of diversification (tobacco, grain, livestock, and market garden crops), self-sufficiency, reformism, even prosperity—but it was not universal. One study that examines the agricultural patterns of primarily three counties (but extended to incorporate four adjacent counties) of the lower Shenandoah Valley between 1845 and 1856 provides a useful view of one Virginia subregion's farming and food production on the eve of secession, and before being subjected to Union raiding. Unlike other parts of the state or region, these Virginians produced and ate well. Their work in grain cultivation adorned the Valley with the characterization of being the granary of the Confederacy. Their diet reflected basic Southern foodways fare except in greater abundance, especially with regard to meat, and it included the production of dairy products. Their farms averaged 250 acres in size, much of which was used to provide feed for their animals, livestock, and poultry. With regard to the family's food production, Valley farmers typically put at least 8 acres in wheat, perhaps 5 acres in corn, and less than an acre combined for potatoes and a kitchen garden, while leaving a great deal of the land in its natural wooded state. On the farms overall, they would have raised about 80 acres of corn, 120 acres in small grain (winter wheat was preferred), and they would have kept approximately sixty-five head of cattle, five cows, fifteen horses, twenty sheep, and ninety hogs. Smaller-scale farmers with farms of half that size usually cultivated about 20 acres of corn, 43 in wheat, and kept a smaller number of animals at hand. Valley farm people grew very little tobacco—wheat was the money crop. As a result, the slave population in these counties was considerably smaller by percentage than the 33 percent slaves comprised of the total population in 1850 in the state of Virginia. Finally, home manufactures centered upon linen making, with the raising of flax, hemp, and sheep for wool.⁹

These successful, general grain-producing Valley farmers were not typical of either Virginia or Southern farmers, although the region's major agricultural paper, the *Southern Cultivator,* would have liked for that to be the case. Just as the Provisional Confederate Congress moved quickly to try to protect an already inadequate food economy, so, too, did the farm press. Farmers were exhorted often to put patriotism over profits and pull back from planting cotton in favor of provision crops, especially corn. "We are cut off from the provision markets of the Northwest, upon which we have been in the habit of relying," the paper lamented. "[N]o other resource is now left us but self-dependence." Farmers and soldiers were presented as waging the same battle, but on different fields: "This war is to be fought out as much with the plow as with the sword." Initially, it appeared to be only a matter of logistics. That is, farmers needed simply to transfer their efforts and labor force from cotton production toward cultivating corn, along with double and triple amounts of oats, hay, potatoes, beets, peas—"all possible supplies for man and beast." Plantation crops of rice and sugar were still important to the food economy, but increasingly the call was for more wheat, garden vegetables, livestock feed, or provision crops for the armies and the home front. Confederate state governments were not as inclined to depend upon patriotic voluntarism alone. Saltworks, invaluable for meat preservation, were seized and subjected to rationing. Whiskey distilleries were shut down, probably less out of concern for temperance than for keeping grain crops freed for bread-making instead of whiskey distilling.¹⁰

The war compelled change not only to the dynamics of Southern farming and food production, but also to its dimensions, prompting new considerations, methods, and routines. For example, the *Southern Cultivator* now strongly advocated the added cultivation of winter crops, which many agriculturists had long avoided in the belief that these would interfere with the chief summer crops. With the exception of cotton, the paper insisted, this would not be the case given the South's climate; moreover, the time was at hand to pursue (at least for the short term) a "circle of continuous production" in the face of a "wasting war," blockaded ports, and the ruinous prices of meat and breadstuffs. A suggested basic cropping strategy was to plant an early corn crop, succeeded by a hay crop, then followed by wheat, rye, turnips, carrots, or winter grass. An obvious advantage of this scheme was the harvesting of winter crops at a time when the usual provision crops were getting low. At the same time, cultivating an increased amount of food crops meant that farm people would be harvesting more of those crops than usual and would need to deal with the abundance to ensure the produce remained edible and did not spoil. The farm press urged greater efforts at drying fruits and vegetables, especially those headed for the armies. "Beets, carrots and other roots, may be grated and dried," the *Southern Cultivator* recommended, "and tomatoes, okra, etc., sliced and dried, then packed away in cloth bags or boxes."[11]

Guarding against and dealing with impending shortages and scarcity colored everything, altering routines, uses, and more. "Save Everything," proclaimed the *Lynchburg Republican* in 1863; "every imaginable kind of edibles will command high prices this winter, and our country friends should make it a point to save as much of everything of the kind as is possible." In all of this, the gender implications are quite apparent. Home front women found their food ingenuity challenged in the need to continue feeding their families without the usual items at hand. Families still had to be fed. Home manufacture of scarce but necessary nonfood items such as soap, candles, dyes, ink, and clothing articles also needed to be increased and kept up. As the war dragged on and access to foodstuffs became more difficult, mainly due to inflation and the military's competing need for available foodstuffs, women's ideas for substitutes became an important commodity in themselves, and their recipes were published in farm and local papers as well as shared and exchanged among family and friends. Substitutes for flour (rice, sorghum seed, cornmeal) and coffee (ground sweet potatoes, rye, acorns) were among the most common, as were suggestions for how to preserve meat without the usual amount of salt. Similarly, waste involving the precarious food supply was denounced wherever it was found. Deteriorating conditions provoked a sense of helplessness over the situation, such as the criticism that corn was being wasted as a result of having to be shipped in rotten bags. The *Southern Cultivator* reported that not a day passed "that it cannot be seen trailing from the drays and wagons, as it is hauled through the streets." This was in addition to the "almost incredible" level of waste observed at railroad depots and warehouses, which was hard for starving

Richmonders to accept. One such observer grieved at knowing that some 40,000 bushels of sweet potatoes sat rotting at depots between Richmond and Wilmington.[12]

Shifting agriculturists' efforts toward increased production of provision crops had a racial dynamic as well, as slave owners manipulated their enslaved population in a number of ways. Plantation agriculture was by its nature more labor intensive than was general farming and food production. The pressure to shift attention away from planting cotton and tobacco, then, caused concern among slave owners about the potential for their labor force to become idled. More time on their hands, writers to *Southern Cultivator* theorized, meant that they would be susceptible to troublemaking, perhaps especially in Virginia, where the frequent battles with Union forces suggested the possibilities for escape and freedom. Some slave owners approached the new labor circumstance with a degree of optimism in completing new tasks, as seen in the words of one overseer, who volunteered: "We shall fix our fences and hedges; we shall move the negro cabins, and put them up right, and in order, and with brick chimneys. We shall do a heap, that we have heretofore left undone." Dealing with food shortages, at least ostensibly, also caused slave owners to contemplate ways to feed their slaves with less—for example, how to cook "Negro Food" in a way that would reduce the amount of bacon previously allotted them. "Of course it is impossible now to give out the old rations of meat to our negroes," the paper complained, "but the improvidence of our people heretofore, in raising home supplies, is at the bottom of the whole matter." In early 1864, to enable more subsistence to go to the army, slave owners were urged to reduce slave rations further by substituting molasses syrup (made from sorghum) for bacon to accompany the corn bread and whatever plantation vegetables could be found. No doubt increasing famine conditions gave added incentive to many slaves to flee toward Union lines.[13]

From 1863 to the war's end, the urging of farmers to plant more food and the assurances that the Confederacy still could produce more than a sufficiency had a hollow ring to it—as hollow and empty as the stomachs of Southern soldiers and civilians. Thoughts of spring planting brought forth a closer scrutiny of the food crisis. "[T]his year, owing to the fact that a considerable portion of country, from which last year supplies were drawn, is now in the hands of the enemy," the *Southern Cultivator* warned, "and that a still larger extent of country has been desolated and laid waste by the contending armies, greater exertions will be necessary, or the people will suffer and the cause perish." Conditions were serious. The previous wheat crop had failed, and most other crops had been "greatly diminished" because of the past summer's "extraordinary drought." Then there was the matter of the shortage of seed, which increasingly had to be obtained by blockade-runners. "Surely," the paper's next issue remarked, "the considerate mind must see, and the honest mind ought to admit, that here is to be found the weakest point in our defences." Indeed, fields were largely unmanned due to the fact that such a disproportionately large number of men were away serving as soldiers, a fact that elicited harsh criticism from this point forward in the farm and local press. Among the policies that angered Southerners the most (and there were many), judging by the frequent condemnations in 1864, were those involving military exemptions. The calls to repeal all exemptions in order to put every able-bodied man in the army had severe implications for an already withering food supply. They caused many to wonder who, then, would be left to cultivate the crops, raise the livestock, and produce the supplies. "We need every man in the field, it is true;" an observer remarked, "but it is the 'corn field,' chiefly." At the same time, the *Richmond Daily Dispatch* reported that 114,000 applications had been made for agricultural details in the Confederacy, and that "very many of them" had been rejected. Its effect was apparent to one government clerk, who noted in October that farmers whose details had been rejected were arriving in the city on a daily basis to head back to the battlefields.[14]

The crucible of war and its miseries, especially as they related to food scarcity, had been enacted upon Richmond well before 1864; their conse-quences were easily discernible throughout the Confederate capital. The most notorious incident was the Bread Riot of April 2, 1863, involving from several hundred to upward of a thousand participants, mainly women, the so-called woman mob. The context for the riot was a dangerous accumula-tion of factors—generally not confined to Richmond—that contrived to keep food at arm's length from the hungry city dwellers. These factors included competing demands between the military and civilians for the diminished food supply, the disruption of food production as a result of nearby military actions, a dramatic upsurge in the population as a result of the war's refugees and more (that is, bureaucrats, military prisoners, opportunists of all kinds), the presence of many soldiers' wives with families having difficulty obtaining food and surviving, the much-maligned food speculators and "extortioners," who by withholding items from the market jeopardized many, and a significant snowfall less than two weeks previously that affected the movement of food into the city. As historian Michael B. Chesson demonstrates, Richmond's Bread Riot was neither isolated nor spontaneous. More than a dozen other food riots and raids, usually comprised of women, have been documented, from as early as December 1862 (Greenville, Alabama) and February 1863 (Bladensboro, North Carolina) to the weeks immediately preceding Richmond's Bread Riot—March 16 (Atlanta), March 18 (Salisbury, North Carolina), March 25 (Mobile), and April 1 (Petersburg). Prior organization is evident. The Richmond Bread Riot had been preceded by a meeting the evening before at a church in the working-class community of Oregon Hill involving a number of the riot's leaders, such as Mary Jackson and Martha Fergusson. There, the women determined to demand food from the governor the next day and to bring along axes and hatchets so that, should they be denied, they would have the means to take it from the merchants. In fact, their demands for "Bread or Blood" were dismissed by the authorities, upon which the rioting and looting commenced in the business district. Two hours later it was over; however, the "Cry for Bread," threats and acts of mobbing, and the "Bread Question" persisted throughout 1864.[15]

Given the extreme circumstances, the prevalence of crime involving food in Richmond throughout 1864, from vandalism to stealing, is not surprising. Confederate clerk and Richmond diarist John B. Jones recorded on February 26 that "writings upon the walls of the houses at the corners of the streets were observed this morning, indicating a riot, if there be no amelioration of the famine." The *Richmond Daily Dispatch*, in reporting the cases in front of the Mayor's Court and other "Local Matters," was replete with accounts of incidents of food stealing. To a notable degree, in 1864 many of those reported involved slaves or free blacks, prompting the paper to warn about "Negro Street Thieves." For example, on April 1 two slaves were charged with cow stealing. Three days later, three slaves (who had been armed with pistols) were charged with robbing a meat house, another slave stole a half peck of flour, for which he was whipped, and a "negro fellow named William" was charged with having stolen ten pounds of beef from a market stall. Along with meat houses and market stalls, common targets for stealing foodstuffs were domestic larders, storehouses, gardens, dairy yards, and city-bound carts on the outskirts. Quite often these robberies took place at night, such as the taking of $1,000 worth of bacon from a private storeroom that one man kept above his store, and the midnight raiding of one woman's larder. A kitchen servant in the household of a Mrs. Trowbridge was awakened by the sound of footsteps in the yard, but her movement caused the potential thieves to run away. Believing that they would not return, the servant went back to bed. In the morning, however, the family discovered that a "successful haul" had been made upon its larder, "and all the groceries on hand, consisting of about half a bushel of meal, five or six pounds of bacon, some coffee and sugar, and other articles of lesser value" had been stolen. In another instance (which was noted as being identical to one the day before), a servant of Samuel Ayres was alerted to an outside noise after midnight. He discovered a black man pulling up onions from the garden, who then ran away. The servant demanded that he stop, and when he did not, he repeatedly fired a gun at him. The next morning, the onion stealer, "about whom nothing could be ascertained," was found dead.[16]

By all accounts, these depredations on private property were occurring on a daily and nightly basis. No one was overlooked by the food thieves. An elderly black couple who lived in a shanty came face-to-face with a group of thieves making off with their small stock of provisions. Exemplifying the social unrest that pervaded famine-stricken Richmond, the paper reported that "the perpetrators of this outrage were black skins, but it is believed that they were white persons in disguise." Groups of young white boys also committed food-related robberies, such as the three (the oldest of whom was about twelve) who robbed an ambulance cart of liquor, sugar, powder, shot, a pistol, and a box of pistol cartridges, and the two who absconded with a jar of pickles. Most distressing, according to the *Richmond Daily Dispatch,* was thieving committed by Confederate soldiers on the property of Confederate citizens. Numerous complaints had been made about soldiers raiding gardens and plundering carts of produce on the way to market in Richmond and in other areas of the state such as Lynchburg. "No good soldier," the paper asserted, "would be guilty of acts of this description." Yet, these acts were so disruptive that the commander at Lynchburg, Gen. Raleigh Colston, proclaimed that hereafter offenders would be prosecuted under the fifty-second Article of War—namely, "Any officer or soldier who shall quit his post or colors to plunder and pillage . . . being duly convicted thereof, shall suffer death, or such other punishment as shall be ordered by the sentence of a general court-martial." The paper wondered aloud if perhaps the commander at Richmond should follow Colston's lead.[17]

Many Virginians, especially Richmonders, believed that the most serious depredations were occurring daily at the markets, at the hands of hucksters (peddlers), merchants, and the oft-derided "extortioners" and speculators. Indeed, a public appeal for a market police was made. The problem of the markets, however, was more complex and was really the convergence of the ills of the South's food economy, war-related actions and Confederate policies, out-of-control inflation, a broken-down, ineffectual transportation system, and, apparently, opportunistic greed, self-interest, and official incompetence. "There is madness in our counsels!" war clerk Jones concluded at the end of 1864. More than Unionist sympathizers and plotters, these factors represented the enemy from within, for all of the suffering and demoralizing they caused civilians and soldiers alike.[18]

The Richmond food markets were grim places. Typically, after 1862, as one woman remarked, "the markets were so ill supplied that they had almost as well been closed." Another stated that "the storerooms became almost empty and our fare was very frugal." A review of the published market prices of the major food items in 1863 illustrates the dilemma going into 1864. In early January 1863, corn sold for $3.50 per bushel, corn meal for $3.50–$3.75 per bushel, molasses (for a sweetener) for $7 per gallon (scarce), rice for 9¢ per pound (for old), bacon for 65¢–70¢ per pound, Irish potatoes for $3–$4 per bushel, and sweet potatoes for $5–$7 per bushel. By March, one month before the Bread Riot, the *Richmond Daily Dispatch* was reporting that the city's supplies were "very limited" and that prices were "enormously high." In June, corn (scarce) had risen to $10 per bushel, corn meal (scarce) was going for $11–$12 a bushel, molasses for $10.50–$11 per gallon, and rice for 18¢–20¢ per pound. August saw some decline in prices, but not enough. Corn sold for $9–$10.50 per bushel, corn meal for $9.25–$9.50 per bushel, molasses for $14 per gallon, rice for 20¢–25¢ per pound, and bacon for $2–$2.10 per pound. The scarcity of flour, believed to be caused by speculators, provoked the paper to ask, "Will the Government and people stand by and see the country overrun and ruined by these vampyres [*sic*] in trade?" and suggest that they be rounded up and marched to the front. By the end of October, there was virtually no supply of flour, and the only known sale of corn meal was at $13 per bushel. Molasses sold for $18 per gallon, bacon for $2.60–$2.75 per pound, Irish potatoes for $8–$12 per bushel, and sweet potatoes for $15–$17 per bushel, all of which constituted a significant increase since January.[19]

City market prices continued their steady advance in 1864. In mid-March the paper reported that the supply of breadstuffs was more abundant than it had been for six months, although the prices remained out of reach for many. Flour was selling for $230–$275 a barrel, while corn meal was now $40 a bushel. Bacon sold for $7–$7.50 per pound, molasses for $41.50 per gallon, rice for 90¢–95¢ per pound, dried apples for $2.10 per pound, and $5 for a half pint of snap beans to plant. Confederate clerk Jones noted famine's arrival that month, and that the market houses, though somewhat stocked, were deserted because of the unobtainable prices. In April he wrote that the famine was becoming "more terrible" with each day's passing; "soon," he added, "no salary will suffice to support one's family." By June, the *Dispatch* no longer itemized market prices and instead began inserting only a brief descriptive paragraph that simply noted the supply levels and a general statement about prices—and the exorbitant price of butter, at $15 per pound, which was regularly denounced. City markets were not only grim but acrimonious and hostile places as well, whenever a merchant's or huckster's behavior appeared to be suspiciously or outright egregiously designed to gain a profit in the midst of widespread starvation. Reported incidents included short-weighting butter, "forestalling the market" (the practice of buying market-bound foodstuffs and immediately reselling at a higher price in the market), the near mobbing and lynching of a man in May who priced a barrel of flour at $500 and three bushels of corn meal at $100 each, and the city council's expulsion of unscrupulous merchants.[20]

Virginians' constant public outcry in 1863 and 1864 was that they were being denied the "necessaries of life," specifically foodstuffs. While they had legitimate grievances about the food crisis against the government and those who manipulated the markets, their harsh accusations against the farmers seem more the result of the desperate situation than grounded in fact. Farmers throughout the Confederacy were roundly and repeatedly accused of hoarding their produce and meat and keeping them off the market in order to obtain a better price, either from the commissary agents procuring food for the army or from market sales to civilians. Typical of the condemnations and blame was the January 11, 1864, *Richmond Daily Dispatch* sarcasm: "If the farmers of Virginia prefer the condition of the people of Culpeper, Norfolk, and New Orleans, to their present state, they have only to keep fast their grip on their corn and wheat, and their desires can be gratified." Confederate clerk Jones believed that Richmonders were "starving in the midst of plenty," and that hoarding farmers had best take heed or the Union raiders would take it all anyway. Indeed, they did that summer. And when rural Virginians sent in letters to the *Dispatch* detailing how the raiders, for example, "took every vegetable and gooseberry, [and] walked into the house and deliberately stole all the flour we had and carried it off," they were blindsided again. The *Dispatch* followed these up on July 9 with a cynical profession of surprise to hear that such large quantities of provisions had actually been taken by the Yankees since prior to this none had been made available to the starving Richmonders or the army. It had "no pity to spare for hoarders and extortioners."[21]

Virginia's farm population was unfairly blamed for the situation. In reality farmers were truly squeezed in a number of ways. At every turn their harvests, commodities, livestock, feed, and draft animal power (horses and mules) were threatened with being impounded—by either side. And what there was to sell was subject to the vicissitudes of the markets, poor transportation, and the commissary agents. Very early on the Confederate government and the army pursued an impressment policy that theoretically gave officials the power to seize whatever was deemed necessary to support the military effort. Farmers were usually paid considerably less than open market prices. As the gap between government price and market price widened, compounded by shortages and worthless currency, some Virginia farmers (and others in the Confederacy) resisted the squeeze and apparently reduced their planting to subsistence levels or withheld produce from the market. "Everywhere," war clerk Jones noted, "the people are clamorous against the sweeping impressments of crops, horses, etc." Market-bound carts were frequently impressed, thus diverting food headed for famine areas like Richmond to the equally hungry soldiers. Farmers were singled out again by the tithing tax incorporated into the Revenue Act of April 24, 1863, in which they had to pay a 10 percent tax in kind on their produce after setting aside a reserve of foodstuffs, according to designated amounts, for home consumption. Virginia farmers resisted this as well. Understandably, then, Confederate farmers and planters were stung by the wholesale accusations against them. We are "farmers not extortioners," a *Southern Cultivator* writer insisted. While conceding that some planters were not blameless, he asserted that producers as a whole did not deserve the "severe censure" that had been heaped upon them. "People have got a very foolish idea in their heads," he explained, "that whatever is made by a farmer at home, costs him nothing."

Moreover, the paper publicly admonished the "provision hoarders" among them and had emphatically urged from the beginning that "we ought to feed the poor" and soldiers' families.[22]

"We are all good scavengers now," quipped war clerk Jones in early 1864. By then Virginia's complex and devastating food crisis had proven the reality of the fatal disadvantage arising from the South's agrarian history. Yet, Virginians met the crisis emboldened by courage, remarkable endurance, a creative food ingenuity, and an insistence that their government ensure that the "necessaries of life" not be denied them because of profit or mismanagement. In the end, and for a variety of reasons, the Confederate government and its agents failed the people. But the war gave agriculturists pause for reflection. The reformers had been right to seek progressive change, contended G. D. Harmon, a soldier who had served two years in Virginia before becoming disabled. Addressing his fellow farmers in the *Southern Cultivator,* Harmon wrote: "Time has demonstrated the fact, that the doctrine which you and I, and many of your old correspondents advocated so long and earnestly, of making the South agriculturally independent of the North and North west, was correct." Had such a policy been followed, the urgent legislative actions and appeals for subsistence would not be, he argued, what they currently were. For now, though, attention would have to focus upon surviving both the food crisis and the war. Thoughts about a new Southern agricultural economy would have to wait for another day.[23]

Notes

1. John B. Jones, *A Rebel War Clerk's Diary* (1866; repr., Alexandria, Va.: Time-Life, 1982), 2:78.

2. William C. Davis, "The Virginian Wartime Scrapbook: Preserving Memories on Paper," in William C. Davis and James I. Robertson Jr., eds., *Virginia at War, 1863* (Lexington: University Press of Kentucky, 2008), 111.

3. See Emory M. Thomas, *The Confederate Nation, 1861–1865* (New York: Harper and Row, 1979), 199–200.

4. *Acts and Resolutions of the First Session of the Provisional Congress of the Confederate States* (Richmond, 1861), 41; the only book specifically on the subject is Paul W. Gates, *Agriculture and the Civil War* (New York: Knopf, 1965), 5 (quote) and chap. 1; a useful though limited study is John Solomon Otto, *Southern Agriculture during the Civil War Era, 1860–1880* (Westport, Conn.:

Greenwood, 1994), chap. 2; also useful but in need of updating is Lewis Cecil Gray, *History of Agriculture in the Southern United States to 1860,* vol. 2 (1933; repr., Gloucester, Mass.: Peter Smith, 1958), see especially chap. 34.

　5. Gray, *Agriculture in the Southern United States,* chaps. 38, 39; Avery Odelle Craven, *Soil Exhaustion as a Factor in the Agricultural History of Virginia and Maryland, 1606–1860* (1925; repr., Columbia: University of South Carolina Press, 2006), chap. 4; the desperate conditions throughout the South are depicted in William C. Davis, *Look Away! A History of the Confederate States of America* (New York: Free Press, 2002), chaps. 7, 10; the Virginia perspective as it relates to food shortages, the dissent it provoked, and subsequent responses is found in William Blair, *Virginia's Private War: Feeding Body and Soul in the Confederacy, 1861–1865* (New York: Oxford University Press, 1998); Gates, *Agriculture and the Civil War,* 18.

　6. Blair, *Virginia's Private War,* 9; James M. McPherson, *Battle Cry of Freedom: The Civil War Era* (New York: Oxford University Press, 1988), chaps. 24–26; Mark Grimsley, *The Hard Hand of War: Union Military Policy toward Southern Civilians, 1861–1865* (Cambridge: Cambridge University Press, 1995); Scott Reynolds Nelson and Carol Sheriff, *A People at War: Civilians and Soldiers in America's Civil War, 1854–1877* (New York: Oxford University Press, 2007), chap. 7.

　7. Gray, *Agriculture in the Southern United States,* 919; Sam Bowers Hilliard, *Hog Meat and Hoecake: Food Supply in the Old South, 1840–1860* (Carbondale: Southern Illinois University Press, 1972), 21, 23, 199; Sam Bowers Hilliard, *Atlas of Antebellum Southern Agriculture* (Baton Rouge: Louisiana State University Press, 1984). On a historiographic note, one must take care in accepting uncritically the major argument in Michael G. Mahon, *The Shenandoah Valley, 1861–1865: The Destruction of the Granary of the Confederacy* (Mechanicsburg, Pa.: Stackpole, 1999). Mahon contends that "the Shenandoah Valley was not the granary that historians have alleged," and that Maj. Gen. Philip Sheridan's raiding in 1864 was not as devastating because the region's food supply had been depleted by 1862. His bibliography indicates that he did not consult sources on agricultural history such as the foundational works by Gates, Gray, and Hilliard noted above. Agriculturalists, though stymied, never stopped planting, even in the face of repeated attacks, confiscation, and difficulty in obtaining seed. Moreover, Sheridan's memoirs point out the existing potential in 1864 in the Valley, that "though for three years contending armies had been marching up and down it, the fertile soil still yielded ample subsistence for Early's men, with a large surplus for the army of Lee." Philip H. Sheridan, *Personal Memoirs of P. H. Sheridan* (New York: Charles L. Webster, 1891) 1:470; see also James O.

Lehman and Steven M. Nolt, *Mennonites, Amish, and the American Civil War* (Baltimore: Johns Hopkins, 2007), chap. 10; by comparison, early midwesterners' market ambitions are described in Ginette Aley, "A Republic of Farm People: Women, Families, and Market-Minded Agrarianism in Ohio, 1820s–1830s," *Ohio History* 114 (2007): 28–45.

8. Hilliard, *Hog Meat and Hoecake*, 23, 213, and chaps. 3–6; Hilliard argues (unconvincingly) against Gates's contention that the South was significantly dependent upon the western states (now the Midwest) for food, and asserts that the South could feed itself, despite the fact that some parts of the region could not. While Hilliard's study is undeniably important, his argument is weakened by his chapter 10, entitled, "Making up the Shortage," and it does not explain why the major farm press, the *Southern Cultivator,* repeatedly lamented the South's agricultural dependence on both the North and the Old Northwest states, as cited in this essay.

9. John T. Schlebecker, "Farmers in the Lower Shenandoah Valley, 1850," *Virginia Magazine of History and Biography* 79 (October 1971): 462–76; Schlebecker focuses on Warren, Frederick, and Shenandoah counties, but to round out the story he looks at Clarke, Rockingham, Augusta, and Berkeley counties as well. In addition, while he uses the year 1850 as his focal point, he incorporates source material spanning 1845 to 1856 for a broader interpretation; Emmett B. Fields, "The Agricultural Population of Virginia, 1850–1860" (Ph.D. diss., Vanderbilt University, 1953), chaps. 2, 3; an excellent study for its focus on wheat production in the Valley in the postwar period is Kenneth E. Koons, "'The Staple of Our Country': Wheat in the Regional Farm Economy of the Nineteenth-Century Valley of Virginia," *Proceedings of the Rockbridge Historical Society* 12 (1995–2002): 505–38.

10. *Southern Cultivator,* February 1862, 36 (first and second quote), 48 (third quote), 68, 76, and March–April 1862, 80, 83, 85; Davis, *Look Away!* chap. 10. Note that wartime exigencies caused the *Southern Cultivator* to periodically alter its publication frequency.

11. *Southern Cultivator,* September–October 1862, 181, and May–June 1863, 81.

12. An important study, though also in need of updating, is Mary Elizabeth Massey, *Ersatz in the Confederacy: Shortages and Substitutes on the Southern Homefront* (1952; repr., Columbia: University of South Carolina Press, 1993). For examples of how women coped with food scarcity, see the following: Confederate Receipt Book, Eleanor S. Brockenbrough Library, Museum of the Confederacy, Richmond; Alice Allen, "Recollections of War in Virginia," *Confederate Veteran* 23 (1915): 26–69; Danielle M. Torisky, "Comfort Foods and Food Remedies

in 19th-Century Cooking Manuals," in Dorothy A. Boyd-Bragg, ed., *Portals to Shenandoah Valley Folkways* (Staunton, Va.: Lot's Wife, 2005): 99–129. A fascinating compendium is Edward D. C. Campbell Jr. and Kym S. Rice, eds., *A Woman's War: Southern Women, Civil War, and the Confederate Legacy* (Richmond: Museum of the Confederacy; Charlottesville: University of Virginia Press, 1996). *Southern Cultivator,* July 1861, 243, January–February 1863, 12 (for the *Lynchburg Republican* quote), 18, May–June 1863, 78, 84 (last quote), and November–December 1863, 133; Jones, *Rebel War Clerk's Diary,* 2:89.

13. *Southern Cultivator,* December 1861, 310, July–August 1862, 132 (first quote), November–December 1863, 129 (second quote), and January 1864, 20.

14. Ibid., March–April 1863, 61 (first quote), May–June 1863, 74 (second quote), January 1864, 26, March 1864, 56 (third quote), and August 1864, 129; *Richmond Daily Dispatch,* September 12, 1864; see also *Richmond Daily Dispatch,* January 11, 1864, and September 20, 1864; see Massey, *Ersatz in the Confederacy,* 60, for the seed shortage reference.

15. *Richmond Daily Dispatch,* April 13, 1863; Mary Elizabeth Massey, *Refugee Life in the Confederacy* (1964; repr., Baton Rouge: Louisiana State University Press, 2001), 75. On the changing character of the Richmond population, mostly for the worse, as a result of the influx of others besides the refugees, see Sallie Brock Putnam, *Richmond during the War: Four Years of Personal Observations* (1867; repr., Lincoln: University of Nebraska Press, 1996); Nelson Lankford, *Richmond Burning: The Last Days of the Confederate Capital* (New York: Viking, 2002), 19. Michael B. Chesson, "Harlots or Heroines? A New Look at the Richmond Bread Riot," *Virginia Magazine of History and Biography* 92 (April 1984): 131–75; Gates, *Agriculture and the Civil War,* 38–40; *Southern Cultivator,* January 1864, 14; *Richmond Daily Dispatch,* July 13, 1864; Jones, *Rebel War Clerk's Diary,* 2:305, 307; Blair incorrectly asserts that only one food riot erupted in Virginia in Blair, *Virginia's Private War,* 74, but see the preceding Chesson and Gates references.

16. Jones, *Rebel War Clerk's Diary,* 2:59; *Richmond Daily Dispatch,* August 3, 1863, 1, April 4, 6, 10 (Trowbridge quote), 13, 21 (onion-stealer quote), June 30, July 29, 1864; see also Sallie Brock Putnam's opinion on the matter of crime and mischief committed by the black population in Putnam, *Richmond during the War,* chap. 50.

17. Jones, *Rebel War Clerk's Diary,* 2:101; *Richmond Daily Dispatch,* June 21, 22 (shanty couple quote), August 12 (stealing soldiers quote), September 15, 1864.

18. *Richmond Daily Dispatch,* October 28, 1863. The farm and local press, especially the latter, are full of accusations against the so-called extortioners

and speculators, such as "Enemies at Home," *Southern Cultivator,* May–June 1863, 107. Jones, *Rebel War Clerk's Diary,* 2:107, 131, 136, 188, 255, 347 (quote), 353; a useful explication of these factors is Gates, *Agriculture and the Civil War,* chaps. 1–5; Davis, *Look Away!* chap. 7.

19. Putnam, *Richmond during the War,* 113; Mrs. Mark Valentine, "A Girl in the Sixties in Richmond," *Confederate Veteran* 20 (1912): 280; *Richmond Daily Dispatch,* January 7, March 2, June 10, August 6 (vampyres quote), 28, October 30, 1863.

20. *Richmond Daily Dispatch,* March 19, June 7, 9, 13, August 1, 25, September 5, 1864; Jones, *Rebel War Clerk's Diary,* 2:168–69, 170, 189 (quote). That Virginians and the Confederacy were aware in 1864 that the war had reduced them to living a life of starvation is evident in *Richmond Daily Dispatch,* July 30, 1864; see also March 3, May 20, 28, July 18, 1864.

21. *Richmond Daily Dispatch,* January 11, May 20, July 5 (first quote), 9 (second quote), August 25, 1864; Jones, *Rebel War Clerk's Diary,* 2:165, 180 (quote).

22. Gates, *Agriculture and the Civil War,* chap. 3; Jones, *Rebel War Clerk's Diary,* 2:95, 103 (quote), 104, 118, 255, 259, 260, 286, 287; *Southern Cultivator,* January 1864, 13 (quote), and August 1864, 129; see also Blair, *Virginia's Private War,* 69–74.

23. Jones, *Rebel War Clerk's Diary,* 2:154; *Southern Cultivator,* May–June 1863, 77.

The Struggle to Learn

Higher Education in Civil War Virginia
Peter Wallenstein

It is somehow fitting that the best-known episode from the story of higher education in Civil War Virginia took place not in the classroom but on the battlefield, when the cadets of the Virginia Military Institute (VMI) marched north in mid-May 1864 to engage Union forces in the battle of New Market. Cadets from that military school marched in a body, nearly 250 strong, to contribute to Confederate efforts to secure the Shenandoah Valley. One objective was to maintain control of an important source of food supply for the Confederate military as well as for Virginia civilians. Another was to keep Union forces from bringing still more pressure to bear on Lee's troops to the east, on the other side of the Blue Ridge. To this day, countless VMI cadets and alumni cherish the thought of that most memorable day.[1] It takes nothing away from that day's exploits to observe that many lesser stories can also be told, and that collectively they paint a portrait of political crisis and military developments that provide context for the VMI heroics.[2]

Virginia's institutions of higher education, public and private, shared some common features of their wartime experience, though they differed in others. As the war ground on, or even at the beginning, some institutions adapted to the changing conditions, or their facilities and personnel were adapted to new purposes. School buildings often served as military hospitals. Teachers sometimes joined the military effort. Students often left behind their schoolbooks to carry a weapon off to war. In school after school, but not everywhere, the number of enrolled students dropped sharply. Early or late, some colleges entirely suspended operations.

Everywhere could be seen, as the officers of Wytheville Female College observed of their school in spring 1861, an "extraordinary pressure . . .

growing out of our political troubles." Final exams, they announced, would be "omitted" in June 1861, and "TWO CONCERTS" substituted, as "the minds of the pupils are more or less unhinged by the excitement of the times." A few months later, concerned that the trustees might not reopen Randolph-Macon College for fall classes, one writer lamented: "There is scarcely any other feature of this wicked war which is, to my mind, so disastrous to the future of our country as that of the partial suspension of the educational enterprises of the land."[3]

On the eve of the Civil War, Virginia had two public institutions of higher education—the University of Virginia, which had enrolled its first students in 1825, and the Virginia Military Institute, which opened its doors in 1839—as well as the Medical College of Virginia, an institution in Richmond that had originated as the medical department of Hampden-Sydney College. More college students in Virginia attended private institutions, like Washington College in Lexington and the College of William and Mary in Williamsburg. The students of public and private schools alike were white men, or in some cases white women, but almost never both, and never together in the same classrooms; nowhere could black Virginians, whether slave or free, attend even elementary schools, let alone college.

Most of these private institutions had been founded by people associated with one Protestant denomination or another. Young men might attend Hampden-Sydney College, founded by Presbyterians; Richmond College, founded by Baptists; Roanoke College, founded by Lutherans; or Randolph-Macon College or Emory and Henry College, both founded by Methodists. Their sisters could attend Augusta Female Seminary in Staunton, Farmville Female College in Farmville, Union Female Seminary in Danville, or Hollins Institute near Roanoke (which for a time, under the name Valley Union Seminary, had enrolled boys as well as girls, though in separate departments). Higher education was simply not the same during the Civil War era as it later became; many of these schools had preparatory programs as well as collegiate courses, or simply operated at more or less a high school level. All these schools were tiny by today's standards. Every one of them faced extraordinary challenges during the war, certainly by 1864.

The crisis of the Union affected institutions of higher education in Virginia well before Virginia seceded. Shortly after the events at Harpers Ferry, Virginia, in October 1859—a couple of months after the hanging of white abolitionist John Brown in December—nearly 250 medical students from the South abandoned their studies in Philadelphia and headed south. Of the 244 who arrived on December 22 in Richmond—where they were greeted with a tremendous celebration—144 enrolled in the Medical College of Virginia. The other 100 headed on to the Deep South, where 13 enrolled at the Medical College of Georgia in Augusta, and another 28 at the Medical College of the State of South Carolina in Charleston.[4]

And how did prominent Virginians respond to the return of the prodigal medical students? Such leading pro-slavery and Southern nationalist radicals as George Fitzhugh and Edmund Ruffin celebrated the medical students' "secession" from the Philadelphia school. Fitzhugh wrote: "The Southern medical students who lately deserted Northern colleges deserve immortal honor. It is time the South should educate her sons." Indeed, the day after the students' arrival in Richmond, a bill to provide $30,000 in new funds for the Medical College of Virginia (MCV) was introduced into the General Assembly, which early the next year approved it—the basis for the institution's becoming a state facility. Arthur E. Peticolas, professor of anatomy at the Medical College of Virginia, told the new students at his school that they had earned "the gratitude of every man, woman and child in a slaveholding State," for, he said, they had collectively "struck the heaviest blow that has ever yet been aimed at that hideous hydra-headed monster known to us as abolition fanaticism."[5]

Late the next year, on about December 10—so after Lincoln's victory in the 1860 presidential contest, but even before South Carolina had seceded—seven students at Washington College in Lexington hoisted a flag one night that one of the seven, H. Rutherford Morrison, described as "blue with one blood red star in the middle and DISUNION painted in large letters above it." Fellow student Frank Willson observed that this flag had been "raised on the roof of the college endowed by the father of his country." As for school president George Junkin, a native of Pennsylvania, he wished to identify the perpetrator so he could, as Willson reported, "cane the traitorous fellow." Revealing that the students were by no means of one mind on the subject, a number of them threatened to pull the flag down, but Morrison wrote: "[W]e told them that if they tried it there would be a war." President Junkin ordered removal of the flag, but the disunionist seven had hidden all the ladders to be found on campus, and once one had been obtained from town, winds were at first too strong to climb it. Through the night, pro-secession students guarded the flag against assaults by pro-Union classmates.[6]

Similar incidents at the school cropped up in the four months that followed, and ever more of the students sided with the "traitorous fellow"—in fact, saw the question of loyalty in a manner radically different from President Junkin. On George Washington's birthday in February 1861, the Washington Literary Society at the college voted 43–8 that Virginia should secede and join the Confederacy. In March, some thirty students organized a military company, "the Southern Blues." When yet another in a series of secession banners was pulled down in early April 1861, the president set it on fire: "So *perish* all efforts to dissolve this glorious Union!" In emphatic dissent, one student after another tore off a strip from the burned flag and wore it as an insignia of his political identity and loyalty.[7]

In short order came news of the firing at Fort Sumter, Lincoln's call for volunteer troops to help put down the rebellion in South Carolina, and the vote in the Virginia convention to secede and join the Confederacy. Students at Washington College then brought to the president a petition—they said it was "unanimous"—in support of keeping a secession flag waving over the campus. Speaking of "treason against Virginia," they insisted that there could no longer be any "opposition" to flying such a flag except from "enemies of Virginia." The faculty voted for "*the present*" to side with the students and let the flag wave, whereupon President Junkin declared: "I never will hear a recitation or deliver a lecture under a rebel flag." He resigned his post and left Virginia for his native state in the North.[8]

Similar incidents unfolded across the Blue Ridge at the University of Virginia. Students there from the Deep South demonstrated a zeal for secession that, especially in the first months after Lincoln's win, contrasted with many of their in-state classmates, who typically hoped for compromise, Union, and peace. In late November, a few weeks after Lincoln's victory in the polls, George K. Miller wrote back home to his girlfriend, Cellie McCann. Describing himself as "truly proud that I am a South Carolinian" and "an uncompromising secessionist," Miller expressed the hope that his home state "will be the first to secede." Moreover, if South Carolina did secede, he said, and if Lincoln mobilized troops against it, Miller would "be there in two days" to help defend against such an attack. He told her that "most of the Carolina and Alabama students have donned the blue cockade," symbolizing their separate Southern political identity. Even more earnest than his Deep South colleagues, however, Miller was such a purist that, hearing that the cockades had been "made by special order in a northern city," he refused to wear one. His girlfriend quickly sent him a homemade version, and he became the envy of the other pro-secession students, he assured her, "when they heard it was all the way from So. Carolina & from one of its fair daughters."[9]

Whatever was the case back in November and December, whether at Washington College, the University of Virginia, or elsewhere, by sometime in February any number of college students in Virginia had largely adopted secession as the unavoidable next step. Even more so had they when they saw in Lincoln's inaugural speech in early March no space left for Virginia in a Union governed by Republicans. Thus they were in advance of the center of public opinion in Virginia, as Civil War historian Peter Carmichael observes of college students in Virginia throughout the secession crisis. Randolph-Macon College student Richard H. Bagby, for example, wrote his father back home in Powhatan County about Lincoln's inaugural speech: "I think it is an open declaration of war against the South, and I . . . am for going *out* of the *Union* now."[10]

Students at the University of Virginia by that point had reached the same conclusion, and they were very public and emphatic in declaring their renovated political loyalty. They made "strong Secession speeches; and strong resolutions to the same effect were adopted unanimously," reported one of the students there; and one week later the University of Virginia students published a pro-secession proclamation in various Virginia newspapers. During the month *before* Fort Sumter, secession flags went up at Roanoke College, William and Mary, VMI, and elsewhere, as they had at Washington College. In other words, these students had adopted a posture that one-third of Virginia's secession convention delegates in Richmond had reached before the Confederate firing on Fort Sumter, and that another third would reach in its aftermath. Writing again from Randolph-Macon College, immediately after Fort Sumter and Lincoln's call for troops, Richard H. Bagby said: "Virginia, the most powerful of the slave states, the mother of states," had been "kicked out" of the nation it had once dominated. But of course he had taken a pro-secession stance weeks earlier.[11]

The emergence of a pro-secession stance among college students in Virginia seems to reveal an alteration of identities and a shifting of behavior among them tracking the broader shift toward secession, a shift that lurched forward in the aftermath of Fort Sumter and Lincoln's call for troops, including troops from Virginia, to put down what Lincoln saw and termed as a rebellion. Or it might be something else. George K. Miller, writing back in November with such enthusiasm about secession, had identified himself as from South Carolina, and many other students came from that or some other Deep South state. Even the Virginia students at the university mostly came from east of the Blue Ridge, the part of Virginia where pro-secession leanings were the most pervasive and pronounced.[12] Therefore, college students might have been unrepresentative not just in that they adopted the true faith of secession in advance of the state convention, but because they came from families and areas that leaned that way.

After the call for troops, nonetheless, the tilt toward secession was suddenly even more pronounced, and, as the students at Washington College had put it to their president, political loyalties had come to require an identity with the Confederacy, not the Union. As Virginians began preparations in spring 1861 for a possible war, cadets from the Virginia Military Institute made their way to Richmond to train volunteers. After arriving at Camp Lee on April 22, just five days after Virginia's convention voted to take the state out of the Union, 185 VMI cadets went to work training recruits to the Confederate forces. Effective they were, and Robert E. Lee himself wrote VMI superintendent Francis H. Smith in May about the cadets and their efforts at training an army: "They are wanted everywhere."[13]

Hampden-Sydney college president John M. P. Atkinson had no military experience, but the student volunteers there elected him captain. Novice as he was, he chose to drill his students far from curious eyes, in the dead of night and in the basement of a campus building. It was not easy to see him at his work, but it is easy to see why he took such precautions, in view of how one of the cadets, seminary student G. T. Lyle, described President Atkinson's instructions regarding the "double quick": "Gentlemen, when I count one, you will bring up the right foot until the thigh is perpendicular to the body, and when I count two, you will bring the other up beside it." The "Hampden-Sydney Boys" were mustered into service in May 1861 and soon received more practical instruction at Camp Lee in Richmond from the VMI cadets.[14]

Meanwhile, back at Washington College, the Liberty Hall Volunteers called upon their school leaders to suspend academic work so they could concentrate on military training. Called into service in early June, as one source states, they were "the only distinctively college company that served as such throughout the entire war," or, as the university historian puts it, they "fought as a unit from First Manassas to Appomattox." While those students were otherwise occupied, the school limped along. Professors went off to war or, on the home front, oversaw soldiers' relief work and organized donations to military hospitals. Campus buildings were used briefly for quartering soldiers or designated a military hospital. Especially during 1862 and 1863, Washington College occasionally suspended classes, and, responding to shortages of both students and teaching materials, established a preparatory department in which most wartime students were enrolled, sought enrollment on the basis of the town's sheltered position, and urged prospective students to bring their own textbooks.[15]

The University of Virginia was unusual among state universities and other public institutions of higher education in the Confederate South in that it remained open throughout the war. By contrast, such institutions as the University of Mississippi, together with its counterparts in Alabama, Georgia, South Carolina, and North Carolina, suspended operations for much of the war. Attending the Charlottesville school during the war were mostly students too young to serve or former soldiers who had been severely wounded, among them George L. Christian, who later became a prominent lawyer and judge.[16]

At least 5 of every 6 of the students who had been enrolled at the University of Virginia during the 1860–1861 school year joined Confederate units. In fact, more than 2,000 former students of the school fought for the Confederacy, and some 500 of these men died. Dozens of former students at the university became Confederate generals—26 of them—or leading figures in the Confederate government. These men include Robert Toombs of Georgia, Confederate secretary of state and brigadier general; Louis T. Wigfall of Texas, Confederate senator and (briefly) brigadier general; and James L. Orr of South Carolina, a senator in the Confederate Congress; as well as such officeholders or generals from Virginia as James A. Seddon and Roger A. Pryor.[17]

Faculty from the University of Virginia played multiple roles. Dr. James L. Cabell, who had attended the University of Virginia as a youth, in 1837 joined the faculty as a professor of anatomy and surgery. Still in that position when the Civil War came, he served as the chief surgeon of the Charlottesville General Hospital, which was organized to treat wounded soldiers not long after the fighting at First Manassas. Mathematics professor Albert T. Bledsoe served the Confederacy as assistant secretary of war. History and general literature professor George F. Holmes joined other volunteers in May 1863 amid rumors that a Federal force was nearing Charlottesville. Greek and Hebrew professor Basil L. Gildersleeve joined the cavalry and in 1864 suffered a serious wound, and Latin professor Lewis M. Coleman died in 1862 of wounds suffered during the battle of Fredericksburg.[18]

Roanoke College offers glimpses of how a Virginia school might be affected by the war, or how it might escape some effects. In the spring of 1861, most of the students left the college to go to war, as did Professor Simon Carson Wells. Later that year, school president David Bittle negotiated with the Confederate secretary of war to keep the school open and let students, if they wished, complete the semester in which they turned eighteen, while younger students would drill, and form a home guard, with another professor, George Holland, who had gone off to fight but then returned wounded. In 1862, the college advertised for students with the attractive claim that the Salem area was "free from the invasion of the enemy." The college soon responded to the dearth of male students by enrolling female students for a time, although they met in separate classes. By continuing to enroll male students under the age of eighteen as well as reaching across the gender line, the college was generally able to maintain an enrollment of at least 100, although with no regular college classes—virtually all the students during the war years were in the school's preparatory programs—and no degrees conferred. At one point, President Bittle learned of plans to seize the campus and convert it into a hospital for wounded Confederate soldiers, but he was able to prevent that from happening, although meanwhile Confederate troops ransacked the college and carried off or destroyed some equipment. For a few weeks in 1864, the administration building was in fact used as a military hospital, although not while the college was in session. Late in the war, too late, President Bittle tried to convert more than $1,000 in the college's Confederate currency into the purchase of books for the school library.[19]

Not far from Roanoke College was Hollins Institute, a school for young ladies. Intent on erecting an expansive, elegant new residence hall, complete with a chapel and a dining hall, Hollins began construction on Main Building on the very day the Virginia convention in Richmond passed the secession ordinance. The walls nonetheless went up, and the roof, but then funds and supplies dried up, and "the Wilderness," as students soon named it, stood uncompleted through the late 1860s. Interrupted though the construction was, the school continued in operation through the end of the war. An

enrollment figure of 159 at one point in 1864 included a number report-
edly sent to the institution as a sanctuary generally far the fighting. School
principal Charles Lewis Cocke reported at the close of the war that "amidst
so much excitement, anxiety and gloom," students had found it hard to
focus on their studies, but "it is a source of gratification that we have made
out as well as we have."[20]

In Staunton, the Augusta Female Seminary limped along until midway
in the war, when school principal J. Brown Tinsley decided to close the
school rather than try to reopen for the 1863–1864 session. But then the
trustees persuaded Mary Julia Baldwin to head up the school, and under
her leadership the school picked up and persisted through the war and then
far beyond. It reopened in 1863 with twenty-two boarding students, fully at
capacity, as well as fifty-eight day students, for a total enrollment that may
have surpassed the highest prewar figure. One wartime student wrote that
she had been enrolled "I suppose for safe keeping." Another wrote, years
later: "Yet with all their interruptions and inconveniences[,] these young
girls steadily trod the path of learning. What cared they if every girl in the
arithmetic class did have a different textbook, as long as they had teachers
capable of surmounting the difficulty?" Wartime brought many an adventure,
many a scare, many a hardship, but the future Mary Baldwin College came
out of the war stronger than it had gone in.[21]

Another women's school, Farmville Female College, in Southside Virginia, announced in 1863 that its location was "in daily communication by
railroad" with Lynchburg to the west and Richmond and Petersburg to the
east: "It is therefore, easily accessible from all parts of the State, and at the
same time so remote from the seat of war as to be both safe and quiet." The
school offered both a preparatory department and a collegiate department,
and completion of requirements for the latter would qualify a student for
"the degree of Mistress of Arts." Prospective students and their parents
were advised that "the President and his Lady." had charge of "the Boarding Department" and were assured that all the teachers resided on campus.
The school warned, however, that "the number of applicants" for boarding
status had "of late" been "greater than could be accommodated" on campus,
and apologized for having had to raise boarding fees in view of "the present
price of provisions." In yet another indication of how the war was affecting
the school, all pupils were "earnestly requested to bring with them all the
Text books they can."[22]

The Baptist Female Seminary began operations in Danville in February 1859, and its leaders soon arranged for a college curriculum to be part of the institution's offerings. Reflecting the combined efforts of several Baptist associations, the school was reorganized that year as Union Female College. Four faculty members—Nathan Penick and his wife, the former Jane Elizabeth Averett, together with her brother Joseph Averett and his wife—constituted the faculty for a student enrollment of eighty-three in the year 1860–1861. Both men resigned that spring to become Confederate officers, but the school seems to have remained open, though the main building served as a Confederate hospital in early 1865. The name Union Female College proved an embarrassment to Confederate Virginians, however, so by 1864 it had become Roanoke Female College. Eventually it grew into Averett University.[23]

In the weeks that followed Virginia's secession, Emory and Henry College closed its doors as students left for home. A number were preparatory students, many of them at first too young for military service, but most of the students who had been enrolled in the college curriculum soon went to war. Two students on the eve of secession—John Bell Brownlow and James P. Brownlow, sons of Unionist leader "Parson" William G. Brownlow of Tennessee—went on to wear Union blue. Yet six Confederate generals were former students at the college. In May 1861, the trustees rejected a request for use of the college's dormitory space as barracks for training the Washington Mounted Rifles, which included John Singleton Mosby. One year later, however, in May 1862, Confederate authorities seized all the college's buildings, located as they were on the Virginia & Tennessee Railroad, for use as a military hospital for wounded soldiers. The school invested the rental fee in Confederate bonds as a prospective endowment. The college lost the value of those securities but came out of the war with little damage to its physical plant. No sooner had the war ended than the college made plans to reopen in August 1865.[24]

In Lynchburg, the Methodist Protestant Church had established Lynchburg College in 1855, moving operations from Madison College, in Pennsylvania, as sectional tensions grew ever greater. By that year all of the faculty as well as most of the students were from the South. The 1860–1861 year began with fifty-two students in the college program and twenty-five in the preparatory program, but by the last week of April 1861, many of the college students had left school for military service; so had some faculty, including

Professor James E. Blankenship, VMI class of 1852. On April 26, the trustees suspended operations and offered the institution's buildings to the Confederate army. Nothing happened for about a year, but the "College Hospital" was one of six military hospitals established in Lynchburg in spring 1862. When the trustees of Randolph-Macon College—which had been founded by another Methodist group, the Methodist Episcopal Church—began looking for a new venue for operations in 1863, a delegation from Lynchburg lobbied for Randolph-Macon to move to Lynchburg and take over Lynchburg College. That did not happen. Sectional and sectarian developments of the 1850s brought to Lynchburg a college that sectional developments of the 1860s destroyed. The Lynchburg College of the twentieth century, founded a generation later, was an entirely different institution.[25]

Randolph-Macon College, a men's institution then located in the Southside's Mecklenburg County in the town of Boydton, had an enrollment of 134 at the time of Lincoln's election. A year later, enrollment had fallen to 56, and three-quarters of that number were under the age of nineteen. The board of trustees sought to reinvent the school as a military academy, under the supervision of VMI alumnus James E. Blankenship, who had left Lynchburg College briefly for the army. This initiative failed to return enrollment to anywhere near its prewar level, and moreover most of the students were soon drafted. In 1863 the trustees closed the college. A substantial endowment largely vanished by the end of the war, as some $45,000 invested in Confederate bonds lost its entire value. Federal troops occupied the buildings for a few months shortly after the war, but the school reopened in 1866, albeit with a mere 46 students, many of them so young they were placed in a primary department. In 1868, the school moved its operations to Ashland, north of Richmond. Thus the war brought an end to the old institution, though under the same name it later found new life in another location.[26]

As for higher education in the Confederate capital city, Richmond was home to two main institutions of higher education, Richmond College and the Medical College of Virginia. At Richmond College, students left in droves to join the Confederate military, and the school suspended normal operations. As early as spring 1861, the campus grounds provided a place for housing and training hundreds of Confederate troops, in particular for instructing recruits to the artillery. Beginning in fall 1862, campus buildings served as military hospitals.[27]

Newspapers and other sources tell again and again of the roles played by doctors and medical students at the Medical College of Virginia in treating Confederate soldiers who had been wounded in the Richmond area. Dr. James Brown McCaw, whose father, grandfather, and great-grandfather had all been local doctors, played multiple roles in the medical establishment of late-1850s Richmond. An accomplished practitioner and professor, he had a private practice; he edited the *Virginia Medical and Surgical Journal;* and he was professor of chemistry and pharmacy at the Medical College of Virginia. Then the fighting began. In October 1861, the Confederacy's surgeon general, Dr. Samuel P. Moore, appointed Dr. McCaw to be surgeon in chief at what became Chimborazo Hospital, which Dr. McCaw planned and then directed throughout the war years. The MCV professor ran one of the largest military hospitals the world had ever seen.[28]

Records from MCV itself reveal ways in which the war affected the school and other medical schools across the South. A catalogue published in 1864 observed that, among the medical schools in the Confederate states, only MCV and the University of Virginia remained open. Reflecting many wartime developments, MCV apologized for having had to raise its fees, in view of the enormous inflation of the Confederate currency. The usual textbooks were listed as slated for use in the upcoming session, but prospective students were permitted to rely on substitutes if those particular books proved unavailable, "in view of the present difficulty of obtaining some of these works," and in any case were urged to bring their books with them if possible, "rather than trust to the very doubtful chance of obtaining them in Richmond."[29]

Of the forty-six graduates in 1863, the MCV authorities reported that, according to such information as had reached them, twenty had passed the medical board exams for the Confederate army, another seven for the navy, and others were acting in such capacities as acting assistant surgeon and hospital steward. The school anticipated—in effect, solicited—applications from what it termed "young men who have been disabled for military service by wounds or disease, and who will seek the means of livelihood in the pursuit of an honorable profession."[30] Surely the civilian society was in need of additional doctors, the school noted in its announcement of the upcoming session, as were the military branches. To the extent possible, the Medical College of Virginia would continue its classes, and it did so.

The chief medical school in the Old Dominion trained students from every state in the Confederacy. Enrolled during the 1863–1864 session were 155 students, more than half of them from Virginia, the remainder coming from all the states in the Confederacy, plus Maryland, Kentucky, and Washington, D.C. Some of the 48 medical students who graduated in March 1864 came from Virginia, with others from North Carolina, South Carolina, Tennessee, Georgia, Alabama, Mississippi, Louisiana, and Texas, as well as Kentucky, Missouri, Maryland, and Washington, D.C. As the *Richmond Dispatch* observed soon after the war: "The value of the College, in furnishing the Southern armies with a corps of educated and skillful surgeons, cannot be overrated."[31]

Over in Williamsburg, at the College of William and Mary, President Benjamin S. Ewell opposed secession for as long as he thought possible. But when the news came that the Virginia convention had adopted an ordinance of secession, Ewell signed on in support of the new political world, and he soon became an officer in the Confederate army. When he met with his faculty on May 1, most of the students had already left for the war, and it was assumed that most others would soon follow. The college suspended operations, hoping to reopen in October, but instead the buildings were soon serving as military barracks and a hospital for the Confederacy. Then, in 1862, Federal forces moved into Williamsburg. President Ewell returned in June 1865 only to find a main building burned to the ground, much of the rest of the school in disrepair, if not ruin, and few resources with which to commence operations again.[32] The Civil War had done much to destroy the first institution of higher education Virginia had ever had.

And then, of course, there was VMI. To be highlighted are the sheer numbers of prewar and wartime VMI students who fought for the Confederacy. Before or during the war, approximately 2,000 young men enrolled at the institute, and some 19 of every 20 of them served in the Confederate military. Hundreds upon hundreds of Confederate officers were former VMI cadets, whether trained before the war or as the war continued to rage, including many who commanded Virginia regiments of infantry, cavalry, and artillery. And 259 sons of VMI died under arms of wounds or disease. Moreover, some of the Confederacy's officers had been faculty at the school, chief among them, of course, Stonewall Jackson. Among the institute's former students, 16 served the Confederacy as brigadier generals, including Gabriel C. Wharton '47, and John McCausland '57; and three served as major generals, including William Mahone '47.[33]

Then came the battle of New Market in May 1864. With their commandant, Lt. Scott Ship (later Shipp), some 241 cadets marched north through the Shenandoah Valley to New Market, where they joined Confederate forces under Gen. John Breckinridge. Fighting in the infantry on May 15 were 209 cadets; in the artillery, another 32. Under intense pressure, the cadets acquitted themselves very well indeed, and the Union forces were repulsed. Nearly one-quarter of the cadets were casualties: 10 died during the battle or afterward from wounds they suffered that day; 47 more were wounded.[34]

VMI was, much of it, destroyed by Union troops in mid-June 1864—largely, it seems, in retaliation for the role the cadets had played the month before at the battle of New Market, though perhaps also because the town of Lexington had put up resistance to Union troops when they approached, or because the institute had supplied so much of the Confederacy's military leadership. So the school had to find a new home, at least a temporary one. Such a home looked at first to be at Washington College, which had suffered depredations as well, but it turned out to be in Richmond, beginning in late December 1864. At an opening convocation, Superintendent Francis H. Smith celebrated with the assembled cadets the "brilliant victory of *New Market*" by the institute's "soldier-scholars." There, in the "beleaguered city" of Richmond, each cadet must now "study with his armor on, and his musket by his side, ready for the lecture-room or the battle-field, as duty may call." Enrollment at other institutions, he noted, had become largely restricted to either "the disabled soldier" at the college level or younger students in a "grammar school," but VMI and its counterparts in other Confederate states must continue in operation, as before, as they trained for military leadership in this "great public work" in the "life struggle for our independence."[35]

So Virginia went to war, and all of its people and all its institutions became caught up in the war. The war changed everything and everyone. Virginia's institutions of higher education tracked the shift in sentiment toward secession, from John Brown's raid in October 1859 to Abraham Lincoln's election in November 1860 to the secession of seven Deep South states during a six-week period beginning with South Carolina in December and finally to the events of mid-April 1861. Those institutions played a range of roles in the war: supplying their students and faculty as officers and men; providing their buildings, whether as barracks or hospitals; and lending their expertise, whether military or medical. But by 1864, whatever their contributions to the war effort, most of the schools were in crisis if they had not already closed. Then the war ended; old questions recurred; and new questions arose.

At least three story lines emerge from the war years in Virginia. One might follow individuals in their postwar careers—for example, the VMI cadets who fought at New Market. A VMI historian published a book with biographical sketches of every one of the cadets who marched north in May 1864, including all the survivors of New Market, young men who as they grew older became teachers, farmers, lawyers, and railroad engineers. Another story line might follow the institutions. As things turned out, VMI was restored at Lexington. As for the College of William and Mary, so weakened was it that, resuming operations on a shoestring in the 1870s, it staggered through the decade and then in 1881 suspended operations, leaving great uncertainty that it could ever resume.[36] Eventually it reopened, and during the next century grew into a very different institution—public, comprehensive, coeducational, multiracial. The University of Virginia, too, developed into a far greater institution than it had once been.

Yet a third story line introduces a cluster of new phenomena. Early in the war, at about the time of Second Manassas, the U.S. Congress enacted a law, the Morrill Land-Grant College Act of 1862, to promote studies in agriculture and engineering in each state. When the war ended, and Virginia's state government was back in more or less normal operation and with more or less normal relations with the government of the United States, the Virginia General Assembly turned its attention to the contentious question of how to put to good use the Federal funds that had become available. Virginia accepted the offer from the national government it had fought for four years. Schools across the state sought to benefit from the limited largesse, among them the Virginia Military Institute, the University of Virginia, Hampden-Sydney College, Washington College, Roanoke College, Richmond College, Emory and Henry College, the College of William and Mary, and Randolph-Macon College. The prospect of obtaining that money lured VMI into offering to move permanently to Richmond, on condition of obtaining a new source of public funding.[37]

In the end, the two leading candidates for the fund canceled each other out. VMI went away empty-handed, as did the University of Virginia. So, too, did all the lesser rivals among existing colleges. Instead, a portion of the fund, two-thirds of it, went to an institution in Montgomery County, a former white boys' Methodist academy that had come on hard times on account of the war and now offered to give up its former identity if the state would allow it to rise from the dead and live in a new incarnation: Virginia Agricultural and Mechanical College, a land-grant institution.[38]

But the 1872 law reflected not only a wartime act of Congress *and* the Union's defeat of the Confederacy. It also reflected the advent of universal emancipation, an end to slavery, *plus* the postwar developments that made citizens of former slaves, permitted black men to vote and run for elective office in Virginia, and led to the presence of a number of black delegates and senators in the Virginia legislature that passed the 1872 law. The same law that bestowed a modest largesse on a tiny school just outside the village of Blacksburg *also* gave a small allowance, the remaining one-third, to a new school for black students, Hampton Agricultural and Normal Institute, almost all the way across the state.[39]

In 1920—many years after the state government had established an institution just outside Petersburg for black Virginians—the land-grant designation and money were lifted from Hampton Institute and granted to that public institution, by that time named Virginia Normal and Industrial Institute, a school that became known soon as Virginia State College for Negroes and later as Virginia State University.[40] A century and a half after secession, the continuing influence of the Civil War on higher education in Virginia can be seen in the mere presence of such institutions as Hampton University, Virginia State University, and Virginia Polytechnic Institute and State University, as well as in the campus culture of Virginia Military Institute.

Notes

1. William C. Davis, *The Battle of New Market* (1975; repr., Baton Rouge: Louisiana State University Press, 1983). For accounts of the institute during the war years, see William Couper, *One Hundred Years at V.M.I.,* 4 vols. (Richmond: Garrett and Massie, 1939), 2 (the entire volume) and 3:1–102; Henry A. Wise, *Drawing Out the Man: The VMI Story* (Charlottesville: University of Virginia Press, 1978), 34–45; Richard M. McMurry, *Virginia Military Institute Alumni in the Civil War: In Bello Praesidium* (Lynchburg, Va.: H. E. Howard, 1999), esp. 40–53. This essay excludes colleges in present-day Virginia.

2. For a survey of how institutions of higher education across both the Union and the Confederacy experienced the Civil War, see Willis Rudy, *The*

Campus and a Nation in Crisis: From the American Revolution to Vietnam (Madison, N.J.: Fairleigh Dickinson University Press, 1996), 51–100.

3. *Sixth Annual Circular of Wytheville Female College* (Wytheville: D. A. St. Clair, 1861), 12–13, 15, in *Confederate Imprints, 1861–1865* (New Haven, Conn.: Research Publications, 1974), reel 113, no. 3989-1; *Richmond Dispatch*, September 3, 1861.

4. James O. Breeden, "Rehearsal for Secession? The Return Home of Southern Medical Students from Philadelphia in 1859," in Paul Finkelman, ed., *His Soul Goes Marching On: Responses to John Brown and the Harpers Ferry Raid* (Charlottesville: University Press of Virginia, 1995), 179–89.

5. Ibid., 200–201, 202–3; Virginius Dabney, *Virginia Commonwealth University: A Sesquicentennial History* (Charlottesville: University of Virginia Press, 1987), 8–9.

6. Ollinger Crenshaw, *General Lee's College: The Rise and Growth of Washington and Lee University* (New York: Random House, 1969), 119–20.

7. Ibid., 120–22.

8. Ibid., 123–24.

9. Robert F. Pace, *Halls of Honor: College Men in the Old South* (Baton Rouge: Louisiana State University Press, 2004), 101.

10. Peter S. Carmichael, *The Last Generation: Young Virginians in Peace, War, and Reunion* (Chapel Hill: University of North Carolina Press, 2005), 6–10, 47, 137 (source of quote). Bagby was one of the 121 members of "the last generation" in Carmichael's sample.

11. Ibid., 137, 139, 143.

12. A. Frederick Fleet, a first-year student at the University of Virginia from King and Queen County in the eastern half of the state, wrote his father in February 1861 that the school's well-being depended on Virginia's secession. As he explained, unless Virginia joined the Confederacy, "a good many of the Southern students [that is, from the states that had already formed the Confederacy] say that they will hold a meeting and all go home, & they . . . constitute . . . nearly half of the whole number" of students at the university: Betsy Fleet and John D. P. Fuller, eds., *Green Mount: A Virginia Plantation Family during the Civil War; Being the Journal of Benjamin Robert Fleet and Letters of His Family* (Lexington: University of Kentucky Press, 1962), 48, quoted in John G. Selby, *Virginians at War: The Civil War Experience of Seven Young Confederates* (Wilmington, Del.: Scholarly Resources, 2002), 26. In fact, a full 25 percent of the university's students (151 of 604) came from one or another of the original seven states of the Confederacy; 56 percent (339) came from Virginia; most of the other 114 came from North Carolina, Tennessee, Kentucky, Maryland, Washington, D.C.,

or Missouri. As for the 339 from Virginia, more than four-fifths came from east of the Blue Ridge (with about half of the rest from the Shenandoah Valley, and a mere 10 or so from the vast area that soon became West Virginia): *Catalogue of the University of Virginia, Session of 1860–'61* (Richmond: Chas. H. Wynne, 1861), 9–22 (also 46–47, regarding "state students," one from each senatorial district, admitted tuition-free, on condition of a pledge to teach subsequently for at least two years in a Virginia school), in *Confederate Imprints,* reel 113, no. 4021.

13. James Lee Conrad, *The Young Lions: Confederate Cadets at War* (Mechanicsburg, Pa.: Stackpole, 1997), 39–40.

14. John Luster Brinkley, *On This Hill: A Narrative History of Hampden-Sydney College, 1774–1994* (Hampden-Sydney, Va.: [Hampden-Sydney College], 1994), 273–76, 280–82.

15. Crenshaw, *General Lee's College,* 125–36, 139–41.

16. Virginius Dabney, *Mr. Jefferson's University: A History* (Charlottesville: University of Virginia Press, 1981), 26.

17. Ervin L. Jordan Jr., *Charlottesville and the University of Virginia in the Civil War* (Lynchburg, Va.: H. E. Howard, 1988), 23–24, 103, 122; Dabney, *Mr. Jefferson's University,* 26.

18. Jordan, *Charlottesville and the University of Virginia in the Civil War,* 39, 46–48; Dabney, *Mr. Jefferson's University,* 15, 16, 26; Philip Alexander Bruce, *History of the University of Virginia, 1819–1919: The Lengthened Shadow of One Man,* 5 vols. (New York: Macmillan, 1920–1922), 3:293, 310.

19. Mark F. Miller, *"Dear Old Roanoke": A Sesquicentennial Portrait, 1842–1992* (Macon, Ga.: Mercer University Press, 1992), 29–43.

20. Dorothy Scovil Vickery, *Hollins College, 1842–1942: An Historical Sketch* (Hollins College, Va.: Hollins College, 1942), 13–15; Frances J. Niederer, *Hollins College: An Illustrated History* (Charlottesville: University of Virginia Press, 1973), 15, 24–25. See also Ethel Morgan Smith, *From Whence Cometh My Help: The African American Community at Hollins College* (Columbia: University of Missouri Press, 2000), 12–47.

21. Mary Watters, *The History of Mary Baldwin College, 1842–1942: Augusta Female Seminary, Mary Baldwin Seminary, Mary Baldwin College* (Staunton, Va.: Mary Baldwin College, 1942), 62–65, 72–78.

22. Farmville Female College, "The Next Term of This Institution Will Commence Thursday, October 1st, 1863," broadside in *Confederate Imprints,* reel 113, no. 3989-1; see also Rosemary Sprague, *Longwood College: A History* (Richmond: William Byrd, 1989), 18–31.

23. Jack Irby Hayes Jr., *The Lamp and the Cross: A History of Averett College, 1859–2001* (Macon, Ga.: Mercer University Press, 2004), 19–25.

24. George J. Stevenson, *Increase in Excellence: A History of Emory and Henry College* (New York: Appleton-Century Crofts, 1963), 89–96. Confederate officers who had attended Emory and Henry College included two major generals: Henry D. Clayton, an 1848 graduate, and J. E. B. Stuart, who attended the school before enrolling at West Point, where he graduated in 1854. They also included four brigadier generals: James B. Gordon, who attended in the early 1840s; William E. "Grumble" Jones, who graduated from the college in 1844 and also from West Point in 1848; John C. Moore, who attended Emory and Henry and went on to graduate from the U.S. Military Academy in 1849; and William F. Tucker, an 1848 graduate of the college. My thanks to Edgar V. ("Eddie" or "Sarge") Wheeler for bringing these six generals to my attention, after I gave a talk on the subject of this essay in March 2007 during the Sixteenth Annual Civil War Weekend at Virginia Tech.

25. W. Harrison Daniel, "Old Lynchburg College, 1855–1869," *Virginia Magazine of History and Biography* 88 (October 1980): 446–77, esp. 471–77.

26. James Edward Scanlon, *Randolph-Macon College: A Southern History, 1825–1967* (Charlottesville: University of Virginia Press, 1983), 107–9, 110, 114–20, 124–46; McMurry, *Virginia Military Institute Alumni*, 94.

27. *Richmond Dispatch*, April 29, May 30, June 1, 1861; Louis H. Manarin, ed., *Richmond at War: The Minutes of the City Council, 1861–1865* (Chapel Hill: University of North Carolina Press, 1966), 2. The published history of Richmond College speaks most directly to features of the school's wartime experience that took place after Appomattox. It speaks vaguely to an occupation of the school's buildings by Federal troops shortly after they entered the city in April 1865, and it mentions the loss of institutional funds that were invested in Confederate securities. From the eve of the war, shortly after John Brown's raid at Harpers Ferry, it notes pro-secession sentiment and preparation among students. Reuben E. Alley, *History of the University of Richmond, 1830–1971* (Charlottesville: University of Virginia Press, 1977), 44–45, 46, 48. See also John L. Dwyer, "Adult Education in Civil War Richmond, January 1861–April 1865" (Ph.D. diss., Virginia Polytechnic Institute and State University, 1997).

28. Carol C. Green, *Chimborazo: The Confederacy's Largest Hospital* (Knoxville: University of Tennessee Press, 2004), 7; David J. Coles, "Richmond, the Confederate Hospital City," in William C. Davis and James I. Robertson Jr., eds., *Virginia at War, 1862* (Lexington: University Press of Kentucky, 2007), 71–91.

29. *Catalogue of the Medical College of Virginia, Session of 1863–64; Announcement of Session 1864–65* (Richmond: Chas. H. Wynne, 1864), 12, 13–14, 16.

30. Ibid., 12–13.

31. Ibid., 9, 10–11; *Richmond Dispatch*, December 27, 1865.

32. Susan H. Godson et al., *The College of William & Mary: A History*, 2 vols. (Williamsburg, Va.: King and Queen, 1993), 1:289–90, 333–37; Sean M. Heuvel, "The Old College Goes to War: The Civil War Service of William and Mary Students," *Virginia Social Science Journal* 42 (2007): 32–48.

33. James I. Robertson Jr., *Stonewall Jackson: The Man, the Soldier, the Legend* (New York: Macmillan, 1997); Couper, *One Hundred Years at V.M.I.*, esp. 3:100; Wise, *Drawing Out the Man*, 34–45; McMurry, *Virginia Military Institute Alumni in the Civil War*, 54–61. For an account of VMI faculty killed or wounded in the service of the Confederacy, see Couper, *One Hundred Years at V.M.I.*, 3:100–102. Figures for the numbers of brigadier and major generals from VMI come from McMurry, *Virginia Military Institute Alumni in the Civil War*, 91, 152–53, 264; they include Frederick Samuel Bass but not Alexander Caldwell Jones. In addition, James Brown Hamilton, VMI class of 1851, served as a brigadier general on the Union side (ibid., 64, 138). Among the twenty-six Confederate generals claimed by the University of Virginia, three brigadier generals were former VMI cadets who are therefore also counted on that school's roster: James Henry Lane, '54, William Henry F. Payne, '49, and James Alexander Walker, '52.

34. Among the institute's cadets at the time, 30 were left behind at Lexington or at Staunton, leaving 241 who actually fought. Davis, *Battle of New Market*, 46–192; Couper, *One Hundred Years at V.M.I.*, 2:266–326, esp. 315; Wise, *Drawing Out the Man*, 37–43; McMurry, *Virginia Military Institute Alumni in the Civil War*, 51.

35. Crenshaw, *General Lee's College*, 137–40; Davis, *Battle of New Market*, 178; McMurry, *Virginia Military Institute Alumni in the Civil War*, 52–53; Francis H. Smith, *Introductory Lecture Read before the Corps of Cadets, on the Resumption of the Academic Duties of the Virginia Military Institute, at the Alms House, Richmond, Va., December 28, 1864* (Richmond: MacFarland and Fergusson, 1865), in *Confederate Imprints*, reel 113, no. 4011.

36. William Couper, *The V.M.I. New Market Cadets: Biographical Sketches of All Members of the Virginia Military Institute Corps of Cadets Who Fought in the Battle of New Market, May 15, 1864* (Charlottesville: Michie, 1933); McMurry, *Virginia Military Institute Alumni in the Civil War*, 71–72; Godson et al., *The College of William & Mary*, 1:333–411.

37. Duncan Lyle Kinnear, *The First 100 Years: A History of Virginia Polytechnic Institute and State University* (Blacksburg: Virginia Polytechnic Institute Educational Foundation, 1972), 19–40; Jack P. Maddex Jr., *The Virginia Conservatives, 1867–1879: A Study in Reconstruction Politics* (Chapel Hill: University of North Carolina Press, 1970), 189, 214–15; Couper, *One Hundred Years at V.M.I.*, 3:114–15, 232–37; Wise, *Drawing Out the Man*, 47–48; Bruce, *History*

of the University of Virginia, 4:242–43: Alley, *History of the University of Richmond,* 49; Miller, *"Dear Old Roanoke,"* 46–47; Crenshaw, *General Lee's College,* 163; Brinkley, *On This Hill,* 277–79; Godson et al., *The College of William & Mary,* 1:344, 421n21. Scanlon, *Randolph-Macon College,* does not mention the land-grant fund.

38. Kinnear, *The First 100 Years,* 34–41; Peter Wallenstein, *Cradle of America: Four Centuries of Virginia History* (Lawrence: University Press of Kansas, 2007), 224–28.

39. Robert Francis Engs, *Freedom's First Generation: Black Hampton, Virginia, 1861–1890* (Philadelphia: University of Pennsylvania Press, 1979), 139–60.

40. Wallenstein, *Cradle of America,* 262–65.

Words in War

The Literature of Confederate Virginia
William C. Davis

"We have yet to form a literature," Samuel D. Davies wrote in the *Southern Literary Messenger* in October 1863. He called on fellow Virginians—and Confederates—to "regulate our literature by according to the principles of good taste and sound morality." More than that, he said, "there is no want of a disposition to write and publish, and this disposition was perhaps never so strongly and so generally felt as it is at the present time."[1]

Even in the crisis, Virginians were mindful of the importance of reading. Indeed, articles appeared in the press linking reading to mental health, and not just any reading, either. "Any one who tries it soon finds out how wearying, how disproportionately exhausting, is an overdose of 'light literature' compared with an equal amount of time spent on real work," protested one editorial.[2] Despite that injunction to raise both their eyes and their aspirations in their reading, Virginians throughout the conflict remained typical of the American reading public at large in that era, only with a special focus on the conflict that so dominated every aspect of their daily lives for four years.

Native literature requires publishing, and while Virginians before the war generated a good deal of Southern writing, the Commonwealth itself was never the center of the regional literary industry. Compared to the nation as a whole, Virginia's mechanical component of the literary industry was modest at best, but it dominated some of the manufacturing of print media. As of six months before secession began, Virginia did not even rank in the top two-thirds of the United States in printing and publishing, and from the future Confederate states only Tennessee did so, thanks to Nashville and Memphis.[3] However, of the South's seventeen book binderies in 1861, Virginia had nine, just over half, producing hardbound books, stitched or sewn pamphlets, and softbound so-called paste books. Its fifteen printers were one-tenth of those in the region as a whole, and that did not count the state's eighty-five newspapers, many of which often acted as job printers publishing books and journals. More vital, however, there were only fifteen paper mills in the Confederacy at the outset, and Virginia had two of them, while the Richmond Type Foundry was the only one in the fledgling nation.[4]

In journal and periodical literature Virginia offered a mixed comparison with its fellow Confederate states in 1861. At the war's outset, the Commonwealth's presses turned out one political monthly, as did Georgia, and that was all for the entire region. When it came to literary journals, the Old Dominion lagged far behind, with only one monthly and two weeklies. Georgia alone published eight monthlies and another thirteen weeklies, and faraway Texas produced four times as many literary periodicals as Virginia. In fact, of the eleven Confederate states, the Commonwealth ranked a disappointing seventh overall. Only in religious publishing did the state vie for preeminence, hosting two monthlies and eleven tabloids, more than any other Confederate state.

The number of different publications was one thing, however; their circulation and readership quite another. Virginia's monthly journals distributed at least 43,900 copies in the last year before the war, more than any other future Confederate state, with Tennessee close behind, and both of them combined boasted total circulation almost equal to all the remaining nine Confederate states combined. And when Virginia's newspaper circulation was added, total distribution of all print media in the Commonwealth was more than double that of Tennessee, and more than one-fourth the total for the entire Confederacy. There can be little question that Virginians were the most avid readers in the new nation.[5]

Not surprisingly, most of the Commonwealth's literary publishing centered in Richmond. Besides hosting a third of the state's newspapers, the city had virtually all of the principal book and pamphlet publishers. The firm of West and Johnston at 145 Main Street put out more work than any other house, but competitors included MacFarland and Fergusson, M. A. Malsby, Ayers and Wade's Illustrated News Steam Press, Ritchie and Dunnavant, J. W. Randolph, and James E. Goode. There were other, lesser centers of printing and publishing, most notably Norfolk, Harrisonburg, and Lynchburg.[6] Several of these firms both published work in their own name and acted as job printers for other publishers, and by 1864, when firms had to scour the state for available paper and type, even West and Johnston had to send at least one of its titles to Lynchburg for printing by the *Lynchburg Virginian's* press.[7]

When it came to fiction, Confederate Virginians were no different from any other Americans of the time. They preferred—or at least their publishers gave them—melodramatic and often lurid romances, chiefly reprinted from British originals. West and Johnston offered the sensational novels of Mary Elizabeth Braddon, best known for *Lady Audley's Secret,* which saw several editions throughout the Confederacy, as well as equally melodramatic works such as *Mistress and Maid: A Household Story* by Braddon's fellow Englishwoman Dinah Craik. Far better was *Mrs. Halliburton's Troubles: A Novel* by another Briton, Ellen Wood, which West and Johnston issued near the end of the war in two volumes totaling almost 600 pages. It was perhaps the largest novel published in the Confederacy, truly a remarkably ambitious undertaking for 1865. The firm and its competitors also offered Virginia readers their own editions of classics like Wilkie Collins's *No Name* and Victor Hugo's *Les Misérables* (probably the only Confederate fiction publication longer than *Mrs. Halliburton's Troubles*).[8]

Far more popular, though, were homegrown works, chiefly poetry, humor, and melodrama loosely set in the contemporary context of the war itself. Poems and songs were the first to issue from Virginia presses, some within days of secession, and the majority appeared as one-sheet broadsides, such as Susan Archer Talley's *The Battle of Manassas.* Henry Keeling published his modest four-page *Flight of the Genius of Liberty from the Potomac, Southward* in Richmond in 1861, dedicating it to the youth of the Confederacy. Soon after, in 1862, followed such compilations as John Hewitt's *War: A Poem, with Copious Notes, Founded on the Revolution of 1861–1862 (Up to the Battles Before Richmond, Inclusive),* and James R. Randall's immortal *Maryland, My Maryland* and *There's Life in the Old Land Yet,* "dedicated to the Army of the Potomac by the ladies of Richmond." William J. Shelton's *Confederate Poems* was published in Lynchburg, and so was William G. Shepperson's famed *War Songs of the South.*

This outpouring of patriotic verse and song in book and pamphlet form all but stopped after 1862, for by then Virginia writers had turned their pens to other things. Probably the last substantial verse to appear in a form other than broadside was the sixty-four-page *Beechenbrook: A Rhyme of the War* by Margaret Junkin Preston, which Randolph published in 1865. Preston, who was General Thomas J. "Stonewall" Jackson's sister-in-law by his first marriage, was arguably the best native poet in Virginia, and would achieve national note as a writer after the war. Her 1865 collection included "Under the Shade of the Tree," which took its title from Jackson's dying words.

While waiting for writers to create their own new wartime literature, West and Johnston turned to a former Old Dominion classic to appeal to patriotic ardor. In 1862 the firm published a new edition of Nathaniel Beverly Tucker's *The Partisan Leader: A Novel,* which became a landmark Virginian novel after its original publication in 1836. However, to adapt it for the wartime audience, the Reverend Thomas A. Ware edited and updated the work, adding the subtitle *An Apocalypse of the Origin and Struggles of the Southern Confederacy.* The novel, originally set in the Revolution, now became a metaphor and inspiration for the daring partisans about to emerge on the western periphery of the Army of Northern Virginia.

By 1863 Virginia writers had had time to write their first prose works as Confederates. Even then, the rush to press, combined with shortages of paper and available press time, meant that most Virginia wartime fiction would be novellas under 100 printed pages. The impulse to produce a war literature depicting Confederates fighting for their independence was clear from the outset. Probably the first to see print in Virginia came in 1863 with Napier Bartlett's modest 79-page *Clarimonde: A Tale of New Orleans Life, and of the Present War.* That same year MacFarland and Fergusson published in book form James Dabney McCabe's 113-page *The Aide-de-Camp: A Romance of the War,* which originally appeared in serial in the *Magnolia Weekly.* The Richmond native McCabe had been a friend of Edgar Allan Poe, and was a distinguished poet before the war. When the crisis came he became chaplain of a Virginia regiment, and then served the rest of the war as chaplain at Libby Prison in the city itself. At almost the same time West and Johnston brought out McCabe's *The Guerrillas: An Original Domestic Drama, in Three Acts,* one of the very few dramas published in the Confederacy. More than just a play script, it also included directorial instructions for costume, stage "business," and "blocking."

A year later came *The Step-Sister: A Novelette by a Southern Gentleman,* a genuinely ambitious 260-page novel from an anonymous Virginian. But far more typical by the midpoint of the war was Mary Jane Haw's *The Rivals: A Chickahominy Story,* which ran only to 61 pages, but added the novelty—nearly unique in Confederate fiction—of being illustrated.

Richmond's publishers did not forget the instructive value of patriotic stories for younger Virginia Confederates, and in 1863 West and Johnston brought out Edward M. Boykin's *The Boys and Girls Stories of the War,* a 32-page pamphlet recounting the brave deeds of Jackson and others.

It would be only a part of a considerable juvenile literature to appear in Virginia during the war, most of it published by Richmond's George L. Bidgood and geared toward patriotic instruction as well as practical learning. Several editions of Richard McAllister Smith's *The Confederate Primer* appeared during the war, as well as his *Confederate First Reader* and *The Confederate Spelling-Book.* There also appeared *The Old Dominion Speller,* Kensey Johns Stewart's *A Geography for Beginners, The Virginia Primer,* and *The Virginia Spelling and Reading Book,* and from West and Johnston the *Southern Pictorial Primer,* another of the rare efforts to use illustrations. Meanwhile, old standards like *Cinderella* and *Aladdin's Lamp* and the *Mother Goose* stories came out in Virginian editions.

Arguably the finest novel published in the state during the war by a native Southerner came not from a Virginian but from the Georgian Augusta Jane Wilson. In 1865 West and Johnston published her *Macaria; or, Altars of Sacrifice,* basing it on an 1864 South Carolina edition. She would be one of the genuinely memorable female novelists of the nineteenth century, and *Macaria,* with its themes of Confederate women sacrificing their labor and their lives for their cause made it a popular seller even in the Union, where at least 5,000 copies slipped through the blockade to eager readers.

Not surprisingly, histories of the current conflict and biographies of some of its luminaries were very popular, and there was an instant demand for them as soon as they could appear, even when the war was yet too young for anything definitive to be written. In November 1862 West and Johnston published T. W. MacMahon's 207-page *Cause and Contrast: An Essay on the American Crisis,* and even though the *Richmond Daily Enquirer* noted that it would no doubt be an interesting book by "a writer of fine abilities, large information, and impartial sentiments," still the fact remained that "it is too early to write a history of the war in a higher sense," and a writer at the moment could do little more than construct "a connected narrative of events from the beginning thus far."[9] At the same time, however, for some stories the end was already known with all too much finality. John Esten Cooke was able to publish his *Life of Stonewall Jackson, by a Virginian* in 1863 with Ayers and Wade within months of the death of the general, making it the first—and one of the better—of uncountable biographies of the fallen hero. McCabe followed soon thereafter with his *Life of General Thomas J. Jackson,* published under the pseudonym "An Ex-Cadet."

The concept of "from the beginning thus far" was exactly what lay behind the most ambitious of the histories to appear in Virginia. The prolific Edward A. Pollard published his *The First Year of the War* with West and Johnston in 1862. It went through three editions that year, growing to more than 400 pages, and was published in London and New York as well. It would be reissued in the Confederacy yet again in 1863. Later that same year he published *The Second Year of the War,* which sold out in six weeks and went to a second edition in 1864. In January of that year Pollard advertised that he was gathering materials for his next volume, and appealed to army officers and enlisted men to send him narratives and accounts of engagements and campaigns, and in the spring of 1865 West and Johnston brought out Pollard's *Third Year of the War.*

Pollard was never known for objectivity; his account of military and political events was biased, biting, and decidedly anti–Jefferson Davis, but the three volumes of his history—unfinished at war's end—would be the nucleus of an early postwar history that would be influential for generations to come. As far away as London, England, reviewers during the war acknowledged Pollard's as "one of the best works that has yet appeared upon that universally interesting topic, the American war."[10] Military manuals were also a popular genre from the presses, most notably William Gilham's *Manual of Instruction,* for even civilians bought and read them, especially men anticipating military service.

Other nonfiction by Virginians was sparse during the war, but publisher M. A. Malsby did bring out an updated version of another Commonwealth classic, John Beauchamp Jones's 1856 best seller *Wild Western Scenes,* which went through 100 editions internationally, this one retitled *Wild Western Scenes; or, The White Spirit of the Wilderness: Being a Narrative of Adventures, Embracing the Same Characters Portrayed in the Original "Wild Western Scenes."* Having been one of the most popular Southern antebellum writers, Jones was now a clerk in the Bureau of War in the Confederate War Department, destined to become even more famous for the diary he was keeping at this very moment.

Humor also drank a fair bit of ink in Virginia, and not surprisingly, since Confederates were desperately in need of something to make lighter the burden of war. It was like most Victorian humor in America, neither subtle nor especially clever. Rather, Virginians—and Americans in general—laughed at broad farce, plays on words, and especially distinctive native folk characters who spoke in an ungrammatical dialect, which had characterized American humor since the days of David "Davy" Crockett. George Bagby, that indefatigable Old Dominion journalist, published probably the first Confederate Virginian humor in 1862 in his *The Letters of Mozis Addums to Billy Ivvins.* Starting in 1857 and writing as a semiliterate backwoods character—Addums—Bagby sent a series of letters of his observations in Washington to the editor of the *Southern Literary Messenger,* John R. Thompson—Billy Ivvins—following the popular style of outrageous dialect and spelling. West and Johnston's eighty-seven-page edition was a small one, and most of the copies were bought by soldiers in the field, where laughter was most in demand.[11]

Satire at the expense of Yankees became a naturally popular topic. William Russell Smith aimed his 1863 *The Royal Ape: A Dramatic Poem* at the panic in Washington in the wake of Lincoln's defeat at First Bull Run. An anonymous wag also published in 1863 his satirical verse on the Union's repeated failures to take Richmond in *Old Abe, the Miller; or, The Campaigns of Richmond: A Story.* Witty—and sometimes not so witty—pseudonyms were also popular, as when a writer using the byline "A. Young Rebelle" published yet another poetic jab at Lincoln in *Abram: A Military Poem.* Yet a few writers turned their barbs inward at Confederates themselves, most notably the anonymous author who privately published *Special Service Hero! Self-Detailed* in Richmond in 1863, a brief verse shaft aimed at the men who used every possible subterfuge to avoid service in Confederate armies. And a year later Richmond printer Charles H. Wynne brought out the anonymous *Great Expectations; or, Getting Promoted: A Farce in One Act,* satirizing Confederate officers who seemed to have a greater interest in self-advancement than in Confederate independence.

While humor buoyed the spirit at home and in the army, Virginia writers and publishers also catered to the demand for religious material to sustain the soul. Uncounted hundreds of tracts and essays came from the presses, most of them brief and intended for wide but temporary readership. With titles like *Are You Forgiven?* and *Are You Ready?* these tracts aimed at giving comfort for the moment and trust in what might lie beyond death. Sermons and proceedings of denominational conventions predominated. Then there were the numerous tracts on behavior, such as *Can I Be Religious While I Am a Soldier?* and an 1861 Richmond edition from MacFarland and Fergusson of *"Smoke Not": An Essay.* Chiefly, however, Virginians turned to their Bibles and prewar prayer books. Interestingly, no editions of the Bible itself were published, but then that would have been a gargantuan publishing task for a Confederate press. However, Richmond publishers did issue selected portions: the Gospel of John and the Psalms of David (printed in England and delivered through the blockade).

The publishers advertised their new books in the city's press, the firm of West and Johnston being the most energetic in promoting its books, usually with advertisements appearing on the very day of publication. Buyers who sent payment with their orders were shipped the books postage-free anywhere in the Confederacy. By 1864 West and Johnston was publishing yet another of English novelist Mary Elizabeth Braddon's sensational novels, *John Marchmont's Legacy,* for $6, while announcing at the same time a second edition of C. H. Lee's *The Judge Advocate's Vade Mecum,* a treatise on military law and courts-martial. The manual ran to 251 pages and cost $15, evidence that publishers felt they could charge higher prices for technical manuals and thereby help subsidize the more popular novels, keeping their prices within reach of a wider audience, a publishing practice that both preceded and postdated the war.[12]

As part of their effort to promote their titles, publishers sent copies of their books, especially novels, to the major Virginia newspapers to be reviewed. Sometimes those notices were extensive, especially early in the war. By 1864, with ink and newsprint scarce and the journals shrinking to four and even two pages, editors devoted less and less space to anything other than news and paying advertisements. Thus when the prolific Braddon's *John Marchmont's Legacy* appeared, the *Examiner* noted—and dismissed—it sarcastically with the simple observation that the author was "the machine that manufactured *Aurora Floyd* and the like articles."[13]

Small as it was, the greatest outpouring of native Virginian writing during the Confederacy appeared not in books but in the periodical press, limited though it was. Most appeared in eight-page tabloid format and did not last long, like the *Sentinel* and the short-lived *Bohemian. Smith and Barrow's Monthly,* patterned after the English *Blackwood's Magazine,* lasted but a single issue in 1864. West and Johnston began publication of its weekly periodical the *Record* in the spring of 1862, but had problems getting issues out almost from the first because its press was so occupied with government printing.[14] At least five religious periodicals also came off Richmond's presses during the war.[15]

Consistent with the sense of humor of the age, a magazine devoted almost entirely to satire commenced publication in Richmond on August 29, 1863, modeled after the popular English political journal *Punch,* and titled, not surprisingly, *Southern Punch.* In addition to all the forms of humorous editorial content present in other journals, it took special aim at politicians, draft dodgers, extortioners, and of course all Yankees. It promised readers that its content would be "Rich! Rare! Racy!" so it is somehow fitting that the offices were so close to a "disorderly" house that the magazine's proprietor preferred charges in court.[16] Worse, in January 1864 one of the partners in *Southern Punch* suddenly fled the city with the wife of a local theater treasurer and something like $1,300 from the magazine's coffers.[17]

Only the *Magnolia Weekly* offered any serious competition to the dominant Richmond weekly. The first issue appeared at the beginning of October 1862, and the Richmond press blandly described it as "a neatly printed sheet" with "a variety of pleasing and entertaining articles."[18] The editor promised "intellectual treats," and even though it depended heavily on serialized works by English writers like Dickens and Thackeray, for the sheer quality of its native Virginian contributions, the *Magnolia Weekly* was the finest publication in Virginia or the Confederacy. The *Magnolia Weekly* seemed to change its title as whim took the editors, once becoming *A Home Journal of Literature and General News* and another time appearing as *A Southern Home Journal.* It also lent its editorial offices to the collection of affidavits of heroics in the field, with a view toward publication of a war history of Confederate exploits.[19] Perhaps its greatest contribution to war literature was its serialization of McCabe's *The Aide-de-Camp: A Romance of the War,* which some declared to be "the most brilliant romance of the war."[20] McCabe himself served as editor of the *Weekly* in 1863–1864 when it offered a prize of $500 for the best new serialized work of fiction written during the war, but the *Southern Illustrated News* doubled that with a prize of $1,000. McCabe's writers included William Gilmore Simms, Henry Timrod, John Esten Cooke, and more, and his journal was published more or less regularly until 1865, when its offices were destroyed in the fires following the evacuation of Richmond.[21]

The dominant competitor for weekly readers first appeared on September 6, 1862, with the inaugural issue of the *Southern Illustrated News,* a brave but doomed attempt to emulate the successful illustrated weeklies in New York: *Harper's Weekly, Frank Leslie's,* and the *New York Illustrated News.* The Richmond firm of Ayers and Wade combined relatively timely coverage of war and political news, as well as social pages and serialized fiction, with woodcut engravings. The first issue featured an engraving of General "Stonewall" Jackson, and thereafter almost every front page presented another leading general. Along with its editorial content, the publishers promised that their battle sketches would be accurate, and by eyewitnesses, rather than "fancy sketches originating only in the brain of our artists."[22]

They promised quality, not quantity, in their illustrations. In the end they delivered neither. From the very first there was a problem just securing the illustrations, and the editors advertised repeatedly for "Sketches of Scenes and Incidents connected with our army, such as Views of Camps, Battle-Fields, Maps, &c." They could not afford to sustain artists in the field as did the Yankee weeklies, nor did they have access to the caliber of wood engravers. Their printing let them down as well, producing muddy and indistinct "daubs," as one critic complained.

The words were another matter, though, for the *News* produced an interesting editorial mix. There were satires on Southern writers, especially that "machine" Augusta Evans, whom it suggested probably had never "had an original thought."[23] There was soldier humor, none better than the contribution in the October 18, 1862, issue from a man using the pseudonym "Hard Cracker," titled "Foot-Cavalry Chronicle." Obviously he was a soldier in Stonewall Jackson's command, so famed for its rapid marches that it was called "foot cavalry." Writing just after the retreat of Lee's army from the defeat at Antietam, Maryland, from what he termed the "*Camp of the 'Turned-Over and Used-Ups,'*" he provided a witty catechism for all of Stonewall's soldiers:

Man that is born of woman and enlisteth in "Jackson's army" is of few days and short rations.

He draweth his rations from the commissary and devoureth the same; he striketh his teeth against much *hard bread,* and is satisfied; he filleth his canteen with "aqua pura," and clappeth the mouth thereof upon the "bung" of a whiskey barrel, and after a little while goeth away rejoicing at his strategy.

Much soldiering hath made him sharp; yea, even the sole of his shoe is in danger of being cut through.

His tent is filled with potatoes, pies, corn and other morsels for his delicate appetite, which abound not in said commissary department; and many other borrowed things, which will never be returned. Of a surety, it must be said of "Jackson's foot cavalry," "they take not that which they cannot reach."

He fireth his Minie rifle at the dead hour of night, and the camp is roused and formed in line—when, to his mess he cometh bearing a fine "porker"—which he declareth so resembleth a Yankee that he was compelled to pull trigger.[24]

The *Illustrated News* also published short biographical sketches along with its woodcuts, and not just of generals. The noted—if ineffectual—spy Belle Boyd received such treatment.[25]

Where the weekly excelled was in bringing native Virginian fiction, such as it was, to its readers. It may not all have been very good, but it had the benefit of immediacy—written during the war, by Virginians, and largely about Virginia's experience. The short novella *A Summer Idyl* by someone using the nom de plume "Refugitta" ran across three issues at the close of 1862, with its story of women's social life in the mountains of southwest Virginia.[26] There were frequent contributions from women, ranging from musings on the changing roles of ladies in wartime to a blast at that "combination of hog bristles and ox marrow," a man who preferred whiskers to shaving. A good deal of discussion went on for some time about women exchanging crinolines and silks for simple homespun dresses as a sign of frugality and patriotism.[27] Indeed, the greatest strength of the editorial content of the *Illustrated News* was its continuing publication of letters and memoir-novellas dealing with the woman's side of the conflict. "Refugitta" would write several other multipart contributions for the paper, all dealing with what women endured. The contribution that won the $1,000 prize offered by the editors was Mary Jane Hawes's *The Rivals*, which soon afterward appeared as a short novella from West and Johnston.

The paper's editor declared on January 2, 1864, that "*Literature*, too, pure and undefiled—free from the contaminating and detestable *isms* of

Yankeedom—has already asserted itself, and grown amongst us from a tender shoot to almost giant proportions, and now gives healthful instruction and amusement to the old as well as the young."[28] He was being more than a bit hyperbolic, since he referred only to his own weekly and some recent dramatic works written for the Richmond stage. The facts, moreover, belied the editor's rosy declaration. As the war dragged on, the *Illustrated News* had trouble simply coming out on time, and many a week was missed entirely. Its last issue came January 28, 1865, and it seems a miracle that the sheet lasted that long. Yet even in that last number a farcical society satire aimed at Virginia women was a final feature.

It remained to Virginia's lone literary monthly to seek to promote higher forms of literary creation. The *Southern Literary Messenger* had an unmatchable pedigree. Founded in 1834, with Edgar Allen Poe taking on the editorship a year later, it established the benchmark for Southern literary monthlies. By 1861 it stood alongside the *North American Review* and the *Atlantic Monthly* as one of America's three premier literary journals. When the war came its editors frankly addressed the great problem facing them and all Confederate publishing. "In times like the present, very little interest is felt in literature," the editor confessed. "Nothing that does not relate to the war itself is read."[29]

The *Messenger* nevertheless managed to remain a monthly in spite of the scarcity of paper and printers, the declining quality of available ink, and a dramatic growth in the failure of subscribers to pay their bills. In the first issue after Virginia's secession, editor George W. Bagby published heroic poetry such as "Men of the South" and an essay titled "The One Great Cause of the Failure of the Federal Government" by an Alabamian. By the end of the year the *Messenger* continued to publish articles supporting the Confederacy and the ideology behind secession, including such musings as "Characteristics and Capabilities of the Negro Race," which reinforced the necessity for slavery. Satire aimed at the North was always popular, too, as in "The Man about Washington," whom it described as "a prodigiously smart fellow, but utterly useless."[30]

And yet, thoughtful contributions did come to Bagby's office, few more so than the article "The Fine Arts at the South" by Samuel D. Davies, which appeared in the December 1862 issue. "It might be supposed that the present disturbed and anxious condition of the public mind, would be ill adapted to encourage any pursuit of a purely intellectual character," wrote Davies.

Nevertheless, he thought the arts to be the best measurement of a civilization, even a new one such as the Confederacy. "Who has not been gratified
at the exhibitions of poetical talent, which have lately appeared among us?"
he asked. Not immodestly, he actually believed that Confederate verse was
launching a new age of poetry. "If we are to be a cultivated, and at the same
time, a warlike people, then the arts become the most appropriate and efficient auxiliaries of science in accomplishing this twofold purpose." Davies
went on to call for the creation of a Confederate foundation for the arts to
award "premiums" to artists in all media for creating work that inspired
both pleasure and patriotism.[31]

E. S. Joynes wrote an article titled "Education After the War" for the
August 1863 issue, calling on his fellow Virginians and other Confederates
to plan now for the intellectual needs of a postwar generation, including the
men who were now soldiers who would be released into a new Confederate
polity that would need their intellectual strength as much as now it needed
their martial sinews. He called for "a *right* and *wise education,* which, taking hold of the youth, shall rightly form the man."[32] Bagby also published
occasional travel pieces, such as "The Mountain Scenery in Virginia" in the
September 1863 issue, though the strain on the *Messenger* was showing well
by then, as much of the print was almost too faint to be legible thanks to poor
ink. In his editorial column closing out 1863, Bagby began not with literary
comment, but simple business. All subscriptions came to an end with the
close of the year. Only those who paid for 1864 in advance would be sent
any further issues. Nor would the editor respond to any correspondence
unless it came with return postage. Even at $10 a year the *Messenger* was
still, he believed, the most inexpensive publication in the Confederacy for
the quantity of its content. But the tragic imperatives of wartime scarcity
were closing in.

Despite the fact that the ambition to write is a constant in human society,
even submissions from would-be and established writers began to decline.
In his October 1863 article on Confederate literary aspirations, Davies
credited the editor with being central, but added that "of course he must
do the best he can with what his contributors furnish."[33] Trying to evolve
with the times, the *Messenger* began to leaven its pages with war songs,
poetry, humor, and feminine literature, but that only slowed the decline.
Somehow it struggled through the first two years of the war, but soon the
editor was forced to resort to republishing essays from English periodicals

since Confederate contributions had become so scarce. Its problems were only exacerbated in the fall of 1862 when the Confederate government took over the Richmond paper mills. Thereafter the *Messenger* had no choice but to cut back to a bimonthly issue.[34]

Even as the life of the *Southern Literary Messenger* slowly ebbed away, its owners, MacFarland and Fergusson, made every effort to revive it by promotion. They advertised in the Richmond press to announce the contents of forthcoming issues, including the usual serialized novels, and especially highlighting a series of articles written by War Department bureaucrat R. R. Howison beginning with First Bull Run in the May 1863 issue.[35] MacFarland and Fergusson not only sold the *Southern Literary Messenger* by mail subscription and at bookstores, but also invited readers to purchase copies at the firm's office at the corner of Bank and Twelfth streets.[36] By late 1863, however, nothing seemed to work for the publishers, and in December they sold the journal to Thomas Alfriend and George Wedderburn, who announced that they would regain for the *Messenger* "its old supremacy among Southern journals." The new proprietors promised to revitalize the journal with "the very best writers in the South" and with "a series of brilliant Novelettes, Romances, Criticisms, &c.," appealing to the continuing appetite for sensational fiction.[37]

Even this, and the continued editorship of Bagby, could not overcome the shortages of paper and printing facilities, while by 1864 too few readers could afford $10 a year for a discretionary entertainment. Alfriend and Wedderburn's first issue was promised on January 1, but it did not appear until mid-January, almost a fortnight late, and thereafter problems both of supply and demand plagued the magazine. Worse, the advance of Union armies toward Richmond disrupted Bagby's editing and all the other routines of the magazine, so that when the June issue finally came out, Bagby had not even had time to write his usual editorial, and instead was forced back on a simple narrative of the war to date that year. "We have gone to work, however," he promised, assuring readers that they would have their next issue of the *Messenger* "at the earliest possible moment." That moment never came, and with its June 1864 issue, the *Southern Literary Messenger* finally died for good.[38]

As the *Southern Literary Messenger* was dying, along with most other periodicals, publishers still tried to give birth to new ones. Richmond publisher Ernest Lagarde announced in December 1863 that in the following

January he would print the first issue of *The Age: A Southern Monthly Eclectic Magazine* to promote literature, education, and industrial development. Most of its content, however, as with most other Virginia and Confederate wartime periodicals, would be drawn from European magazines, leavened with some homegrown articles. *The Age* died after only three issues.[39]

Meanwhile, book publishers kept occasional titles coming off the presses almost to the end of the war, but with escalating difficulty. On March 2, 1865, West and Johnston announced publication of Ellen Wood's *Mrs. Halliburton's Troubles*, another British work—and an ambitious one, at two volumes and $12 for the set. On the same day the firm also published a more typical work for this stage of the war, *Prisoner of War; or, Five Months among the Yankees*, by Anthony M. Keiley, published under the pseudonym "A. Rifleman."[40]

In fact, *Prisoner of War* may have been the very last book published in the Confederacy. At 120 pages, it was ambitious for this stage of the conflict, and was only the third prisoner of war memoir published in the wartime South. It may also have been the last Virginian—and Confederate—book to be reviewed in the Confederacy. On March 24, 1865, the *Evening Courier* noted that it was "invaluable in arriving at accurate conclusions respecting the opinions, hopes, prospects, and designs of the Northern people in their war for subjugation. It has all the thrilling interest of a legend of romance."[41]

The fall of Richmond on April 2, 1865, ended Confederate publishing and Virginia wartime literature in the capital, and almost all the other centers of publishing in the state had already fallen to the Federals. Perhaps the very last known publication anywhere was a modest memorial to a twenty-year-old partisan killed on March 14 while fighting under Col. John S. Mosby's command. Cornelia Jordan finished her memorial poem "The Death of a Young Partizan" on March 31, 1865, and it was published probably in Lynchburg even as Lee's army was retreating toward Appomattox. It is fitting that the death and destruction that had sapped and destroyed Virginia's literary media should be the subject of their dying contribution to print.[42]

The new Confederate literature that Davies predicted never came to be, of course. The life of the new nation was too brief, and too beset by the draining effects of the war. Virginia literature left few lasting memorable contributions. The poetry and humor were too temporal, and too trapped in Victorian mores and tastes to break free of their sentimental and farcical bonds. The wartime writings of John Esten Cooke would outlive the war, to be overshadowed by his postwar histories. Only Pollard's wartime histories would enjoy a long postwar life, though increasingly as artifacts of wartime sentiment rather than for their historical content. Margaret Junkin Preston's poetry would be the only verse to outlast the war and achieve increasing note as work of enduring quality. But the war failed to produce a memorable Virginian novel with a life beyond Appomattox. The war was probably just too enervating for the most talented to focus their attention on a sustained act of creation, while all too many who might have been memorable writers were swallowed into the armies—to cover battlefields with their blood rather than shed ink on paper.

Notes

The author is indebted to John M. Coski for valuable advice and assistance in preparing this essay.

1. Samuel D. Davies, "Observations of Our Literary Prospects," *Southern Literary Messenger,* October 1863, 622, 624.

2. *Richmond Daily Examiner,* March 20, 1863.

3. Joseph C. G. Kennedy, *Preliminary Report on the Eighth Census, 1860* (Washington, D.C.: Government Printing Office, 1862), 174.

4. Ibid., 211; Department of the Interior, *Manufactures of the United States in 1860; Compiled from the Original Returns of the Eighth Census* (Washington, D.C.: Government Printing Office, 1865), 604, 607, 608, 610, 613, 616, 617, 618, 622, 623, 624, 629, 630, 632, 634, 715, 717; Alice Fahs, *The Imagined Civil War: Popular Literature of the North and South, 1861–1865* (Chapel Hill: University of North Carolina Press, 2001), 21.

5. Kennedy, *Preliminary Report on the Eighth Census,* 211–13.

6. Department of the Interior, *Manufactures of the United States in 1860,* 623, 624, 629.

7. The book was Dinah Maria [Muloch] Craik, *Mistress and Maid: A Household Story* (Richmond: West and Johnston, 1864; printed at Lynchburg Virginian Book and Job Office).

8. Full bibliographic data on these and all other Virginia titles cited in this essay may be found in T. Michael Parrish and Robert M. Willingham Jr., *Confederate Imprints: A Bibliography of Southern Publications from Secession to Surrender* (Austin, Tex.: Jenkins, 1987).

9. *Richmond Enquirer,* November 22, 1862.

10. *Richmond Daily Examiner,* December 31, 1863, January 13, 1864.

11. George W. Bagby, *Selections from the Miscellaneous Writings of Dr. George W. Bagby* (Richmond: Whittet and Shepperson, 1885), 2, 40–41.

12. *Richmond Examiner,* November 29, 1864.

13. *Richmond Daily Examiner,* December 6, 1864.

14. *Richmond Enquirer,* December 2, 1863.

15. Samuel J. T. Moore Jr., *Moore's Complete Civil War Guide to Richmond* (Richmond: privately published, 1973), 76–77.

16. *Richmond Examiner,* September 2, October 24, 1863.

17. Ibid., February 2, 1864.

18. *Richmond Enquirer,* October 10, 1862.

19. *Richmond Examiner,* March 21, 1864.

20. Ibid., September 10, 1863.

21. L. J. Vance, "Dixiana," *Bachelor of Arts,* December 1895, 77–79.

22. Harold Holzer, "Virginians See Their War," in William C. Davis and James I. Robertson Jr., eds., *Virginia at War, 1862* (Lexington: University Press of Kentucky, 2007), 94.

23. *Southern Illustrated News,* January 21, 1865.

24. Ibid., October 18, 1862.

25. Ibid.

26. Ibid., November 22, 29, December 6, 1862.

27. Ibid., November 29, December 6, 13, 20, 1862.

28. Ibid., January 2, 1864.

29. Fahs, *Imagined Civil War,* 20.

30. *Southern Literary Messenger,* December 1861, 445.

31. Ibid., December 1862, 657–60.

32. Ibid., August 1863, 486–88.

33. Davies, "Observations," 624–25.

34. Fahs, *Imagined Civil War,* 28.

35. *Richmond Daily Examiner,* May 9, 1863.

36. Ibid.

37. Ibid., December 31, 1863, January 13, 1864.

38. "Editor's Table," *Southern Literary Messenger,* June 1864, 378.

39. *Richmond Daily Examiner,* December 28, 1863; Vance, "Dixiana," 77.

40. *Richmond Daily Examiner,* March 2, 1865.

41. *Evening Courier,* March 24, 1865.

42. *In Memoriam: John Tyler Waller, of Virginia* (N.p.: privately published, 1865).

Rehearsing Reconstruction in Occupied Virginia

Life and Emancipation at Fort Monroe

J. Michael Cobb

In 1864 Maj. Gen. Benjamin F. Butler commanded the Department of Virginia and North Carolina, headquartered at Fort Monroe, a formidable and strategic Union stronghold in eastern Virginia. Butler was known for his inability to manage his Army of the James in the field, and he was repeatedly criticized.[1] However, Butler spent much of the war as an administrator, with tours of duty at Fort Monroe before and after one in New Orleans. Lt. Gen. Ulysses S. Grant said that "as an administrative officer," Butler "has no superior"; when there was "a dissatisfied element to control, no one could manage it better than he."[2] Certainly he demonstrated the truth of that in his handling of the Union's most prominent enclave inside Confederate territory.

Fort Monroe is the largest masonry fortification in the United States, moated and covering sixty-three acres. The crown jewel of forty-two new bastions forming a coastal defense system built at huge expense following the debacle of British invasion during the War of 1812 and named for President James Monroe, the fort, near the town of Hampton, was designed by Simon Bernard, onetime aide de camp to Napoleon Bonaparte, and was completed by 2nd Lt. Robert E. Lee in 1834. This citadel was sited on Old Point Comfort, at the tip of a peninsula carved by the James and York rivers commanding the entrance from the Chesapeake Bay into the fine harbor of Hampton Roads. Fort Calhoun, built simultaneously with Fort Monroe and named for John C. Calhoun, Monroe's secretary of war, was situated on a man-made island a cannon shot into the roadstead entrance to complete military control of the harbor's mouth.[3] Edmund Ruffin, agriculturalist and arch-Secessionist, said of Fort Monroe: "It is a beautiful place, independent of its military strength, and imposing appearance as a fortress."[4]

Due to its strength, Fort Monroe remained in Union hands during the entire conflict, a Federal bastion less than 100 miles from the Confederate capital at Richmond. Fort Monroe became known as "Freedom's Fortress" among the slaves who flocked to the Union army there, and who inhabited settlements dubbed Slabtowns in the vicinity of the fort and, eventually, throughout the Hampton Roads area.[5] They came because of the courage and ingenuity of three enslaved men and of General Butler, who in May 1861 was serving his first tour as commandant. Rumors came to the blacks of the area that Hampton would be evacuated and they would be taken south. While engaged in building Confederate earthworks opposite Fort Monroe, at Sewell's Point near Norfolk, Frank Baker, Shepard Mallory, and James Townsend made the fateful decision to secede from slavery, clandestinely traveling by boat to the fort.

Butler immediately granted the daring fugitives an interview at his headquarters. Butler, an astute lawyer, progressive Massachusetts politician, friend of abolitionists, and presidential aspirant, concluded that Baker, Mallory, and Townsend were "contraband of war" under the conventions of international law. That is, they were the property of the enemy, and as such were being used against the United States. They would be entitled to shelter at the fort. After the interview the three men were fed and put to work. Union commanders at Port Royal, South Carolina, and elsewhere eventually would follow Butler's lead.[6] Throughout the South thousands of contrabands flocked to the campaigning Federal armies.

The day following the action of Baker, Mallory, and Townsend, Confederate lieutenant colonel John B. Cary, acting as agent for the escapees' owner, Col. Charles King Mallory, requested their return under the provisions of the Fugitive Slave Law. Butler refused, adding to his "contraband property" argument the statement that, due to Virginia's secession from the Union, he was under no obligation to return slaves to the foreign country that Virginia now claimed to be. He would only return the slaves of any person who took an oath of loyalty to the Union, for the slaves would then no longer be contraband, nor would the owner be part of a foreign country. Cary withdrew.[7]

Soon afterward, hundreds of black people began claiming asylum at

"Freedom's Fortress." A Massachusetts soldier reported, "Slaves are brought in here hourly."[8] Laura Wright Hildreth, General Butler's sister-in-law, said: "One day as many as forty came into the backyard; of all ages, from babies up to old men and women . . . homeless, not knowing when or where they were to get their next meal . . . we call them the Virginia Volunteers."[9] By midsummer 1861, 900 contrabands had found asylum at Fort Monroe. They were comprised of 300 able-bodied men, 225 women, 30 elderly persons, 175 children aged ten or under, and 170 young people.[10] Slave owners did not wish to believe that chattels spontaneously desired freedom. Ruffin found an alternative answer in Fort Monroe's white Northerners. "The ignorant slaves of the neighborhood," he said, "have long been exposed to the contaminating influence of the abolition garrison and Yankee crews of vessels."[11] In fact, the contrabands had not been legally set free, and even the Emancipation Proclamation did not do so, freeing only those slaves in areas under Confederate control. However, the promise of freedom surely lay ahead, as Butler foresaw; slaves were soon to be "sent forth from the hand that held them, never to be reclaimed."[12]

Butler's decision was a military necessity, as he explained to Gen. Winfield Scott. The Sewell's Point batteries threatened Butler's naval operations. His action deprived the enemy of its labor force and at the same time provided Butler with badly needed laborers. The men were put to work and a rudimentary wage system was established. Secretary of War Simon Cameron approved, and later Congress, inspired by Butler's action, in the Confiscation Act of August 6, 1861, resolved that contrabands could not be restored to their masters and that slaves performing work on Confederate military sites would be contraband. Later, Butler would entertain doubt that international law sanctioned human property as contraband. He would expound the concept that fugitive slaves should be treated as shipwrecked human beings on a civilized coast: all their social ties and means of living were thereby gone, and they were to be cared for because of their humanity.[13] Even though Abraham Lincoln's administration was troubled by the influx of thousands of contrabands and moved cautiously, the news from Virginia elated abolitionists and the radical wing of the Republican Party. Montgomery Blair, Lincoln's postmaster general and previously an attorney for Dred Scott, advised Butler to pursue a moderate course by limiting the effect of his "fugitive slave law" to actual working people, leaving the Secessionists to expend their limited resources caring for the nonworking classes.[14]

One "Slabtown" was on the border of Camp Hamilton, which contained the overflow of Fort Monroe's troops. Another expansive contraband camp existed on the edge of the ruins of the town of Hampton. Capt. Charles B. Wilder, assistant superintendent of freedmen, oversaw the camps, furnishing provisions and clothing. By May 1863, about 10,000 fugitives had gathered, hailing mainly from eastern Virginia and northeastern North Carolina. Captain Wilder erected a steam sawmill that milled 5,000 feet of boards daily. Butler delivered 3,000 feet of lumber to be used in completing the cabins of destitute families, and the contrabands also scavenged building material from Hampton's ruins. Within rough-hewn walls, enslaved black people experienced a measure of freedom for the first time.

The right to own land was what contrabands desired most.[15] Some, awarded the use of Confederate farmland, were furnished with seed, tools, and horses; they toiled for "halves," with the government receiving the rest of their produce. Many on such plots of ground sustained themselves. A few others were allowed to rent land and farm it with some independence. Butler made some into Union soldiers and sailors. Most contrabands, however, did not receive land. Pressed into service as laborers, they were awakened early and formed into soldierlike squads to be marched off to work on wharves as blacksmiths and carpenters, and in storehouses. They were required to put in long hours, day and night. Officers assigned some to themselves as personal servants. The women served as seamstresses, laundresses, and cooks. They were supposed to be paid at least $8 per month for men, $4 for women, but wages were often long in coming into their hands.

By 1864, Butler had organized the Slabtowns into relatively orderly cabins and streets. They were populated mostly by women and children, as most of the men had been taken elsewhere, to work for the government or as members of the Union forces. The treatment of contrabands by most Northerners was at best paternal and was often abusive, as most of the Union soldiers were no less prejudiced than their Southern counterparts. Reconstruction and the uncertain conditions of wage labor were thus foreshadowed in the contraband situation.

Many Northerners held reservations that enslaved people were prepared for freedom or capable of benefiting from formal education. The American Missionary Association made Hampton the first experiment to prove that blacks could become citizens once slavery was ended, sending teachers and founding several schools. While, as historians Willie Lee Rose and Robert

F. Engs show, more teachers were sent to Port Royal and the good results there had a greater impact upon Federal policies, nevertheless major inroads were made in Hampton.[16]

Union troops venturing through Hampton in early 1861 noted shady dusty streets, "its venerable church, [and] its trees and gardens," in the words of Edward Pierce. "Several old houses, with spacious rooms and high ornamented ceilings, gave evidence that at one time they had been occupied by citizens of considerable taste and rank."[17] They encountered a historic, small, pretty village on the water's edge. The town and surrounding county had about 3,100 whites, 2,400 enslaved persons, and 200 free persons of color in 1860.

"The war came as suddenly as a flash of lightning," Fanny Worsham of Hampton recalled years later. "Nobody a month before it started believed for a minute that there'd actually be a war."[18] Although the situation was more complicated than Worsham remembered, no one wanted war, and Hampton's populace was of a mixed mind in the years before secession. Many Hamptonians were Unionists, and the town's vote was cast for union at the April 1861 Virginia Secession Convention. However, there was much Southern nationalist sentiment, too. Walter Monteiro's 1857 address at the Hampton Academy called the novel *Uncle Tom's Cabin* "vicious" and untruthful, and warned that Northerners would abolish slavery.[19] John Brown's 1859 raid on the arsenal at Harpers Ferry shocked the town and reinforced white Hamptonians' fear of slave uprising, deriving from still-vivid memories of Nat Turner's nearby 1831 insurrection. Summertime Hamptonian and former president John Tyler thought that the specter of war had arrived when the garrison at Fort Monroe swiveled a heavy gun to landward, looming over "the sacred soil of Virginia."[20]

The tide turned when news of the Confederate bombardment of Fort Sumter on April 12, 1861, reached Hampton. Men, women, and children gathered under the secession flag as cheer after cheer rose on the breeze. Rain began to fall and lightning filled the sky. The pilot's cannon on the town wharf was hauled by men and boys along muddy King Street past the town center, past the courthouse, and to the northern edge of town. They placed it in the road near the slaughterhouse, and amid cheers and fireworks the cannon was fired by Secessionists once for each of the states that had seceded.[21] No doubt Hamptonians in their excitement contrasted Fort Sumter and its fate with the presence of Abraham Lincoln's Union army at

Fort Monroe, its garrison within earshot of the cannon's report. Hampton soon voted 360-6 for secession.

The Jefferson Davis administration nullified Federal law and proclaimed the confiscation of Federal property. It viewed the occupation of Fort Monroe as a transgression of Virginia's sovereignty. Winfield Scott, in the spring of 1861, made the fort's reinforcement a paramount objective. Scott understood that holding Fort Monroe was the key to suppressing the rebellion in Virginia, the Confederacy's most influential state. Abraham Lincoln rejected the constitutional legitimacy of secession and was determined to "hold, and occupy, and possess the property and places belonging to the government."[22] With reinforcement, this citadel became impregnable to Southern attack.

White Hamptonians were aghast at Butler's overthrow of slavery in his contraband decision. They understood how defenseless Hampton was, and there had been talk of abandonment. Now Confederate brigadier general John B. Magruder took a violent step forward. Knowing the fort's strength and fearing that Butler would seize the town to quarter troops and contraband, Magruder ordered the town razed. On August 7, 1861, Confederates, some of whom resided nearby, ran through the town with torches.[23] With little recent rain and a strong wind, a huge conflagration ensued. While many structures survived (at least in part), 500 buildings were destroyed. The flames illuminated the whole area.

The immediate impact of the burning of Hampton was dramatic. Lasting impressions were made on all witnessing the destruction. Reminiscences by Union soldiers give vivid pictures of the devastation. "No pen of the most romantic of novelists, or pencil of the finest artist, could . . . portray a scene half as picturesque as was this," a Yankee soldier named Cyrus wrote to his sister.[24] The *Philadelphia Enquirer* described it: "[N]othing [is left] but a forest of bleak sided chimneys and walls of brick houses tottering and cooling in the wind . . . a more desolate site can not be imagined than is Hampton today."[25] Southern sentiment patriotically found the burning a model for the rebels to follow. "Better in ashes, than let it stand to be the home, the protection and the provision house of the invader," intoned the *Charleston Courier*.[26] Butler, however, found the destruction unnecessary.[27]

Many of Hampton's white inhabitants had left town at the war's outbreak. Most of those who remained were now forced to depart. They found shelter in Richmond, Petersburg, and throughout Confederate Virginia and North

Carolina where relatives might take them in. Richmond citizens established a relief fund for displaced Hamptonians. Johanna "Nannie" Semple, for instance, went to work in Richmond at the treasury, signing Confederate currency and holding one of the few positions open to women. Her pay exceeded that of the average soldier. Along with other inhabitants of Richmond, exiles suffered shortages of food and clothing, plus inflated prices.[28]

Butler's job of pacification of Fort Monroe's environs was thus made easier. Few "seceshes" were left there to pacify, and, as at Port Royal, the absence of whites made socialization of the contrabands much easier. Butler was at first conciliatory to whites. Col. Abram Duryée, commander of the Fifth New York Zouaves, issued a special order directed to the Hampton area's remaining white inhabitants: they and their property would be respected, but they should reconsider their position to "obliterate the national existence."[29] When farmers complained of harassment by Federal troops, Butler ordered that the troops be severely punished. Some soldier interaction with locals was compassionate. Eugene Goodwin of the Ninety-ninth New York Infantry described how he "went to Hampton and took a lot of crackers to a poor white woman, 80 years old. I also bought ¼ lb. of green tea, ½ lb. of butter, 1 lb. sugar[,] and tobacco for her. She thanked me a thousand times and seemed very glad."[30]

Times were tough for the few civilians left. Union soldier Henry Lamoreaux heard from an old planter in the countryside near Hampton that he "did not know where the next [meal] was coming from" and said, "O how poor he was." However, thinking to himself, "you liar," Lamoreaux stole a twenty-five-pound pig and six hams (the latter carefully hidden deep inside the planking of an outbuilding). The next day others stole "some fish—they got 15[—]and I got a peck of potatoes."[31]

However, Southern Secessionist sentiment did not much dim, and many found the Northern troops and their insistent Union ideology oppressive. Soldiers at Fort Monroe were among the most Republican and Unionist in the Northern army, and they perceived their enclave as a monolithic stronghold not to be yielded to the slave power.[32] Ann E. Hope, residing near Fort Monroe, expressing sentiments prevalent in southeastern Virginia, sent reassurance to her aunt: "She must not think because I am down here with the Yankees that I have turned Yankee. I grow stronger southern every day[.] I am a rebel. Rebel is the righteous name that Washington bore and why should not we have the same."[33]

White intransigence forced the Federal government to change its policies. Civilian movement was strictly controlled; in a common occurrence, Parthenia Bloxom of Fox Hill was required to obtain a pass from the provost marshal to buy a bag of salt and take it home.[34] The "abandoned" property of those in the Confederate armed forces and the property of civilians who refused to embrace the loyalty oath were now to be confiscated and rented to loyalists or contrabands. Eleven Confederate soldiers' farms near Fort Monroe were seized in the spring of 1863, including Jefferson B. Sinclair's extensive property on the edge of ruined Hampton, Sherwood; George Booker's plantation near Back River, one of the finest in the county; and Lamington, the home of Robert Hudgins, who participated in Hampton's burning. Neighboring holdings in the possession of Unionists were not disturbed.[35] Blacks, however, were not spared. The War Department directed the Fort Monroe commandant to impress 1,000 able-bodied black men from Hampton and Norfolk to work in Washington at the Quartermaster Department. Asa Prescott lamented that Henry Tabb, Miles Hope, and Anthony Armistead, carrying the names of prominent Hampton families, were "taken away from their family and farms with no one to care for them, they will lose everything."[36]

With the capture of Norfolk during the Peninsula campaign of 1862, and amphibious expeditions launched earlier from Fort Monroe against North Carolina's coast, Federal authority spread south of Hampton Roads to Norfolk, Portsmouth, and the surrounding countryside. There, pacification matters were considerably different than in Hampton, since no major structures had been destroyed by the Confederates, and much of the population stayed. The military assumed that normal trade would continue to support subjugated residents. Commanders were assigned to oversee the populace. In Norfolk and Portsmouth, where the largest concentration of civilians existed, there was a large protective force of Federal soldiers, while detachments were posted in other small towns.

Expecting trouble, Butler enacted tough regulations and eventually (unlike in Hampton) instituted martial law. Butler's experience as Federal administrator of a recaptured New Orleans from May to December 1862 had prepared him in many ways for the similar task of governing a truculent and rebellious civilian population in Tidewater Virginia. He had also instituted martial law in New Orleans. On his first day, he had brought in artillery pieces to cow and disperse a blustering mob, showing the locals that no challenges to national authority would be tolerated. He happily concluded that the scene was as "quiet as a children's playground."

A Jacksonian Democrat, then Breckinridge Unionist, now Radical Republican, Butler inflicted punishment on all who refused to take the oath of allegiance to the United States. A civilian who had torn an American flag off the U.S. Mint in New Orleans and had "trailed it on the ground" was tried and executed for treason, while in Norfolk a prominent doctor was executed for murdering a white Federal officer who commanded black troops that had jostled him.[37] Butler's sentiments on ending the war were equally hard-nosed: "[P]rosecute the war, bring every part of the country into submission," he said, "then there will be no place for rebellion, no parties for compromise, no occasion for reconstruction, and clemency may be shown and amnesty offered to individual citizens who deserve it. Is there any other way to restore the Union?"[38] As the hostilities escalated and became more bitter, many Northerners welcomed Butler's uncompromising treatment of the "seceshes." He retained a letter from Thomas J. Moore of Springfield, Illinois, castigating "Lincoln and many others in high authority" for being "too angelic in this devilish rebellion." "I still hope and trust," Moore told Butler, "you will give both the 'he' and 'she' devils of the rebellion their just desserts."[39]

In Norfolk and Portsmouth Butler did not disappoint the Yankees who cheered him on or the Confederates who branded him an outlaw, liable to being shot on sight. Citizens were subjected to the aggravation of obtaining a permit to purchase necessary domestic articles such as spools of cotton, a pound of starch, or a yard of cloth. In Norfolk's Kimberly's Store, a sign read, "[N]o goods sold to citizens except by a special permit of the Provost Marshal."[40] Butler judged that alcohol was dangerous, facilitating pauperism and crime as well as obstreperousness, and he strictly regulated the liquor trade. Only twelve establishments, all hotels, were granted coveted permits to sell alcohol. Since he found Norfolk's houses run down and the city "the filthiest place I ever saw," Butler ordered Norfolk property owners to maintain all structures, in order to prevent the outbreak of yellow fever. Further, they were forbidden to put ashes and other debris into the streets. All of this was under pain of fine or imprisonment. He had previously ordered that New Orleans be similarly cleaned up, since he knew that yellow fever "had always within the memory of man been the scourge of New Orleans."[41]

Speech and symbols considered disloyal were prohibited. In Norfolk, Butler's subordinate Brig. Gen. E. L. Viele forbade gathering in the streets to discuss political matters, while rebel flags and badges were not tolerated. Parents were held strictly accountable for their children's behavior. Butler censored opinion, particularly punishing criticism of his actions and what he considered disloyal commentary. He regulated the distribution of "treasonable sheets" such as the *Catholic Depository* and the *Boston Courier*. He justified this by noting that since everyone agreed on controlling trade in "liquors and drugs that kill the body" "how much more ought there to be a regulation of the sale of poisonous and pernicious writing[s] that kill the soul."[42] Censorship reached into the pulpit when Butler replaced Norfolk's Presbyterian pastor Rev. James D. Armstrong with C. L. Woodworth, the chaplain of the Twenty-seventh Massachusetts Volunteers, a "true loyalist."[43]

To make sure that his version of the truth was disseminated, Butler published the *New Regime,* with the unabashed design of promoting the cause of Union. He had previously commandeered a New Orleans newspaper, *True Delta,* and after jailing its editor for disloyalty had used the sheet for similar purposes. The *New Regime* also made public actions taken to reestablish order in Norfolk and Portsmouth. Accounts were regularly printed of disloyal activity and civil trials, including lengthy lists of soldiers charged with desertion, and of civilians or soldiers charged with intoxication, brawling, theft, or the sale of liquor and other contraband. Finally, the mail was also tightly controlled. Letters could not exceed one page in length, while content was limited strictly to domestic matters. All correspondence had to be signed by the sender and delivered to the provost marshal's office, whence it passed directly to Butler's headquarters.

All property was at hazard. Mrs. Lavinia Holt, mother of two Confederate soldiers, had sent her U.S. money to a friend in Norfolk County for safekeeping when Hampton was evacuated in 1861, hedging her bets on the viability of the then-new Confederacy. In 1863 the friend's house was broken into and all was lost. General Viele said he would do what he could, but "if they find that any of it is for soldiers' [relatives,] they will cease all efforts in its behalf." The friend caused herself fear and danger, accusing her former slaves of theft and having some of them arrested; she is "[now] in constant dread of being burned out by them."[44] Blacks provoked whites by enthusiastically celebrating what they estimated to be the end of their enslavement with a large procession on the first anniversary of the issuance of the Emancipation Proclamation. Viele was aware this would "be a source of deep mortification to the insolent secessionists," but it was not suppressed.[45]

Many residents continued their stout resistance to Butler and the troops. Secessionists who detested the reminders of occupation ripped down the Yankees' posted orders. Pvt. William H. Osborne spoke of two very different sorts of civilian actions:

> There were, however, among the people of Portsmouth, the loyal people there [who] welcomed [us] by a display of American flags. The whole settlement was radiant with bunting—streamers, ship's flags, jacks, and pennants—the poor people had managed to keep these emblems of loyalty during the war. They had hidden them under carpets, in attics, and cellars. One old gentleman stated that his had been boxed up tightly and buried in his garden. . . .
>
> Some of the women of Norfolk and Portsmouth were quite spiteful towards the soldiers. The scene was not infrequent of a bevy of finely-dressed ladies parading the streets with small Confederate flags pinned to their breasts. . . . Another more fiendish manifestation of hatred of the soldiers consisted in politely presenting them with beautiful bouquets filled with needles . . . and wait patiently for the soldier to press the flowers to his face, when up would go a loud shout of exultation.[46]

Butler had more trouble with women than with men. In New Orleans, he had notoriously issued an order mandating that women who disrespected Northern soldiers be treated as women of the street, earning him international condemnation, outlaw status decreed by the Jefferson Davis regime, and the sobriquet "Beast." He remembered, "These women, she-adders, more venomous than he-adders, were the insulting enemies of my army and my country, and were so treated."[47]

Butler's pacification of these areas of high-density Confederate population was as successful as it could have been. He kept the streets clean and the population by and large free from infection, he maintained order, and he demonstrated an unmitigated loyalty to the Union that he hoped would rub off, though of course it did not.

Observers often described wartime Fort Monroe and its vicinity as a city. Thousands of troops were stationed there. The mighty granite fortress dominating the Chesapeake and the harbor, along with Camp Hamilton's cluster of buildings and storehouses plus the grand flotilla of ships, made it look like more than a military camp. Indeed, the sight of Fort Monroe inspired patriotic fervor among the legions tramping through during four bloody years, evoking a belief that the Union would be sustained. Voices in many Northern dialects expressed sentiments symbolizing the overwhelming might produced by the growing mobilization of Northern industry, manpower, and determination. Nathaniel Morton of the Third Massachusetts Volunteers conveyed this sensibility vehemently: "The secession devils dare not come within the roar of Union artillery on this magnificent bulwark of American civilization and freedom."[48]

Butler's Army of the James was made up chiefly of native-born men from the Northeast, containing a higher percentage of New Englanders than any other Union army. Many others were from New York, Pennsylvania, and New Jersey. A relatively rural command, its recruits were drawn from small cities, towns, and villages. Numerous Irish and German immigrants filled the ranks. These soldiers suited their commandant, since Butler's antebellum political career had championed the urban working class. One student of the army has concluded that "more than any other federal army it was a bastion of the republican and union party sentiments."[49]

The fort itself was huge and imposing. Four narrow portals in its thick walls gave access. At the east entrance facing out to sea, Quarters Number One was the commandant's headquarters. Officers resided in three stately buildings lining the parade ground. Many officers, their families, and enlisted men were billeted in damp casemates (built as gun emplacements) in the walls. Troops drilled daily on the broad parade ground. At first the only water supply was rain draining from the ramparts into cisterns. A lighthouse built during Thomas Jefferson's administration was outside the moat on the shore, near which stood the menacing "Lincoln" and "Union" guns. The waterfront became thick with utilitarian buildings: barracks, warehouses, stables, and a signal station. The Quartermaster's Department built two large two-story buildings for contrabands, equal to the soldiers' barracks. Another building was built for the families. Nearby was Northerner John B. Kimberley's massive store, crowded with soldierly customers—only those of undoubted loyalty could purvey to the army.

Fort Monroe's main outlet to the sea was a heavy-timbered wharf, laden with the industrial North's abundant equipage awaiting transport or storage. The fort was a base for the North Atlantic Blockading Squadron. "We arrived safe at Fort Monroe," a New Jersey soldier recounted during the 1862

Peninsula campaign, "when a site [*sic*] met our eyes that put us in the mind of New York. Ships were here in swarms."[50]

The fortification could not house all the troops sent there, and thousands went to Camp Hamilton, situated within the fort's shadow and connected by a narrow isthmus across Mill Creek. It had been established in the spring of 1861 when Butler had confiscated the large farm Roseland, ironically owned by Unionist Joseph E. Segar, an antebellum member of the Virginia General Assembly. The Second New York Volunteers and the First Vermont Militia had settled in Segar's pastures, while the Fifth New York Volunteers had later ransacked the lovely home. Camp Hamilton contained 5,000 residents by winter 1862. Fortunately, a productive well on the nearby property of Rubin Clark produced daily up to 1,000 gallons of water of the best quality.[51]

The lasting occupation transfigured Fort Monroe's pastoral setting. Camp Hamilton possessed the characteristics of a small Northern town, its garrison often exceeding Hampton's antebellum population. It was composed of orderly streets lined with wooden storehouses, shops, stables, and "the white tents of the various regiments . . . were spread out . . . like toys in the distance."[52] The bakery produced well over 1,000 loaves of bread daily. The men built a gymnasium, and officers and their wives attended balls there. Camp Hamilton exhibited a curious mélange of building materials "liberated" from local "secesh" houses, with green blinds, lattice work, and carved woodwork ornamenting rough log houses. Four magnificent peacocks made life more beautiful and noisier.[53]

The invaders were drawn to Old Point Comfort's natural attributes. The sea breeze and mild climate made it "one of the healthiest places in the world," thought one soldier; the men swam in "nature's great bath-tub."[54] Sarah H. Butler, the general's wife, went into raptures: "[T]he wind sweeps over the ramparts, carrying along mist and a soughing, sighing sound, melancholy and bodeful . . . the breakers roll in splendidly tonight. . . . the beach here is one of the finest I ever saw . . . the most agreeable thing is to drive on the beach, and look at the green and foamy waves as they roll in and break to pieces."[55]

Winfield Scott extolled to Butler the area's soft-shelled crabs and waters renowned for an abundance of oysters. Union soldiers from coastal regions knew how to capture these delicacies, and their land-bound comrades eagerly adapted. A Massachusetts soldier found that, "in crossing Hampton [River], our mouths watered to see soldiers digging for oysters."[56] At least one civilian entrepreneur erected a shanty on the strand to vend oysters and crabs to the army and navy.[57] Officers quartered in the casemates consumed vast quantities of oysters and tossed the white shells through the embrasures into the moat.

Billy Yank was an avid sightseer, with a keen appreciation of the area's sights, climate, and history. President Tyler's holiday spot Villa Margaret received much attention.[58] Special homage was paid to the 1728 building housing Hampton's St. John's Church. Fort Monroe provided an excellent vantage point from which to witness the epic encounter between *Monitor* and *Virginia* miles out in the roadstead on March 9, 1862. Thereafter the *Monitor*, the most popular attraction, "was lying not far from [Fort Monroe's] wharf, the little cloud of steam issuing from her pipe, showing that she was ready for instant action," reported a Massachusetts soldier. "The men crowded to the sides [of a ship] and went into the rigging to get a sight of the wonderful vessel."[59] Soldiers and sailors also loved to have their pictures taken, parading through the unpretentious "Monitor Gallery" established by an enterprising veteran from Maine, William Larrabee, and assuming patriotic stances for the camera.

The Northern soldiers were ostentatiously patriotic at Fort Monroe, rituals celebrating the Union occurring frequently on the "sacred soil of Virginia." The largest building near Hampton, the four-story Chesapeake Female Seminary overlooking Hampton Roads, was in 1861 occupied by the Fifth New York Zouaves. Their band went to its roof to play "The Star-Spangled Banner" as the flag was raised, easily visible and likely audible from the center of rebel Hampton.[60] With each passing year the Fourth of July was ever more avidly commemorated, trumping the 1861 activities of the Zouaves, who built huge bonfires around which one soldier said they "danced, sang and yelled like so many Comanche Indians" in their picturesque uniforms of turbans, blue jackets, and baggy red trousers; they proudly earned the sobriquet "red devils."[61]

Two large hospitals were in operation for Union troops wounded in the campaigns against Petersburg and Richmond. The Hampton Military Hospital cared for enlisted men, having thousands of patients per month in 1864–1865; next door the Chesapeake Military Hospital (recently the Female Seminary) cared for officers. Jacob Heffelfinger, a member of the Seventh Pennsylvania Reserve Corps wounded during the Peninsula campaign, was in the Chesapeake Military Hospital in early August 1862. "Two men were buried today," he sadly noted on August 7, 1862. "Their discharge is final and never will the long drum or shrill fife waken them from their slumber."[62]

Under Butler's command and thanks to his ingenuity, significant inroads toward the abolition of slavery were made at Fort Monroe. In addition, he molded a solidly Unionist encampment of freedmen and soldiery there, while in the Norfolk and Portsmouth area, Butler proved an equally proficient and inventive governor of a rebellious citizenry and countryside. Vilified by the white populace because of his heavy-handedness, Butler as military governor of an enlarging Federal domain was a fountainhead of policies of emancipation, union, and grudging loyalty to the conquering government. Ben Butler may have been incompetent in the field, but he performed well his task of pacifying and making orderly the areas of recaptured Confederate territory under his command, always demanding obedience to the Union he loved.

Notes

1. After May 1864, he was at the battlefront in military command, and got his troops almost completely cornered on a peninsula near Petersburg, rendering them less than useful in the last crucial months of war. Grant, disgusted, noted that Butler's bottled-up troops were "strongly corked." Benjamin F. Butler, *Autobiography and Personal Reminiscences of Major-General Benjamin F. Butler* (Boston: A. M. Thayer, 1892), 855.

2. Ibid., 852.

3. In 1862 the Secessionist John C. Calhoun's name was removed and the fort was renamed for Gen. John E. Wool. See John R. Weaver, *A Legacy in Brick and Stone: American Coastal Defense Forts of the Third System, 1816–1867* (Missoula, Mont.: Pictorial Histories, 2001), 49–50, 133–35, 135n5.

4. Edmund Ruffin, *The Diary of Edmund Ruffin*, 3 vols., ed. William Kauffman Scarborough (Baton Rouge: Louisiana State University Press, 1972–1989), 1:84 (entry for June 28, 1857).

5. For the events related in this and the succeeding paragraphs, see Robert F. Engs, *Freedom's First Generation: Black Hampton, Virginia, 1861–1890* (New York: Fordham University Press, 2004), 13–16, 26–27.

6. Willie Lee Rose, *Rehearsal for Reconstruction: The Port Royal Experiment* (Indianapolis: Bobbs-Merrill, 1964), 14–15.

7. Butler, *Autobiography*, 256–58.

8. Nathaniel Morton to "Dear Friend," May 29, 1861, collections of the Hampton History Museum, Hampton, Va.

9. Laura Wright Hildreth to Harriet H. Heard, June 6, 1861, in Benjamin F. Butler, *Private and Official Correspondence of Gen. Benjamin F. Butler, during the Period of the Civil War,* 5 vols., ed. Jessie Ames Marshall (Norwood, Mass.: Plimpton, 1917) 1:128.

10. Engs, *Freedom's First Generation,* 16; U.S. War Department, *War of the Rebellion: A Compilation of Official Records of the Union and Confederate Armies* (Washington, D.C.: Government Printing Office, 1880–1901), series 1, vol. 2, 53 (hereafter cited as *OR*).

11. Ruffin, *Diary,* 2:50 (entry for June 22, 1861).

12. Butler, quoted in Ira Berlin et al., *Slaves No More: Three Essays on Emancipation and the Civil War* (New York: Cambridge University Press, 1992), 22.

13. Scott Reynolds Nelson and Carol Sheriff, *A People at War: Civilians and Soldiers in America's Civil War, 1854–1877* (New York: Oxford University Press, 2007), 78; Benjamin F. Butler to Edwin M. Stanton, May 25, 1862, in Butler, *Correspondence,* 1:516–17.

14. Montgomery Blair to Benjamin F. Butler, May 29, 1861, in Butler, *Correspondence,* 1:116–17.

15. Testimony of Hon. F. W. Bird, December 24, 1863, in Ira Berlin et al., eds., *Free at Last: A Documentary History of Slavery, Freedom, and the Civil War* (New York: Free Press, 1992), 282.

16. Engs, *Freedom's First Generation,* 32–33, 45; Rose, *Rehearsal,* 85–89, 203, 229–35, 372–75.

17. Edward L. Pierce, "Contrabands at Fortress Monroe," *Atlantic Monthly,* November 1861, 630, 631.

18. Worsham, quoted in Les Jensen, *32nd Virginia Infantry* (Lynchburg, Va.: H. E. Howard, 1990), 9.

19. Walter Monteiro, "Address Delivered before the Neotrophian Society of the Hampton Academy on the Twenty-eighth of July, 1857," quoted in Gary W. Gallagher, *The Confederate War* (Cambridge, Mass.: Harvard University Press, 1997), 99. On February 22, 1861, some citizens of Hampton presented Col. Charles King Mallory's 115th Virginia Militia with a flag containing Patrick Henry's words "Give me liberty or give me death" embossed in gold on a field of blue. They viewed the impending conflict as a second American Revolution. See William R. Taylor, *Cavalier and Yankee: The Old South and American Character* (Cambridge, Mass.: Harvard University Press, 1979), 262–65. The flag is in the collections of the Hampton History Museum.

20. Butler, *Autobiography,* 167.

21. W[illiam] H[ope] Peek to George [Meredith Peek], April 15, 1861, Marrow Family Papers, Virginia Historical Society, Richmond.

22. Phillip Shaw Paludan, *The Presidency of Abraham Lincoln* (Lawrence: University Press of Kansas, 1994), 53.

23. One of the torchers had parents living on the edge of Hampton. The parents were Unionists. After giving his parents fifteen minutes to leave, the son, "now filled with frenzy," put the flames to their house. The parents escaped to Fort Monroe, where they told their story. William H. Osborne, *The History of the Twenty-ninth Regiment of Massachusetts Volunteer Infantry* (Boston: A. J. Wright, 1877), 79–80.

24. Cyrus ? to "Dear Sister," March 1, 1862, collections of the Hampton History Museum.

25. *Philadelphia Enquirer,* August 8, 1861.

26. *Charleston Courier,* August 14, 1861.

27. "I confess myself so poor a soldier not to be able to discern the strategical importance of this movement," he said. Benjamin F. Butler to Winfield Scott, August 8, 1861, in Butler, *Correspondence,* 1:198.

28. Edward D. C. Campbell Jr. and Kym S. Rice, eds., *A Woman's War: Southern Women, Civil War, and the Confederate Legacy* (Charlottesville: University of Virginia Press, 1996), 17.

29. Alfred Davenport, *Camp and Field Life of the Fifth New York Volunteer Infantry* (New York: Dick and Fitzgerald, 1879), 37.

30. Civil War Diaries of Dr. Eugene A. Goodwin, entry for November 11, 1861, http://iagenweb.org/jasper/military/goodwin_diary/1861/.

31. Hank [Lamoreaux] to George ?, 102nd New York Volunteers, February 13, 1863 (datelined Newport News, Va.), collections of the Hampton History Museum.

32. Edward G. Longacre, *Army of Amateurs: General Benjamin F. Butler and the Army of the James, 1863–1865* (Mechanicsburg, Pa.: Stackpole, 1997), 45.

33. Ann E. Hope to "Dear Aunt," June 22, 1863, quoted in Gallagher, *Confederate War,* 79. In early February 1864, all Williamsburg, Virginia, citizens were ordered to take an oath of allegiance to the Union at risk of losing their homes, because too many leaks had occurred concerning Union troop movements. Williamsburg resident Sally Galt demurred: "It would almost make me crazy to take any oath to any government . . . I could not promise to support. You know slavery I have always said I did not like, but I can't take an oath." Sally M. Galt to Dorothea Dix, [February 1864], quoted in Carol Kettenburg Dubbs, *Defend This Old Town: Williamsburg during the Civil War* (Baton Rouge: Louisiana State University Press, 2002), 327.

34. Provost Marshal, Fort Monroe, [Pass], October 24, 1863, collections of the Hampton History Museum.

35. Headquarters Department of Virginia, Seventh Army Corps, [Authorization], March 28, 1863, *OR*, series 1, vol. 18, 570.

36. Asa Prescott to Edwin M. Stanton, July 11, 1863, in Berlin et al., *Free at Last*, 202.

37. Butler, *Autobiography*, x, 209, 370.

38. Benjamin F. Butler to James Concklin, September 1, 1863, in Butler, *Correspondence*, 3:110.

39. Thomas J. Moore to Benjamin F. Butler, April 11, 1864, in ibid., 4:61–62.

40. William F. Keeler to Anna E. Keeler, November 25, 1862, in Robert W. Daly, ed., *Aboard the USS Monitor, 1862: The Letters of Acting Paymaster William Frederick Keeler, U.S. Navy, to His Wife, Anna* (Annapolis, Md.: U.S. Naval Institute, 1964), 234.

41. Butler, *Autobiography*, 410, 394.

42. Benjamin F. Butler to President, American News Company, April 11, 1864, in Butler, *Correspondence*, 4:58–59.

43. *New Regime*, April 27, 1864.

44. Almedia White to [Lavinia] Holt, May 6, 1863, collections of the Hampton History Museum.

45. *OR*, series 1, vol. 18, 502.

46. Osborne, *Twenty-ninth Regiment*, 134–35.

47. Longacre, *Army of Amateurs*, 5–6, 421.

48. Nathaniel Morton to "My Dear Friend," May 17, 1861, collections of the Hampton History Museum.

49. Longacre, *Army of Amateurs*, 45, 50.

50. David Herbert Donald, ed., *Gone for a Soldier: The Civil War Memoirs of Private Alfred Bellard* (Boston: Little, Brown, 1975), 51.

51. Davenport, *Camp and Field Life*, 33–34 (Roseland confiscated and ransacked); Benjamin F. Butler to Winfield Scott, May 24, 1861, in Butler, *Correspondence*, 1:104–5 (Second New York and First Vermont with equipage at Segar's; 1,000 gallon figure).

52. Davenport, *Camp and Field Life*, 75–76.

53. William F. Keeler to Anna E. Keeler, May 3, 1862, in Daly, *Aboard the Monitor*, 96–97.

54. Davenport, *Camp and Field Life*, 41.

55. Sarah H. Butler to Harriet H. Heard, June 2, 1861, in Butler, *Correspondence*, 1:122.

56. John L. Parker, *Henry Wilson's Regiment: History of the 22nd Massachusetts Infantry, the Second Company Sharpshooters, and the Third Light Battery in the War of the Rebellion* (1887; repr., Boston: Butternut and Blue, 1997), 77.

57. Thomas A. Scott to John E. Wool, Sept. 27, 1861, collections of the Hampton History Museum.

58. It also received much desecration because of the avid Secessionist sentiment of its owner. It became a residence for the Fifth New York Zouaves, then was the headquarters and dormitory of the American Missionary Association. Davenport, *Camp and Field Life,* 39. On August 8, 1861, following Hampton's destruction, the Zouaves replaced the Stars and Bars (a gift from retreating Hamptonians) with the Stars and Stripes on top of the villa's roof, easily visible from Confederate-occupied Hampton. Osborne, *Twenty-ninth Regiment,* 81.

59. Parker, 22nd *Massachusetts Infantry,* 76.

60. Davenport, *Camp and Field Life,* 36.

61. Ibid., 86–87.

62. Jacob Heffelfinger, Diary, vol. 1, entry for August 7, 1862, collections of the Hampton History Museum.

Diary of a Southern Refugee during the War, June 1863–July 1864

Judith Brockenbrough McGuire

Edited by James I. Robertson Jr.

The thirteen months in this installment of Judith McGuire's diary give a revealing picture of a Confederacy losing the Civil War while with equal slowness falling apart internally. In July, following the battle of Gettysburg and a Union raid on her temporary home at Ashland, Mrs. McGuire wrote of the war: "Sometimes I wish I could sleep until it was over—a selfish wish enough; but it is hard to witness so much sorrow which you cannot alleviate."

Suffering among Virginia citizens was widespread by the midway point of the conflict. In this portion of the McGuire diary are four accounts of acquaintances driven into refugee life by Union occupation of home areas. Another friend provided a narrative of a little-known but destructive raid in the Tappahannock area. Mrs. McGuire also reported a social call she made on Mrs. Robert E. Lee shortly after Gettysburg.

In late October 1863, the McGuires were forced to leave the Ashland cottage that had been their home for many months. Mrs. McGuire was extremely fortunate to obtain rooms not only in Richmond but in the home where she had lived as a young woman. She and her husband resided there through the remainder of the Civil War.

Two positive developments occurred for Mrs. McGuire during this time. When it appeared that the diary might end for lack of writing material, she found "some nice wrapping-paper" on which to make future entries. Then, in November 1863, Mrs. McGuire obtained a clerkship in the C.S. Commissary Department. Her salary was $125 monthly—at a time when a merino dress cost $150 when available.

Spring 1864 entries centered on U. S. Grant's Overland campaign. Following the battles of the Wilderness, Spotsylvania, Cold Harbor, and in the Petersburg area, Mrs. McGuire could only react each time with heartbreak at the loss of family members and beloved friends. Found here will be a lengthy account of the death and funeral of Lee's cavalry chief, Gen. "Jeb" Stuart.

This highly sensitive and deeply devout lady never grasped the fact that the Civil War became history's first total war—that the Union armies became as intent to break the will of the Southern people as they were dedicated to defeating Southern armies.

Some long gaps appear in this part of the diary. Mrs. McGuire apologized to herself by confessing: "[A]fter looking over commissary accounts for six hours in the day, and attending to home or hospital duties in the afternoon, I am too much wearied to write much at night."

Diary of a Southern Refugee

June 1 [1863]—L. and B.[1] went up to Mr. Marye's near Fredericksburg to-day, to visit their brother's grave. They took flowers with which to adorn it. It is a sweet, though sad office, to plant flowers on a Christian's grave. They saw my sister, who is there, nursing their wounded son.[2]

News from Vicksburg cheering.

5th—Our household circle has been broken to-day, by Mrs. S[tuart] and her daughter B[ella] leaving it for South Carolina. We are grieved to give them up.

6th—We have been interested lately by a visit to this village of our old friend, Mrs. T.[3] of Rappahannock County. She gives most graphic descriptions of her sojourn of seven weeks among the Yankees last summer. Sixty thousand surrounded her house, under command of General Siegel.[4] On one occasion, he and his staff rode up and announced that they would *take tea with her*. Entirely alone, that elegant old lady retained her composure, and with unruffled countenance rang her bell; when the servant appeared, she said to him, "Jim, tea for fourteen." She quietly retained her seat, conversing with them with dignified politeness, and submitting as best she could to the General's very free manner of walking about her beautiful establishment, pronouncing it "baronial," and regretting, in her presence, that he had not known of its elegancies and comforts in time, that he might have brought on Mrs. Siegel, and have made it his head-quarters. Tea being announced, Mrs. T[hornton], before proceeding to the dining-room, requested the servant to call a soldier in, who had been guarding her house for weeks, and who had sought occasion to do her many kindnesses. When the man entered, the General demurred: "No, no, madam, he will not go to table with us." Mrs. T[hornton] replied, "General, I must beg that you will allow this *gentleman* to come to *my table,* for *he* has been a friend to me when I have sadly wanted one." The General objected no farther; the *man* took tea with the master. After tea, the General proposed music, asking Mrs. T[hornton] if she had ever played; she replied that "such was still her habit." The piano being opened, she said if she sang at all she must sing the songs of her own land, and then, with her uncommonly fine voice, she sang "The Bonnie Blue Flag," "Dixie," and other Southern songs, with great spirit. They listened with apparent pleasure. One of the staff then suggested that the General was a musician. Upon her vacating the seat he took it, and played in grand style; with so much beauty and *accuracy,* she added, with a twinkle in her eye, that I strongly suspected him of having been a music-master. Since that time she has heard that he was once master of that beautiful art in Mobile. Well, he was at least a more innocent man then than now. Almost every woman of the South, or at least of Virginia, will have her tale to tell when this "cruel war is over."[5] The life of too many will be, alas! as a "tale that is told;" its interest, its charm, even its hope, as far as this world is concerned, having passed away.[6] Their crown of rejoicing will be in the public weal, which their loved and lost have fought, bled, and died to establish; but their own hearts will be withered, their hearths deserted.

Mrs. G. D.,[7] of Fredericksburg, has been giving some amusing incidents of her sudden departure from her home. She had determined to remain, but when, on the night of the bombardment, a shell burst very near her house, her husband aroused her to say that she must go. They had no means of conveyance, and her two children were both under three years of age, and but one servant (the others having gone to the Yankees), a girl twelve years old. It so happened that they had access to three straw carriages, used by her own children and those of her neighbours. They quickly determined to put a child in each of two carriages, and to bundle up as many clothes as would fill the third. The father drew the carriage containing one child, the mother the other child, and the little girl drew the bundle of clothes. They thus set out, to go they knew not whither, only to get out of the way of danger. It was about midnight, a dark, cold night. They went on and on, to the outskirts of the town, encountering a confused multitude rushing pell-mell, with ever and anon a shell bursting at no great distance, sent as a threat of what they might expect on the morrow. They were presently overtaken by a respectable shoemaker whom they knew, rolling a wheelbarrow containing a large bundle of clothes, and *the baby.* They were attracted by the poor little child rolling off from its elevated place on the bundle, and as Mrs. D[aniel] stopped, with motherly solicitude for the child, the poor man told his story. In the darkness and confusion he had become separated from his wife and other children, and knew not where to find them; he thought he might find them but for anxiety about the baby. Mrs. D[aniel] then proposed that he should take her bundle of clothes with his in the wheelbarrow, and put his child in the third straw carriage. This being agreed to, the party passed on. When they came to our encampment, a soldier ran out to offer to draw one carriage, and thus rest the mother; having gone as far as he dared from his regiment, then another soldier took his place to the end of the line, and so on from one soldier to another until our encampment was passed. Then she drew on her little charge about two miles farther, to the house of an acquaintance, which was wide open to the homeless. Until late the next day the shoemaker's baby was under their care, but he at last came, bringing the bundle to safety. As the day progressed the cannon roared and the shells whistled, and it was thought advisable for them to go on to Chancellorsville. The journey of several miles was performed on foot, still with the straw carriages, for no horse nor vehicle could be found in that desolated country. They remained at Chancellorsville until the 2d or 3d of May, when that house became within range of cannon. Again she gathered up her little flock, and came on to Ashland. Her little three-years old boy explored the boarding-house as soon as he got to it, and finding no cellar he became alarmed, and running to his mother, exclaimed, "This house won't do, mother; we all have no cellar to go into when they shell it!" Thus our children are born and reared amid war and bloodshed! It seemed so sad to me to see a bright little girl, a few days ago, of four years old, stop in the midst of her play, when she heard distant thunder, exclaiming, "Let me run home, they are firing!"

Poor little child, her father has been a sacrifice; no wonder that she wanted to run to her mother when she thought she heard firing. Tales far more sad than that of Mrs. D[aniel] are told, of the poor assembled by hundreds on the roadside in groups, having no shelter to cover them, and often nothing to eat, on that dark winter's night.

June 7—We are living in fear of a Yankee raid. They have a large force on York River, and are continually sending parties up the Pamunky and Mattapony Rivers, to devastate the country and annoy the inhabitants.[8] Not long ago a party rode to the house of a gentleman on Mattapony; meeting him on the lawn, the commander accosted him: "Mr. R.,[9] I understand you have the finest horses in King William County." "Perhaps, sir, I have," replied Mr. R[oane]. "Well, sir," said the officer, "I want those horses immediately." "They are not yours," replied Mr. R[oane], "and you can't get them." The officer began to curse, and said he would burn every house on the place if the horses were not produced. Suiting the action to the word, he handed a box of matches to a subordinate, saying, "Burn!" In half an hour, Mr. R[oane] saw fourteen of his houses in a light blaze, including the dwelling, the kitchen, corn-houses, and barn filled with grain, meat-house filled with meat, and servants' houses. Scarcely any thing was saved, not even the family clothes. But he did not get the horses, which were the objects of his peculiar wishes; the faithful servants had carried them away to a place of safety. How strange it is that we can be so calm, surrounded as we are by danger!

8th—We have had a cavalry fight near Culpeper Court-House.[10] We drove the enemy back, but I am afraid that our men won no laurels, for we were certainly surprised most shamefully.

16th—The morning papers gave a telegram from General Lee, announcing that General [Jubal A.] Early's Brigade had taken Winchester by storm.[11] So again Winchester and all that beautiful country, Clarke [County], etc., are disenthralled.

21st—We hear of fights and rumours of fights. It is said that Ewell's Division captured 6,000 prisoners at Winchester, and that General Edward Johnson went to Berryville and captured 2,000 that were on their way to reinforce Millroy.[12] They have driven the enemy out of the Valley, so that now we have possession of it once more. Our cavalry have been as far as Chambersburg, Pennsylvania, but I do not know what they have accomplished.[13]

While in the midst of preparation to visit my sisters at W[estwood] and S[ummer] H[ill], we have been startled by the account of Yankees approaching. They have landed in considerable force at the White House, and are riding over the country to burn and destroy.[14] They have burned the South Anna Bridge on the Central Railroad, and this evening were advancing on the bridge over the South Anna, on this railroad, which is but four miles above us. We have a small force there, and a North Carolina regiment has gone up to-night to reinforce them. We are, of course, in considerable excitement. I am afraid they are ruining the splendid wheat harvests which are now being gathered on the Pamunky. Trusting in the Lord, who hath hitherto been our help, we are going quietly to bed, though we believe that they are very near us. From our army we can hear nothing.[15] No one can get farther than Culpeper Court-House in that direction. Why this has been ordered I know not, but for some good military reason, I have no doubt. It is said that Stuart's cavalry have been fighting along the line of the Manassas Gap Railroad with great success. We can hear no particulars.[16]

Saturday Evening—Just heard from W[estwood] and S[ummer] H[ill]; both terribly robbed by the raiders in the last three days. All of my brother's horses and mules taken. Some of the servants were forced off, who staid so faithfully by them, and resisted all the Yankee entreaties twice before. They attempted to burn the wheat, which is shocked in the field, but an opportune rain made it too wet to burn. The raiders came up the river, destroying crops, carriages, etc., stealing horses and cattle, and carrying off the servants from every plantation, until they got to Hickory Hill (Mr. W. F. Wickham's,)[17] where they found a prize in the person of General W. F. Lee,[18] who was wounded at the cavalry fight of Beverley's Ford, and was at Mr. W[ickham]'s, unable to move. Notwithstanding the remonstrances of his wife and mother, they took him out of his bed, placed him in Mr. Wickham's carriage, and drove off with him. I can't conceive greater hardness of heart than it required to resist the entreaties of that beautiful young wife and infirm mother. E[mily McGuire] has just received a note from the former, written in sorrow and loneliness. She fears that the wound may suffer greatly by locomotion; beyond that, she has much to dread, but she scarcely knows what.

Wednesday—Many exciting rumours to-day about the Yankees being at Hanover Court-House, within a few miles of us. They can be traced everywhere by the devastation which marks their track. There are also rumours that our army is in Pennsylvania. So may it be! We are harassed to death with their ruinous raids, and why should not the North feel it in its homes? Nothing but their personal suffering will shorten the war.[19] I don't want their women and children to suffer; nor that our men should follow their example, and break through and steal. I want our warfare carried on in a more honourable way; but I do want our men and horses to be fed on the good things of Pennsylvania; I want the fine dairies, pantries, granaries, meadows, and orchards belonging to the rich farmers of Pennsylvania, to be laid open to our army; and I want it all paid for with our *Confederate money, which will be good at some future day.* I want their horses taken for our cavalry and wagons, in return for the hundreds of thousands that they have taken from us; and I want their fat cattle driven into Virginia to feed our army. It amuses me to think how the Dutch farmers' wives will be concealing the golden products of their dairies, to say nothing of their apple-butter, peach-butter, and their wealth of apple-pies.

July 3—The scarcity of blank books, and the very high prices, make them unattainable to me; therefore I have determined to begin another volume of my Diary on some nice wrapping-paper which I happen to have; and though not very pleasant to write on, yet it is one of the least of my privations.

We are still worried by reports that the Yankees are very near us, and we are constantly expecting them to raid upon Ashland. We have a good force at "The Junction," and the bridge just above us,[20] which they may respect, as they are dreadfully afraid of our forces.

Spent yesterday in the hospital; the wounded are getting on well. The city was put into a blaze of excitement by the report that General Dix was marching on it from the White House.[21] I dare say that they think that General Lee has left it undefended, in which surmise they are vastly mistaken. Our troops seem to be walking over Pennsylvania without let or hindrance. They have taken possession of Chambersburg, Carlisle, and other smaller towns. They surrendered without firing a gun. I am glad to see that General Lee orders his soldiers to respect private property;[22] but it will be difficult to make an incensed soldiery, whose houses have in many instances been burned, crops wantonly destroyed, horses stolen, negroes persuaded off, hogs and sheep shot down and left in the field in warm weather—it will be difficult to make such sufferers remember the Christian precept of returning good for evil. The soldiers in the hospital seem to think that many a private torch will be applied "just for revenge." It was in vain that I quoted to them, "Vengeance is mine; I will repay, saith the Lord."[23] One stoutly maintained that he would like to go North "just to burn two good houses; one in return for my own house on [the] Mississippi River; the other for that of my brother-in-law, both of which they burned just after landing from their boat, with no pretence at an excuse for it; and when I think of my wife and children homeless, I feel as if I could set all Yankeedom in a blaze." Poor fellow! He became so excited that he arose in his bed, as if impatient to be off and at his work of vengeance. I am glad to hear that quantities of horses and fat cattle are driven into Virginia.

July 4—Our celebration of this day is more serious than in days gone by. Our military have no time for dress-parades and barbecues. The gentlemen could not get home yesterday evening; the trains were all used for carrying soldiers to the bridge on this railroad just above us, upon which the Yankees are making demonstrations. The morning papers report that General D. H. Hill had a skirmish near Tunstall's Station on Thursday evening, and repulsed the enemy.[24] Nothing from our armies in Pennsylvania or Vicksburg.

July 4, Eleven o'Clock P.M.—Heavy musketry to-night, for two hours, at the bridge above this place. It has ceased, and we hope that the enemy are driven back.

Mr. [McGuire] came home this evening; the other gentlemen are absent. We are going to bed, feeling that we are in God's hands. The wires are cut between this and "The Junction," and there is every indication that the Yankees are near. The telegraph operator has gone off, and great anxiety is felt about the village. There are no Government stores here of any sort; I trust that the Yankees know that and will not think us worth the trouble of looking after.

Monday Morning—The hope I expressed in my last line on Saturday night was delusive. About one o'clock I was awakened by E[mily McGuire] leaning over me, and saying in a low, tremulous tone, "Mother, get up, the Yankees are come." We sprang up, and there they were at the telegraph office, immediately opposite.[25] In an instant the door was broken down with a crash, and the battery and other things thrown out. Axes were at work cutting down the telegraph-poles, while busy hands were tearing up the railroad. A sentinel sat on his horse at our gate as motionless as if both man and horse had been cut from a block of Yankee granite. We expected every moment that they would come to the house, or at least go into the hotel opposite to us; but they went off to the depot. There was a dead silence, except an occasional order, "Be quick," "Keep a sharp look-out," etc., etc. The night was moonlight, but we dressed ourselves and sat in the dark; we were afraid to open the window-shutters or to light a lamp, lest they might be attracted to the house. We remained in this way perhaps two hours, when the flames suddenly burst from the depot. All parts of the building seemed to be burning at once; also immense piles of wood and of plank. The conflagration was brilliant. As soon as the whole was fairly blazing the pickets were called in, and the whole party dashed off, with demoniac yells. Soon after, as the dawn began to break upon us, doors were thrown open, and the villagers began to sally forth to the fire. In a short time all of us were there, from every house—even the babies; and as it became daylight, an amusing group was revealed. Every one had dressed in the dark, and all manner of costumes were to be seen—dressing-gowns, cravatless old gentlemen, young ladies in curl-papers, collars pinned awry, etc. Some ladies presented themselves in full costume—handsome dresses, lace collars, ear-rings and breastpins, watches, etc.—giving as a reason, that, if they were burnt out, they would at least save their best clothes—forgetting, the while, that a Yankee soldier has an irresistible *penchant* for watches and other jewelry. Some of us were more cautious, and had put all our valuables in *unapproachable* pockets—the pockets to a lady's dress not having proved on all occasions a place of safety. The loss to the railroad company will be considerable; to the public very small, for they are already replacing the broken rails, and the telegraph was put in operation yesterday.

The morning papers give the Northern account of a battle in Gettysburg, Pennsylvania. It gives the victory to the Federals, though it admits a very heavy loss on their side; announces the loss of Major-General Reynolds and Brigadier-General Paul by death.[26] We pause for the truth.

8th—Accounts from Gettysburg very confused. Nothing seems to be known certainly; but Vicksburg has fallen![27] So says rumour, and we are afraid not to believe. It is a terrible loss to us; but God has been so good to us hereto-fore that we can only say, "It is the Lord." A victory is announced to the War Department by General Loring in the West;[28] and another gained by General Taylor over Banks.[29] For these successes I thank God from my heart. Many troops have passed here to-day, for what point we know not. Our anxiety is very great. Our home is blessed with health and comfort.

July 11—Vicksburg was surrendered on the 4th of July. The terms of capitula-tion seem marvelously generous for such a foe. What can the meaning be?

General Lee has had a most bloody battle near Gettysburg. Our loss was fearful.[30] We have heard of no casualties except in general officers. General Richard Garnett, our friend and connection, has yielded up his brave spirit on a foreign field. He was shot through the head while standing on the fortifications, encouraging his men and waving them on to the fight.[31] How my heart bleeds to think of his hoary-headed father, of whom he was the stay! General [William] Barksdale, of Mississippi, is another martyr. Also General [Lewis A.] Armistead, of Virginia. Generals [James] Kemper and [W. Dorsey] Pender wounded. I dread to hear of others. Who of our nearest kin may have ceased to live? When I think of probabilities and possibilities, I am almost crazy. Some of our men are reported wounded and in the enemy's hands. They took many prisoners. The cars are rushing up and down with soldiers. Two trains with pontoons have gone up within the last two days. What does it all portend?

July 12—The enemy is again before Charleston. Lord, have mercy upon the efforts of our people! I am miserable about my poor little J. P., who is on board the *Chicora*, in Charleston harbor.[32]

14th—To-day spent in the hospital; a number of wounded there from the fatal field of Gettysburg. They are not severely wounded, or they could not have been brought so far. Port Hudson has fallen![33] It could not be retained after losing Vicksburg. General Lee's army is near Hagerstown. Some of the casualties of the Gettysburg fight which have reached me are very distress-ing. The death of James Maupin,[34] of the University of Virginia—so young, so gentle, so brave! He fell at his gun, as member of the Second Howitzers of Richmond. My heart goes out in warmest sympathy for his parents and devoted grandmother. Colonel James Marshall,[35] of Fauquier, has fallen. He is yet another of those dear ones over whose youth we so fondly watched. Yet another was Westwood McCreery,[36] formerly of Richmond. \nother was Valentine Southall.[37] They all went with bright hope, rem... ...ing that every blow that was struck was for their own South. Alas! alas! the South now weeps some of her bravest sons. But, trying as it is to record the death of those dear boys, it is harder still to speak of those of our own house and blood. Lieutenant B. H. McGuire,[38] our nephew, the bright, fair-haired boy, from whom we parted last summer at Lynchburg as he went on his way to the field, full of buoyancy and hope, is among the dead at Gettysburg. Also, captain Austin Brockenbrough,[39] of Essex County. Virginia has no son to whom a brighter future opened. His talents, his education, his social qualities, his affectionate sympathy with all around him, are all laid low. Oh, may God be with those of whose life they seemed a part! It is hard to think of so many of our warm-hearted, whole-souled, brave, ardent Southern youths, now sleeping beneath the cold clods of Pennsylvania. We can only hope that the day is not too far distant when we may bring their dear bodies back to their native soil.

15th—In Richmond, to-day, I saw my old friend, Mrs. E. R. C.,[40] looking after her sons. One was reported "wounded;" the other "missing."[41] This sad word may mean that he is a prisoner; it may mean worse. She can get no clue to him. His company has not come, and she is very miserable. Two mothers, one from Georgia, another from Florida, have come on in pursuit of their sons, and are searching the hospitals for them. They were not in our hospital, and we could give them no information, so they went on to others. There is more unhappiness abroad among our people than I have ever seen before. Sometimes I wish I could sleep until it was over—a selfish wish enough; but it is hard to witness so much sorrow which you cannot alleviate.

July 18—This day two years ago the battle of Bull Run was fought, a kind of prelude to that of Manassas, on the 21st. Since that time what scenes have been enacted! Battles have been fought by scores, and lives, precious lives, have been sacrificed by thousands, and that, too, of the very flower of our country. Again I have heard of the death of one of our dear E[piscopal] H[igh] S[chool] boys—William H. Robb,[42] of Westmoreland. He was with us for four years, and was very, very dear to us all. He died of wounds received in a cavalry fight at Brandy Station. We thought he had recovered, but this evening brought the fatal tidings. The news of the New York riots, which they got up in opposition to the draft, is cheering![43] Oh! that they could not get up another army, and would fight each other! Fitz Lee's cavalry had a fight yesterday at Shepherdstown, and repulsed the enemy handsomely.[44] All eyes turn gloomily to Charleston.[45] It is greatly feared that it will have to succumb to Federal force. I trust that our Heavenly Father may avert so dire a calamity!

19th—When shall we recover from this fatal trip to Pennsylvania? General Pettigrew,[46] of North Carolina, fell on the retreat, at a little skirmish near the Falling Waters. Thus our best men seem to be falling on the right hand and on the left. When speaking of General P[ettigrew]'s death, a friend related a circumstance which interested me. General P[ettigrew] was severely wounded at the battle of "Seven Pines." He was lying in a helpless condition, when a young soldier of another command saw him, and immediately stooping to the ground, assisted him in getting on his back, and was bearing him to a place of safety, when he (the soldier) was struck by a ball and instantly killed. The General fell to the ground, and remained there, unable to move, until he was captured by the enemy. He was subsequently incarcerated in Fort Delaware. Having learned from the soldier, while on his back, that his name was White, from Westmoreland County, Virginia, as soon as the General was exchanged he inquired for the family, and found that the mother was a respectable widow who had had five sons on the field, but one of whom survived. He immediately wrote to her, expressing his deep sense of obligation to her son for his gracious effort to save his life, delicately inquired into her circumstances, and offered, if necessary, to make a liberal provision for her. I did not learn the widow's reply.[47]

We have had this week a visit of two days from Mrs. General Lee. She was on her way to the Hot Springs in pursuit of health, of which she stands greatly in need.[48] She is great sufferer from rheumatism, but is cheerful, notwithstanding her sufferings, bodily and mentally. She is, of course, unhappy about the overpowering responsibilities of her noble husband; but of that you never hear a word from her. She left us this morning, in a box car, fitted up to suit an invalid, with a bed, chairs, etc. She was accompanied by the lovely wife of her captive son, also travelling in pursuit of health. Greater beauty and sweetness rarely fall to the lot of woman; and as I looked at the sad, delicate lineaments of her young face, I could but inwardly pray that

the terrible threats denounced against her husband by Yankee authority might never reach her ear; for, though we do not believe that they will dare to offer him violence, yet the mere suggestion would be enough to make her very miserable.

Yesterday morning we had quite a pleasant diversion, in attending a marriage in the village. Mr. [McGuire] performed the ceremony, and we afterwards breakfasted with the bridal party. We then proceeded to Richmond—they to spend their honeymoon in and around the city, and we to our duties there.

July 23—Spent the day at the hospital. Mr. [McGuire] has just received a post chaplaincy from Government, and is assigned to the Officers' Hospital on Tenth Street. For this we are very thankful, as the performance of the duties to the ministerial office is in all respects congenial to his taste and feeling. I pray that God may give him health and strength for the office!

28th—The girls are in Richmond, staying at Dr. G's.[49] They went in to attend a tournament to be given to-day by General Jenkins's Brigade,[50] stationed near Richmond; but this morning the brigade was ordered to go South, and great was the disappointment of the young people. They cannot feel as we do during these gloomy times, but are always ready to catch the "passing pleasure as it flies," forgetting that, in the best times,

> Pleasures are like poppies spread:
> You seize the flower, the bloom is shed.[51]

And how much more uncertain are they now, when we literally cannot tell what a day may bring forth, and none of us know, when we arise in the morning, that we may not hear before noonday that we have been shorn of all that makes life dear!

July 29—A letter of farewell from the Valley, written as the enemy's lines were closing around our loved ones there. It is painful to think of their situation, but they are in God's hands.

It is said that Lee's army and Meade's[52] are approaching each other. Oh, I trust that a battle is not at hand![53] I feel unnerved, as if I could not stand the suspense of another engagement. Not that I fear the result, for I cannot believe that Meade could whip General Lee, under any circumstances; but the dread casualties! The fearful list of killed and wounded, when so many of our nearest and dearest are engaged, is too full of anguish to anticipate without a sinking of heart which I have never known before.

There was a little fight some days ago, near Brandy Station—the enemy driven across the river.[54] Fredericksburg and Culpeper Court-House are both occupied by our troops. This is very gratifying to our Fredericksburg refugees, who are going up to see if they can recover their property. All moveables, such as household furniture, books, etc., of any value, have been carried off. Their houses, in some instances, have been battered down.

I was in Richmond this morning, and bought a calico dress, for which I gave $2.50 per yard, and considered it a bargain; the new importations have run up to $3.50 and $4 per yard. To what are we coming?

30th—Our good President has again appointed a day for fasting and prayer.

The *Florida* and *Alabama* are performing wonderful feats, and are worrying the North excessively.[55] Many a cargo has been lost to the Northern merchant princes by their skill, and I trust that the Government vessels feel their power.

Several members of our household have gone to the mountains in search of health—Mr. [McGuire] among the rest. Mrs. P.,[56] of Amelia, is here, cheering the house by her sprightliness; and last night we had Mr. Randolph Tucker,[57] who is a delightful companion—so intellectual, cheerful, and God-fearing!

The army is unusually quiet at all points. Does it portend a storm? Many changes are going on in "our village." The half-English, half-Yankee Wades are gone at last, to our great relief. I dare say she shakes the dust from her feet, as a testimony against the South; for she certainly has suffered very much here, and she will not have as many difficulties there, with her Yankee Colonel father. She professes to outrebel the rebels, and to be the most intense Southern woman of us all; but I rather think that she deceives herself, and unless I mistake her character very much indeed, I think when she gets among her own people she will tell them all she knows of our hopes, fears, and difficulties. Poor thing! I am glad she is gone to those persons on whom she has a natural claim for protection.

August 10—Spent this morning in the house of mourning. Our neighbor Mrs. S[tuart] has lost her eldest son.[58] The disease was "that most fatal of Pandora's train," consumption.[59] He contracted it in the Western Army. His poor mother has watched the ebbing of his life for several months, and last night he died most suddenly. That young soldier related to me an anecdote, some weeks ago, with his short, oppressed breathing and broken sentences, which showed the horrors of this fratricidal war. He said the day after a battle in Missouri, in the Fall of 1861, he, among others, was detailed to bury the dead. Some Yankee soldiers were on the field doing the same thing. As they turned over a dead man, he saw a Yankee stop, look intently, and then run to the spot with an exclamation of horror. In a moment he was on his knees by the body, in a paroxysm of grief. It was his brother. They were Missourians. The brother now dead had emigrated South some years before. He said that before the war communication had been kept up between them, and he had strongly suspected that he was in the army; he had consequently been in constant search of his brother. The Northern and Southern soldier then united in burying him, who was brother in arms of the one, and the mother's son of the other!

The Bishop and Mrs. J[ohns] returned home to-day from their long trip to the South-west. They travelled with great comfort, but barely escaped a raid at Wytheville.[60] We welcomed them gladly. So many of our family party are wandering about, that our little cottage has become lonely.

Mr. C. has come out, and reports a furious bombardment of Sumter.[61] This has been going on so long, that I begin to feel that it is indeed impregnable.

Wednesday—We are all pursuing the even tenor of our way, as if there were no war. An order from General Lee is in to-day's paper, exhorting officers and soldiers to a strict observance of fast-day, which is on Friday.[62] In the mean time the enemy is storming Charleston with unprecedented fury. It is an object of peculiar vengeance. Sumter has literally fallen, but it has not yet yielded; its battered walls bid defiance to the whole power of the North.

August 26—A week ago I was called to Camp Jackson[63] to nurse ——, who has been very sick there. The hospital is very extensive, and in beautiful order. It is under the supervision of Surgeon Hancock, whose whole soul seems engaged in making it an attractive home to the sick and wounded.

The beautiful shade-trees and bold spring are delightful to the convalescents during this warm weather. Fast-day was observed there with great solemnity. I heard a Methodist chaplain preach to several hundred soldiers, and I never saw a more attentive congregation.

September 8—The Government employed the cars yesterday bringing Longstreet's Corps from Fredericksburg, on the way to Chattanooga.[64] We all stood at our gate last night to give the soldiers water; we had nothing else to give them, poor fellows, as there were three long trains, and they had no time to stay. They looked healthy and cheerful, and went off hurrahing for Virginia.

The year of our sojourn at this cottage is nearly over. Our mess must be broken up, as some of our gentlemen are ordered away.[65] We have had a very pleasant time, and it is painful to dissolve our social relations. Not one of the families is provided with a home; we are all looking out for lodgings, and find it very difficult to get them. The change of home, habits, and association is very trying to old persons; the variety seems rather pleasant to the young.

September 16—This house is to be sold on the 29th, so we must all find resting-places before that time. But where? Room-rent in Richmond is enormously high. We may get one very small cottage here for forty dollars per month, but it has the reputation of being unhealthy. Our connection, Mr. P[aine], is here looking out for a home, and we may get one together. It would be delightful to have him and the dear girls with us. No one thinks of boarding; almost all the boarding-house keepers rent out their rooms, and refugees keep house in them as cheaply as they choose.

Richmond, 24—We have all been scattered. The Bishop has obtained good rooms; the other members of the household are temporarily fixed. We are here with our son, looking for rooms every day; very few are vacant, and they are too high for our means. We shall probably have to take the little cottage at Ashland, notwithstanding its reputation—either the cottage or a country-house near Richmond, about which we are in correspondence with a gentleman. This plan will be carried out, and work well if the Lord pleases, and with this assurance we should be satisfied; but still we are restless and anxious. Our ladies, who have been brought up in the greatest luxury, are working with their hands to assist the families. The offices given to ladies have been filled long ago, and yet I hear of a number of applicants. Mr. [Secretary of the Treasury Christopher G.] Memminger says that one vacancy will bring a hundred applications. Some young ladies plait straw hats for sale; I saw one sold this morning for twenty dollars—and their fingers, which had not been accustomed to work for their living, plait on merrily; they can dispose of them easily; and, so far from being ashamed of it, they take pride in their own handiwork. I went to see Mrs. —— to-day, daughter of one of our gentlemen high in position, and whose husband was a wealthy landholder in Maryland.[66] I found her sitting at her sewing-machine, making an elaborate shirt-bosom. She said she took in sewing, and spoke of it very cheerfully. "How can we rent rooms and live on captain's pay?" She began by sewing for brothers and cousins, then for neighbours, and now for anybody who will give it to her. She laughingly added that she thought she would hang out her sign, "Plain sewing done here." We certainly are a *great people*, women as well as men. This lady, and all other ladies, have always places at their frugal tables for hungry soldiers. Many ladies take in copying.

25th—There has been a great battle in the West, at Chickamauga, in Tennessee, between Bragg and Rosecranz. We are gloriously victorious![67] The last telegram from General Bragg tells of 7,000 prisoners, thirty-five pieces of cannon, and 15,000 small-arms, taken by our men. The fight is not over, though they have been fighting three days. Longstreet and his corps of veterans are there to reinforce them. A battle is daily expected on the Rapidan; and to use Lincoln's expression, they are still "pegging away" at Charleston.

September 26—Spent this morning seeking information about our plans for living in the country. Nothing satisfactory.

28th—Mrs. M[ason] and myself went to St. John's Church yesterday, and heard an excellent sermon from Bishop Wilmer; service read by Dr. Norwood.[68] Encouraging news continues from the West. I am still anxious about our home. Mr. [McGuire] is sick, and the prospect of getting a house diminishing. Perhaps I should take comfort from the fact that a great many persons are homeless as well as ourselves. If Mr. [McGuire] were well, I should not feel so hopeless. The girls, too, are visiting the country, expecting us to get an *impossible* home, and I do dislike to disappoint them. Oh, that we could be perfectly satisfied, knowing that we are in the Lord's hands!

Cedar Hill, October 4—We came to Ashland on the 29th, to attend the sale of the house in which we lived last year. We got a few pieces of furniture, and determined to rent the little cottage. We spent the night at Mrs. T[hornton]'s, and came here next morning, and are now collecting hops, brooms, and the various *et ceteras* necessary for house-keeping. A refugee friend, who will change her location, has lent us her furniture, so that we expect to be very snug. Of course we shall have no curtains nor carpets, which are privations in our old age, but the deficiencies must be made up by large wood fires and bright faces. The war has taught useful lessons, and we can make ourselves comfortable and happy on much less than we ever dreamed of before.

October 24—Since writing in my diary, our plans have been entirely changed. Our old friend, Mrs. [Catherine] R[owland], offered us rooms in Richmond, on such terms as are within our means, and a remarkable circumstance connected with it is, that they are in the house which my father once occupied, and the pleasant chamber which I now occupy I left this month twenty-nine years ago. It is much more convenient to live in Richmond than in Ashland, so that we have rented the little cottage to another. One room answers the purpose of dining-room and sleeping-room, by putting a large screen around the bed; the girls have a room, and we use the parlour of the family for entertaining our guests. For this we pay $60 per month and half of the gas bill.

But this has been a sad, sad month to me, and I find it very difficult to bring my mind to attend to the ordinary affairs of life. On the 11th of this month, our nephew, Captain William B. Newton, was killed while leading a cavalry charge in Culpeper County.[69] We have the consolation of believing that his redeemed spirit has passed into heaven; but to how many has the earth been left desolate! His young wife and three lovely children; his father, mother, sisters, brothers, uncles and aunts, have seen the pride of their hearts pass away. His country mourns him as a great public loss. The bar, the legislative hall, and the camp proudly acknowledge his brilliant talents. In peace, the country looked to him as one to whom her best interests would hereafter be intrusted; in war, as one of the most gallant officers on the field. An early and ardent Secessionist, he was among the first to turn from the delightful home circle, where he ever sought his happiness, to go to the defence of right. He came into the field as First Lieutenant of the Hanover Troop; shortly after became its Captain, loved and revered by his men; and the commission of Lieutenant-Colonel of his regiment, the Fourth Virginia Cavalry, was on its way to him; but alas! alas! it reached its destination a few hours too late. God be with my precious [Mary Page Newton] and her sweet children! I long and yet dread to go to that once bright home, the light of which has faded forever.

I was shocked to hear that on the fatal Sunday on which my darling William fell, three of the E[piscopal] H[igh] S[chool] boys had come to a glorious, though untimely end, on the same field—Surgeon John Nelson, Lieutenant Lomax Tayloe, and Private J. Vivian Towles;[70] and at Bristow Station a few days afterwards, dear little Willie Robinson,[71] son of my old friends, Mr. Conway and Mrs. Mary Susan Robinson. He was but eighteen. I attended his funeral on Wednesday last, and there learned that he was a devoted Christian. These dear boys! Oh, I trust that they sprang from the din of the battle-field to the peace of heaven! Lord, how long must we suffer such things?

25th—To-day we heard the Rev. Mr. Peterkin, from the text: "Be not weary in well-doing."[72] It was a delightful sermon, persuasive and encouraging. Mr. [McGuire] spends Sunday mornings always in the hospital. He has Hospital No. 1, in addition to the Officers' Hospital, under his care. They occupy a great deal of his time, in the most interesting way.

27th—I was surprised this morning by a precious visit from S[ally] S[mith]. She went to Petersburg this evening, to join her husband, who is stationed there. She seems to think that she can never return to her Winchester home, so completely is every thing ruined. It is strange how we go on from month to month, living in the present, without any prospect for the future. We had some sweet, sad talk of our dear William. She says he was prepared, and God took him. At his funeral, his pastor took out his last letter from him, but became so overwhelmed with tears that he could not read it. It is right, and we must submit; but it is a bitter trial to give up one we loved so dearly.

28th—Our niece, M[ary] P[age], came for me to go with her on a shopping expedition. It makes me sad to find our money depreciating so much, except that I know it was worse during the old Revolution.[73] A merino dress cost $150, long cloth $5.50 per yard, fine cotton stockings $6 per pair; handkerchiefs, for which we gave fifty cents before the war, are now $5. There seems no scarcity of dry-goods of the ordinary kinds; bombazines, silks, etc., are scarce and very high; carpets are not to be found—they are too large to run the blockade from Baltimore, from which city many of our goods come.

November 9—We are now quite comfortably fixed, in what was once my mother's chamber, and most unexpectedly we have a carpet. The other day, while entertaining some friends, in this chamber by night, dining-room by day, and parlour ever and anon, Mrs. Secretary Mallory[74] walked in, who, like ourselves, has had many ups-and-downs during the Confederacy, and therefore her kind heart knows exactly how to sympathize with others. While talking away, she suddenly observed that there was no carpet on the floor, and exclaimed, "Mrs. [McGuire], you have no carpet! My boxes have just come from Montgomery [Alabama], where I left them two years ago, filled with carpets and bedding. I have five, and I will lend you one. Don't say a word; I couldn't be comfortable and think of you with this bare floor. Mr. [McGuire] is too delicate for it, and you are both too old to begin now on an uncarpeted floor." An hour after she left us a servant came with the carpet, which was soon tacked down, and gives a home-like, comfortable air to the room.

11th—Just received a visit from my nephew, W[illoughby] N[ewton], who is on his way to Fauquier [County] to be married.[75] I had not seen him since he lost his leg. He is still on crutches, and it made my heart bleed to see him walk with such difficulty. I believe that neither war, pestilence, nor famine could put an end to the marrying and giving in marriage which is constantly going on. Strange that these sons of Mars can so assiduously devote themselves to Cupid and Hymen; but every respite, every furlough, must be thus employed. I am glad they can accomplish it; and if "the brave deserve the fair,"[76] I am sure that the deeds of daring of our Southern soldiers should have their rewards. My niece, L. B., of Lexington, should have been married to-morrow night, but her betrothed, Captain S., has been ordered off to meet the enemy.[77] The marriage is, of course, postponed. Poor fellow! I trust that he may come safely home.

I have just written to Colonel Northrop,[78] Commissary-General, to ask an appointment as clerk in his department. So many of the young men have been ordered to the field, that this office has been open to ladies. My cousin, Colonel F. G. Ruffin,[79] of the same office, has interested himself for me. They require us to say that we are really in want of the office—rather a work of supererogation, I should say, as no lady would bind herself to keep accounts for six hours per day without a dire necessity.

13th—My appointment to a clerkship in the Commissary Department has been received, with a salary of $125 per month. The rooms are not ready for us to begin our duties, and Colonel R[uffin] has just called to tell me one of the requirements. As our duties are those of accountants, we are to go through a formal examination in arithmetic.[80] If we do not, as the University boys say, "pass," we are considered incompetent, and of course are dropped from the list of appointees. This requirement may be right, but it certainly seems to me both provoking and absurd that I must be examined in arithmetic by a commissary major young enough to be my son. If I could afford it, I would give up the appointment, but, as it is, must submit with the best grace possible, particularly as other ladies of my age have to submit to it.

November 15—Went this morning to —— Church and heard the Gospel preached, but in a manner so dull, and in a voice so monotonous, that I did not hear with much profit. I mourn that I did not, for I believe that some of the most God-serving, and therefore efficient ministers, are those who are not attractive as preachers, and there must be some defect in the listener who is not profited by the Gospel preached in spirit and in truth, though not set forth in an attractive form. I would that our best preachers could be sent to the field, for the soldiers, having such temptations to spending the Sabbath in idleness, should have the Gospel made impressive and interesting, so that they may be induced to attend the services and to enjoy them.

W[illoughby] N[ewton] and his sweet bride passed through town this week. It was very pleasant to see how she understood his wants; how naturally she would open the doors, gates, etc., and assist him in walking up and down steps. I trust he may soon be able to give up his crutches. L[ouisa] B[rockenbrough] is also married and in town, staying at Judge M's.[81] Captain S[emmes] returned *from the wars* a few nights after the one appointed, and was married in quite the old style of bridesmaids and groomsmen, with a bridal supper which I am told reminded one of peace times.

Our army does not seem prospering in the West. Bragg has fallen back.[82] We long to hear better things. A battle seems imminent on the Rappahannock; ninety-three wagons filled with ammunition were yesterday captured by Colonel Rosser—a good capture, at a good time.[83]

December 4—On Friday last there was a severe fight on the Rapidan, at Germanna Ford.[84] The enemy were splendidly repulsed; but my dear Raleigh T. Colston, Lieutenant-Colonel of the Second Regiment, was shot through his left leg, which was amputated on the field. I thank God that he is doing well, and feel so thankful that his life was spared![85] His mother was in Powhatan, on a visit to one of her daughters; but, becoming uneasy at seeing that General Edward Johnson's Division had been engaged, immediately came to Richmond. The cars arrived at night, and she came directly to our rooms. We were surprised to see her, and I, supposing that she had heard of her son's misfortune, was about to say what I could to relieve her mind, when she exclaimed, "I know that my sons are safe, from your countenance." "Yes," said I; "W[illiam][86] is safe, and R[aleigh] is doing well; he was wounded in his leg." "Severely?" she asked. "His left leg has been amputated below the knee; he is at the University, under the care of Mr. and Mrs. Minor[87] and his sisters, and is doing remarkably well. Colonel Ruffin received a telegram to-day, and I a letter." She passed her hand across her eyes for a minute, and said, "Thank God, his life is spared." Next morning she left us for the University.

General Bragg has met with a repulse in the South-west, and was pursued; but, being reinforced, has again attacked the enemy and repulsed them.[88] This occurred in the North-western part of Georgia. The papers say that the enemy under General Grant has retreated towards Chattanooga. Longstreet, when last heard from, was at Knoxville.[89] Meade, on the Rapidan, after having been in line of battle for several days, has fallen back, finding that General Lee was ready to meet him.

December 6—I this morning attended the funeral of Mr. John Seddon,[90] brother of the Secretary of War. It was a most solemn occasion; he was a man of fine talents and high character. The Rev. Dr. Moore,[91] of the Presbyterian Church, preached a most beautiful sermon.

December 12—To-day I was examined on arithmetic—"Denominate numbers, vulgar and decimal fractions, tare and tret," etc., etc., by Major

Brewer,[92] of the Commissary Department. I felt as if I had returned to my childhood. But for the ridiculousness of the thing, I dare say I should have been embarrassed. On Monday I am to enter on the duties of the office. We are to work from nine to three.

We have just received from our relatives in the country some fine Irish and sweet potatoes, cabbages, butter, sausages, chines, and a ham; and from a friend in town two pounds of very good green tea. These things are very acceptable, as potatoes are twelve dollars per bushel, pork and bacon two dollars fifty cents per pound, and good tea at twenty-five dollars per pound.[93] How are the poor to live? Though it is said that the *poor genteel* are the real sufferers. Money is laid aside for paupers by every one who can possibly do it, but persons who do not let their wants be known are the really poor.

Sunday, Dec. 13—The first anniversary of the battle of Fredericksburg, where we lost so many valuable lives, and where the Federals were thoroughly whipped. Since that time we have lost many lives, which nothing can repay; but we hold our own, have had some victories, and have been upon the whole much blessed by God. At St. James's Church, this morning, and heard a very fine sermon from the Rev. Mr. Peterkin, from the text, "Blessed are the poor in spirit."[94] To-night we expect to hear Bishop Lay.[95]

January 1, 1864—A melancholy pause in my diary. After returning from church on the night of the 13th, a telegram was handed me from Professor Minor, of the University of Virginia, saying, "Come at once, Colonel Colston is extremely ill." After the first shock was over, I wrote an explanatory note to Major [Samuel] Brewer, why I could not be at the office next day, packed my trunk, and was in the cars by seven in the morning. That evening I reached the University, and found dear R[aleigh] desperately ill with pneumonia, which so often follows, as in the case of General Jackson, the amputation of limbs. Surgeons Davis and Cabell[96] were in attendance, and R[aleigh]'s uncle, Dr. Brockenbrough, arrived the next day. After ten days of watching and nursing, amid alternate hopes and fears, we saw our friend Dr. Maupin close our darling's eyes, on the morning of the 23d; and on Christmas-day a military escort land him among many brother soldiers in the Cemetery at the University of Virginia. He died in the faith of Christ, and with the glorious hope of immortality. His poor mother is heart-stricken, but she, together with his sisters, and one dearer still, had the blessed, and what is now the rare privilege, of soothing and nursing him in his last hours.[97] To them, and to us all, his life seemed as if part of our own. His superior judgment and affectionate temper made him the guide of his whole family. To them his loss can never be supplied. His country has lost one of its earliest and best soldiers. Having been educated at the Virginia Military Institute, he raised and drilled a company in his native County of Berkeley at the time of the John Brown raid. In 1861 he again led that company to Harper's Ferry. From that time he was never absent more than a week or ten days from his command, and even when wounded at Gaines's Mill, he absented but three days, and was again at his post during the several last days of those desperate fights. His fatal wound was received in his nineteenth general engagement, in none of which had he his superior in bravery and devotion to the cause. He was proud of belonging to the glorious Stonewall Brigade, and I have been told by those who knew the circumstances, that he was confided in and trusted by General Jackson to a remarkable degree.[98]

Thus we bury, one by one, the dearest, the brightest, the best of our domestic circles. Now, in our excitement, while we are scattered, and many of us homeless, these separations are poignant, nay, overwhelming; but how can we estimate the sadness of heart which will pervade the South when the war is over, and we are again gathered together around our family hearths and altars, and find the circles broken? One and another gone. Some times the father and husband, the beloved head of the household, in whom was centered all that made life dear. Again the eldest son and brother of the widowed home, to whom all looked for guidance and direction; or, perhaps, that bright youth, on whom we had not ceased to look as still a child, whose fair, beardless cheek we had but now been in the habit of smoothing with our hands in fondness—one to whom mother and sisters would always give the good-night kiss, as his peculiar due, and repress the sigh that would arise at the thought that college or business days had almost come to take him from us. And then we will remember the mixed feeling of hope and pride when we first saw the household pet don his jacket of gray and shoulder his musket for the field; how we would be bright and cheerful before him, and turn to our chambers to weep oceans of tears when he is fairly gone. And does he, too, sleep his last sleep? Does our precious one fill a hero's grave? O God! help us, for the wail is in the whole land! "Rachel weeping for her children, and will not be comforted, because they are not."[99] In all the broad South there will be scarcely a fold without its missing lamb, a fireside without its vacant chair. And yet we must go on. It is our duty to rid our land of invaders; we must destroy the snake which is endeavouring to entwine us in its coils, though it drains our heart's blood. We know that we are right in the sight of God, and that we must

> With patient mind our course of duty run.
> God nothing does, or suffers to be done,
> But we would do ourselves, if we could see
> The end of all events as well as He.[100]

The Lord reigneth, be the earth never so unquiet.[101]

January 3—Entered on the duties of my office on the 30th of December. So far I like it well. "The Major" [Samuel Brewer] is very kind, and considerate of our comfort; the duties of the office are not very onerous, but rather confining for one who left school thirty-four years ago, and has had no restraint of the kind during the interim. The ladies, thirty-five in number, are of all ages, and representing various parts of Virginia, also Maryland and Louisiana. Many of them are refugees. It is melancholy to see how many wear mourning for brothers or other relatives, the victims of war. One sad young girl sits near me, whose two brothers have fallen on the field, but she is too poor to buy mourning. I found many acquaintances, and when I learned the history of others, it was often that of fallen fortunes and destroyed homes. One young lady, of high-sounding Maryland name, was banished from Baltimore, because of her zeal in going to the assistance of our Gettysburg wounded. The society is pleasant, and we hope to get along very agreeably. I am now obliged to visit the hospital in the afternoon, and I give it two evenings in the week. It is a cross to me not to be able to give it more time; but we have very few patients just now, so that it makes very little difference.

January 15—Nothing new from the armies—all quiet. At home we are in *status quo,* except that we have had a very agreeable accession to our family party in the person of Colonel C. F. M. G.[102] He sleeps in his office, and messes with us. He cheers us every day by bringing the latest news, in the most pleasant form which the nature of the case will admit. My occupation at home just now is as new as that in the office—it is shoe-making. I am busy upon the second pair of gaiter boots. They are made of canvas, presented me by a friend.[103] It was taken from one of our James River vessels, and has been often spread to the breeze, under the "Stars and Bars." The vessel was sunk among the obstructions at Drury's Bluff. The gaiters are cut out by a shoemaker, stitched and bound by the ladies, then soled by a shoemaker, for the moderate sum of fifty dollars. Last year he put soles on a pair for ten dollars. They are blacked with the material used for blacking guns in the navy. They are very handsome gaiters, and bear polishing by blacking and the shoe-brush as well as morocco. They are lasting, and very cheap when compared with those we buy, which are from $125 to $150 a pair. We are certainly becoming very independent of foreign aid. The girls make beautifully fitting gloves of dark flannel, cloth, linen, and any other material we can command. We make very nice blacking, and a friend has just sent me a bottle of brilliant black ink, made of elderberries.

February 15—A pause in my diary; but nothing of importance has occurred, either at home or with the country. The armies are mud-bound—I wish they would continue so. I dread the approach of Spring, with its excitements and horrors.

Prices of provisions have risen enormously—bacon $8 per pound, butter $15, etc. Our old friends from the lower part of Essex [County], Mr. [McGuire]'s parishioners for many years, sent over a wagon 'filled most generously with all manner of necessary things for our larder. We have no right to complain, for Providence is certainly supplying our wants. The clerks' salaries, too, have been raised to $250 per month, which sounds very large; but when we remember that flour is $300 per barrel, it sinks into insignificance.

28th—Our hearts ache for the poor. A few days ago, as E[mily McGuire] was walking out, she met a wretchedly dressed woman, of miserable appearance, who said she was seeking the Young Men's Christian Association, where she hoped to get assistance and work to do. E[mily] carried her to the door, but it was closed, and the poor woman's wants were pressing. She then brought her home, supplied her with food, and told her to return to see me the following afternoon. She came, and with an honest countenance and manner told me her history. Her name is Brown;[104] her husband has been a workman in Fredericksburg; he joined the army and was killed at the second battle of

Manassas. Many of her acquaintances in Fredericksburg fled last winter during the bombardment; she became alarmed, and with her three little children
fled too. She had tried to get work in Richmond; sometimes she succeeded,
but could not supply her wants. A kind woman had lent her a room and a
part of a garden, but it was outside of the corporation; and although it saved
house-rent, it debarred her from the relief of the associations formed for
supplying the city poor with meal, wood, etc. She has evidently been in a
situation little short of starvation. I asked her if she could get bread enough
for her children by her work? She said she could sometimes, and when she
could not, she "got turnip-tops from her piece of a garden, which were not
putting up smartly, and she boiled them, with a little salt, and fed them on
that." "But do they satisfy your hunger," said I? "Well, it is something to go
upon for awhile, but it does not stick by us like as bread does, and then we
get hungry again, and I am afraid to let the children eat them too often, lest
they should get sick; so I tries to get them to go to sleep; and sometimes
the woman in the next room will bring the children her leavings, but she
is monstrous poor." When I gave her meat for her children, taken from the
bounty of our Essex friends, tears of gratitude ran down her cheeks; she said
they "had not seen meat for so long." Poor thing, I promised her that her case
should be known, and that she should not suffer so again. A soldier's widow
shall not suffer from hunger in Richmond. It must not be, and will not be
when her case is known. Others are now interested for her. This evening Mrs.
R[owland] and myself went in pursuit of her; but though we went through
all the streets and lanes of "Butcher's Flat,"[105] and other vicinities, we could
get no clue to her. We went into many small and squalid-looking houses, yet
we saw no such abject poverty as Mrs. Brown's. All who needed it were supplied with meal by the corporation, and many were supporting themselves
with Government work. One woman stood at a table cutting out work; we
asked her the stereotyped question—"Is there a very poor widow named
Brown in this direction?" "No, ladies, I knows two Mrs. Browns, but they
ain't so poor, and ain't no widows nuther." As neither of them was our Mrs.
B[rown], we turned away; but she suddenly exclaimed, "Ladies will one of
you read my husband's last letter to me? For you see I can't read writing." As
Mrs. R[owland] took it, she remarked that is was four weeks old, and asked
if no one had read it to her? "Oh yes, a gentleman has read it to me four or
five times; but you see I loves to hear it, for may-be I shan't hear from him
no more." The tears now poured down her cheeks. "He always writes to me

every chance, and it has been so long since he wrote that, and they tell me that they have been fighting and may-be something has happened to him." We assured her that there had been no fighting—not even a skirmish. This quieted her, and Mrs. R[owland] read the badly written but affectionate letter, in which he expressed his anxiety to see her and the children, and his inability to get a furlough. She then turned to the mantel-piece, and with evident pride took from a nail an old felt hat, through the crown of which were two bullet-holes. It was her husband's hat, through which a bullet had passed in the battle of Chancellorsville, and, as she remarked, must have come "very nigh grazing his head." We remarked upon its being a proof of his bravery, which gratified her very much; she then hung it up carefully, saying that it was just opposite her bed, and she never let it be out of her sight. She said she wanted her husband to fight for his country, and not "to stand back, like some women's husbands, to be drafted; she would have been ashamed of that, but she felt uneasy, because something told her that he would never get back." Poor woman! We felt very much interested in her, and tried to comfort her.

March 10—There has been much excitement in Richmond about Kilpatrick's and Dahlgren's raids, and the death of the latter.[106] The cannon roared around the city, the alarm-bell rang, the reserves went out; but Richmond was safe, and we felt no alarm. As usual they did all the injury they could to country-people, by pillaging and burning. They steal every thing they can; but the people have become very adroit in hiding. Bacon, flour, etc., are put in most mysterious places; plate and handsome china are kept under ground; horses are driven into dense woods, and the cattle and sheep are driven off. It is astonishing, though much is taken, how much is left. I suppose the raiders are too much hurried for close inspection.

20th—Our Lent services in St. Paul's Lecture-room, at seven o'clock in the morning, are delightful. The room is always crowded to overflowing—the old, the young, the grave, the gay, collect there soon after sunrise; also military officers in number. When General Lee is in town, as he now is, he is never absent, and always one of the most devout worshippers. Within a few days I have seen General Whiting there; also Generals Ransom, Pegram,[107] and others. Starred officers of all grades, colonels, majors, etc., together with many others belonging to the rank and file; and civilians of every degree. It is delightful to see them, all bending together before high Heaven, imploring the help which we so much need.

The Transportation Office is just opposite to us, where crowds of fur-loughed soldiers, returning to their commands, are constantly standing, waiting for transportation. As I pass them on my way to the office in the morning, I always stop to have a cheerful word with them. Yesterday morning I said to them: "Gentlemen, whom do you suppose I have seen this morn-ing?" In answer to their inquiring looks, I said: "General Lee." "General Lee," they exclaimed: "I did not know he was in town; God bless him!" and they looked excited, as if they were about to burst forth with "Hurrah for General Lee!" "And where do you suppose I saw him so early?" "Where, Madam—where?" "At prayer-meeting, down upon his knees, praying for you and for the country." In an instant they seemed subdued; tears started in the eyes of many of those hardy, sunburnt veterans. Some were utterly silent, while others exclaimed, with various ejaculations, "God bless him!" "God bless his dear old soul!" etc. As I walked away, some followed me to know where he was to be seen. One had never seen him at all, and wanted to see him "monstrous bad;" others had seen him often, but wanted to see him in town, "just to look at him." I told them where his family residence was, but as they feared that they could not leave the Transportation Office long enough to find "Franklin Street,"[108] I dare say the poor fellows did not see General Lee. This morning I had almost the same conversation with another crowd in the same place. It is delightful to see how they reverence him, and almost as much for his goodness as for his greatness.

April 1—My diary has been somewhat neglected, for after looking over com-missary accounts for six hours in the day, and attending to home or hospital duties in the afternoon, I am too much wearied to write much at night. There are reports of movements in the armies which portend bloody work as the season advances. Oh that the Lord may have me in his holy keeping!

We continue quite comfortable at home. Of course provisions are scarce; but, thanks to our country friends and relatives, we have never been obliged to give up meat entirely. My brother-in-law, Mr. N.,[109] has lately sent us twelve hams, so that we are much better supplied than most persons. Groceries are extremely high. We were fortunate in buying ten pounds of tea, when it only sold for $22 per pound. White sugar is not to be thought of by persons of moderate means. Milk is very scarce and high, so that we have only had

188 *Diary of a Southern Refugee*

it once for many months; and we, the Colonel, Mr. [McGuire], and myself, are very glad to get a cup of tea, night and morning, sweetened with brown sugar, and without milk or cream. Before the war we would have scorned it, but now we enjoy it exceedingly, and feel ourselves very much blessed to have it. The girls have given up tea and coffee; I attempted to do it, and for several days drank only water, but such is the effect of habit upon old people, it made me perfectly miserable; I lost my elasticity of spirit; the accounts in the office went on heavily, everybody asked me if I had heard any bad news, and the family begged me not to look so unhappy. I struggled and strived against the feeling, but the girls pronounced me utterly subjugated, and insisted on my returning to my old beverage. I found myself much more easily persuaded than it is my wont to be, and was happy to resume my brown-sugar tea without cream.

On going down-stairs this evening, I found my friend Mrs. Upshur awaiting me in the parlour. She is the widow of the Hon. Abel P. Upshur, Secretary of War in Mr. [John] Tyler's administration, whose untimely end we remember so well.[110] She is a refugee from Washington, and called to ask me to assist her in finding a room to accommodate herself, her sister, and her little grandson. Her present room, in the third story of a very nice house, suited her very well, but the price was raised every month, until it became beyond her means. She is rich, but it is almost impossible for her to get funds from Washington. To obtain a room is a most difficult task, but I cheerfully promised her to do what I could; but that I must first go up the street to get some flour, for as it was $300 per barrel, we could not get one, but must purchase it at $1.25 per pound, until we could get some wheat, which we were then expecting from the country, and have it ground. She at once insisted on lending me flour until ours was ground; this being agreed to, we continued on our walk in pursuit of the room. We naturally talked of the past. She related to me a circumstance which occurred when I was a young girl, and was a striking illustration of the change which time and the war had brought on us both. She said that during the political Convention of 1829–30, she came to Richmond with her husband, who was a member of it. The first entertainment to which she was invited was given at my father's home.[111] When she entered the room my mother was standing about the centre of it, receiving her guests, and seeing that Mrs. Upshur was young and a perfect stranger, she took her by the hand and seated her by Mrs. [James] Madison, at the same time introducing her to that celebrated woman. She said it was one of the most pleasant evenings of her life, and she looked back upon it with peculiar satisfaction, for she was then introduced to Mr. Madison, Mr. [James] Monroe, Mr. Benjamin Watkins Leigh, and many others of the celebrated men of the day, who were attending the Convention. Could we then have looked through the vista of time, and have seen ourselves in the same city, the one looking for a cheap room in somebody's third story, the other looking for *cheap bread,* would we have believed it? The anecdote saddened us both for a time, but we soon recovered, and went on our way in cheerful, hopeful conversation. But we did not find the room.

April 25—Our family in *statu quo.* The country in great excitement. We have lately had a splendid little victory at Plymouth, North Carolina.[112] We have also had successes in Florida, at Shreveport, and other places in the South and South-west.[113] The God of battles is helping us, or how could we thus succeed? This city is quite excited by Mr. Memminger having ordered off the Note-signing Department, consisting entirely of ladies, to Columbia, South Carolina.[114] It has caused much distress, for many of them, whose living depends on the salary, can't possibly go. Mothers cannot leave their children, nor wives their husbands. No one seems to understand the motive which promoted the order. It seems to be very arbitrary. It is thought by some persons that all the departments will be ordered off. I trust not; for I, among many others, would be obliged to resign, and I cannot imagine how we would live without the salary. I see no reason to believe that any such move is intended, and I will not be unhappy about it. "Sufficient unto the day is the evil thereof."[115]

The enemy threatens Richmond, and is coming against it with an immense arm. They boast that they can and will have it this summer; but, with the help of God, we hope to drive them back again. Our Government is making every effort to defeat them. I don't think that anyone doubts our ability to do it; but the awful loss of life necessary upon the fights is what we dread.

April 27—Another day and night have passed, and nothing of importance has occurred to the country. We are expecting movements in every direction. O God! direct our leaders!

Our daughter M[ary] is with us, quite sick; her husband has just arrived from North Carolina, where he is attached to General Whiting's command.[116]

29th—The country seems to continue quiet, but the campaign on the Rapidan is expected to open every day. Oh, how I dread it! The morning is bright and beautiful; it seems hardly possible that such strife is abroad in the land.

May 2—Just taken leave of J. J., who has gone to Halifax [County], where the Bishop resides.[117] It seems so strange that she does not want to go to the country. If I could only get to some quiet nook, some lodge in a vast wilderness, where rumours of unsuccessful or successful war could never reach me more, I think I should be happy. The Bishop says it is too expensive here for his income, and so it is for everybody's income, but were we to leave it we should have none; our whole dependence is now upon the Government, except the interest on a small amount invested in Confederate bonds.

Our army, it is said, is fighting at or near Newbern, North Carolina. I trust they are following up the Plymouth victory.[118]

Tuesday Morning, May 3—Yesterday passed as usual. We attended Mr. Peterkin's prayer-meeting before breakfast, which we generally do, and which was very interesting. Then came by market for our daily supplies; and at nine I commenced my labour in the office, while Mr. [McGuire] went to his hospital, which occupies a great deal of his time.

Washington, North Carolina, has been evacuated by the Federals, who have retired to Newbern. All quiet on the Rapidan. Six steamers have run the blockade within a few days, laden with ammunition, etc. Surely God is with us. It is a delightful thing to contemplate that so many of our officers of high position, who are leading and giving an example to our soldiers, should be God-fearing men; from the President and General Lee down, I believe a majority of them are professing Christians. On Sunday I saw General R. Ransom (who was lately put in command here) and General Kemper,[119] who has just recovered from the wound received at Gettysburg, both at the communion table.

On Saturday our President had a most heart-rending accident in his family.[120] His little son was playing on the back-portico, fell over, and was picked up apparently lifeless. Both parents were absent, nor did they get home in time to see their child alive. The neighbours collected around him, physicians were immediately called in, but the little fellow could not be aroused; he breathed for about three-quarters of an hour. His devoted parents returned to find their boy, whom they had left two hours before full of "life in every limb," now cold in death. They have the deep sympathy of the community.

May 5—Our army on the Rapidan is in line of battle. [Gen. U. S.] Grant is moving his mighty columns. Where the battle will take place Heaven only knows. I pray that God may be with us, and that the enemy may be driven far from our borders.

We are now attending the prayer-meetings held by the Young Men's Christian Association, which are very interesting; three of them will be held this week for our dear army, and for the battle now pending.

May 6, 1864—The Federals are this morning ascending James River, with a fleet of thirty-nine vessels—four monitors among them.[121] The battle between Lee and Grant imminent. God help us! We feel strengthened by the prayers of so many good people. All the city seems quiet and trusting. We feel that the Lord will keep the city. We were at our own prayer-meeting at St. John's this morning at half-past six. Yesterday evening we heard most fervent prayers from the Young Men's Christian Association.[122] To-day Dr. Reid's Church[123] will be open all day for prayer. I am sorry that I shall not be able to go before the afternoon.

Grant's force is said to be between one hundred and fifty and one hundred and eighty thousand men. The "battle is not always to the strong," as we have so often experienced during the past three years.

We spent last evening at the Ballard House,[124] with Dr. S[mith] and my dear S[ally]. She is hastening to her ill child; he must return to his post; private griefs cannot now be indulged.

Sunday, May 8—By the blessing of God, I now record that, as far as heard from, our arms have been signally victorious. On Thursday and Friday the enemy were driven off, and the telegram of yesterday from General Lee spoke of our cause as going on prosperously, and with comparatively little loss to us.[125] Grant has been driven back, and 10,000 prisoners taken, but how far he has gone is not yet known. General Lee's telegram last night was very encouraging; he speaks of having captured two major-generals and killed three brigadiers. We have not yet heard of our casualties, except in one or two instances. We have been dreadfully shocked by the death of Colonel William Randolph, of Clarke County.[126] He fell on the 6th of May.

The country has lost no more devoted patriot, the army no more gallant officer, and society no more brilliant member. It was but last Sunday that his sister-in-law, Miss M. S.,[127] said to me with natural pride and pleasure: "William Randolph has been promoted; he is now colonel of the Second." I expressed the pleasure which I then felt; but as she passed out of the room, and my thoughts again turned to the subject, a superstitious horror came over me, and I said to those around me, "This is a fatal honour conferred upon W[illiam] R[andolph]," and I could not get rid of the impression. The Second Regiment has invariably lost its field officers. It is one of the most gallant regiments of the Stonewall Brigade, and has frequently had what is called the post of honour. Colonel [James Walkinson] Allen, Colonel [Lawson] Botts, Lieutenant Colonel [Francis] Lackland, Major [Francis Buckner] Jones, and now Colonel Randolph, have fallen! And Colonel [John Quincy Adams] Nadenbousch, of the same regiment, has been so mutilated by wounds as to be obliged to retire from the service.

The fleet upon James River has landed about 30,000 or 40,000 troops. One of their gunboats ran upon a torpedo, which blew it to atoms.[128] We repulsed them near Walthall.[129] Yesterday they came with a very strong force upon the Petersburg Railroad. They were too strong for us, and we had to fall back; the enemy consequently took the road, and, of course, injured it very much; but they have fallen back; why, we do not know, unless they have heard of Grant's failure. The alarm-bell is constantly ringing, making us nervous and anxious. The militia have been called out, and have left the city, but where they have gone I know not. It is strange how little apprehension seems to be felt in the city. Our trust is first in God, and, under Him, in our brave men. At this moment Yankee prisoners are passing by. I do not know where they were captured. Those taken at the battle of "The Wilderness" were sent South.

I went to the Monumental Church this morning. Mr. —— read the service, and Mr. Johnston, of Alexandria, preached.[130]

Wednesday, May 11—The last three days have been most exciting. The enemy on the south side of the river have made heavy demonstrations; their force is perhaps 40,000; ours not half that number. The militia, the City Battalion, and the clerks have gone from Richmond. They have had a heavy fight at Port Walthall, and another near Chester, in which we had, upon the whole, the advantage of them.[131] In the mean time a large body of raiders are going over the country. They have cut the [Virginia] Central Railroad, and burnt three trains of cars, laden with provisions for General Lee's army, and are doing all manner of mischief to public and private property. Not a word can we hear from General Lee, except through private telegrams sent from Guiney's Station. The wires (telegraph) above that place have been cut. Our accounts from Guiney's are very encouraging. It is astonishing how quiet everybody is—all owing, I must believe, to an abiding faith in the goodness of God. Prayer-meetings are held in almost all the churches, and we take great comfort in them. It seems to me evident that the Lord is fighting our battles for us.

The last was a most disturbed night. We knew that the attaches of the War Department had received orders to spend the night there, and our son had promised us that if any thing exciting occurred he would come up and let us know. We were first aroused by hearing a number of soldiers pass up Broad Street. I sprang up, and saw at least a brigade passing by. As we were composing ourselves to sleep, I heard several pebbles come against the window. On looking out, I saw J[ames] standing below. In a moment the door was opened and he was in our room, with the information, brought by a courier, that 7,000 raiders were within sixteen miles of us, making their way to the city.[132] He also said that 3,000 infantry had marched to meet them. Every lady in the house dressed immediately, and some of us went down to the porch. There we saw ladies in every porch, and walking on the pavements, as if it were evening. We saw but one person who seemed really alarmed; every one else seemed to expect something to occur to stop the raiders. Our city had too often been saved as if by a miracle. About two o'clock a telegram came from General Stuart that he was in pursuit of the enemy. J[ames] came up to bring us the information, and we felt that all was right. In a very short time families had retired to their chambers, and quietness reigned in this hitherto perturbed street. For ourselves, we were soon asleep. To-day General Stuart telegraphs that the enemy were overtaken at Ashland by Lomax's Brigade, and handsomely repulsed.[133] We have just heard that they have taken the road to Dover's Mills, and our men are in hot pursuit.

Thursday, May 12—The cannon is now roaring in our ears. It cannot be more than three miles off. The Lord reigneth; in that is our trust. There was a severe cavalry fight yesterday morning, in which our brilliant cavalry leader, General J. E. B. Stuart, was severely wounded. He was brought to the city last night. One of his aides, our relative, Lieutenant T. S. Garnett,[134] has told us with what difficulty they got him here; in an ambulance, going out of the way, hither and thither, to avoid the enemy; of course, every jolt inflicting intense agony. He is now at the house of his brother-in-law, Dr. Brewer,[135] surrounded by the most efficient surgeons and devoted friends. The prayers of the community are with him.

My time, when out of the office, is much absorbed by the hospital. Many wounded are brought in from both sides of the river. This morning, as I entered St. James's Church, I saw the smoke from the cannon distinctly. I stood for a moment on the steps and listened to the continued roaring, and felt that the contest was fearfully near to us. The prayers, hymns, psalms, and address were most comforting. God be praised for his goodness, that we are still surrounded by Christian people, and have the faith and trust of Christians. The town is as calm as if it were not the great object of desire to hundreds of thousands of implacable enemies, who desire nothing so much as its destruction.

General Lee's telegram last night gave us an account of another repulse given General Grant, with great slaughter. "We suffered little in comparison;" such was his telegram, signed "R. E. Lee."[136] His signature is always cheering to our people. For some time we had not seen it, in consequence of cut telegraphic wires. Both armies are now fortifying. The Yankees have such indomitable perseverance, that they will never give up.

May 13—General Stuart died of his wounds last night, twenty-four hours after he was shot. He was a member of the Episcopal Church, and expressed to the Rev. Dr. Peterkin his resignation to the will of God. After much conversation with his friends and Dr. P[eterkin], and joining them in a hymn which he requested should be sung, he calmly resigned his redeemed spirit to the God who gave it. Thus passed away our great cavalry general, just one year after the immortal Jackson. This seems darkly mysterious to us, but God's will be done. The funeral took place this evening, from St. James's Church. My duty to the living prevented my attending it, for which I am very sorry; but I was in the hospital from three o'clock until eight, soothing the sufferers in the only way I could, by fanning them, bathing their wounds, and giving them a word of comfort. Mr. [McGuire] and others of our household were at the funeral. They represent the scene as being very imposing.

14th—The cavalry fight on the Chickahominy was very severe.[137] The Yankees escaped on Thursday night; they should not have been allowed to get off. Our sad deficiency in numbers is always in our way.

The death of another of our beloved E[piscopal] H[igh] S[chool] boys has shocked us greatly—I mean that of Colonel Robert Randolph, of Fauquier [County],[138] for a long time the chivalric captain of the famous "Black Horse Company." After fighting desperately for hours, he was ordered to change his position; he immediately raised himself in his saddle, exclaiming, "Boys, we will give them one round more before we go!" fired, and was at that moment struck in the forehead by a Minie ball, and laid low, a few hours after the fall of his General. Thus our young men, of the first blood of the country—first in character and education, and, what is more important to us now, first in gallantry and patriotism—fall one by one. What a noble army of martyrs has already passed away! I tremble for the future; but we must not think of the future. "Sufficient unto the day is the evil thereof."[139]

General Lee's last telegram tells of a furious fight on Thursday, near Spottsylvania Court-House.[140] The enemy was repulsed, and driven back; and yet General Grant prepares for a fresh attack. It is said that 15,000 wounded Yankees are in Fredericksburg. We have heard cannon all day in the direction of Drury's Bluff;[141] yet we are calm!

Tuesday Morning, May 17—For some days the cannon has been resounding in our ears, from the south side of the James River. Colonel [James Mercer] Garnett has come in to tell us that for the first two days there was only heavy skirmishing, but that on yesterday there was a terrific fight all along the lines. Yesterday a brigadier, his staff, and 840 men, were lodged in the Libby Prison.[142] Nothing definite has been heard since that time. The impression is, that we have been generally successful. Very brilliant reports are afloat on the streets, but whether they are reliable is the question. My nephew, Major B[rockenbrough], has just called to tell me that his brother W[illoughby] is reported "missing."[143] His battery suffered dreadfully, and he has not been seen. God grant that he may be only a prisoner! We suppose that it would have been known to the fragment of his battery which is left, if he had fallen.

18th—W[illoughby] B[rockenbrough] certainly captured. I thank God for it, as the least of casualties.

General Lee and Grant still fighting.

On the south side, Beauregard has driven Butler to Bermuda Hundred, where he is under shelter of his gun-boats.[144] Oh! when will this fearful state of things end?

23d—Our young relative, Lieutenant G[arnett], a member of General Stuart's staff, who was always near his person, has just been giving us a most gratifying account of General Stuart's habits. He says, that although he considered him one of the most sprightly men he has ever seen, devoted to society, particularly to that of the ladies, always social and cheerful, yet he has never seen him do any thing, even under the strongest excitement, unbecoming his Christian profession or his high position as a soldier; he never saw him drink, or heard an oath escape his lips; his sentiments were always high-minded, pure, and honourable, and his actions entirely coincided with them. In short, he considered him, whether on the field or in the private circle, the model of a Christian gentleman and soldier. When speaking of his gallantry as an officer, Lieutenant G[arnett]'s admiration knows no bounds. He speaks of the devotion of the soldiers to him as enthusiastic in the extreme. The evening before his fatal wound, he sent his troops on in pursuit of Sheridan, under the command of General Fitz Lee, as he was unavoidably detained for some three or four hours. General Lee overtook the enemy, and a sharp skirmish ensued, in which Sheridan's rear suffered very much. In the mean time, General Stuart determined to overtake General Lee, and, with his staff, rode very rapidly sixteen miles, and reached him about nightfall. They were halting for a few moments, as General Stuart rode up quietly, no one suspecting he was there, until a plain-looking soldier crossed the road, stopped, peered through the darkness into his face, and shouted out, "Old Jeb has come!" In an instant the air was rent with huzzas. General Stuart waved his cap in recognition; but called out in rather a sad voice, "My friends, we won't halloo until we get out of the woods!" intimating that there was serious work before them. At that hour the next night he was pursuing his weary and suffering way to Richmond. A friend, who knows how much I regretted not being able to serve General Stuart in any way, or even to be at his funeral, has been so kind as to write me a minute account of his sickness, death, and burial. "Perhaps (she says) it is not generally known how entirely General Stuart sacrificed his life to save Richmond. An officer of high rank, who knew the circumstances, told me that in all the war there was not one man more truly a martyr to our cause. In the many raids upon Richmond there was none in which we seemed in such imminent peril as the one in which General Stuart has just fallen. How we listened, and watched, and prayed, as the cannon sounded nearer and nearer, and even the volleys of musketry could be heard out on the roads by which the enemy were approaching! We knew that General Stuart had a band of about 2,000 cavalry against overwhelming odds on the Yankee side,[145] and that he knew that upon this 2,000 men alone it depended to bar the enemy's approach on that side. He met the Yankees, 5,000 strong, beat them back, and fell in the encounter! It was with difficulty that he could be rescued from those who were bearing him away, but one of his own troopers saved him, and with his staff and surgeon (Dr. John Fontaine) bore him to the city.[146] We heard that he was dying, and, in spite of the anxiety and confusion reigning at such a time, many of us rushed to Dr. Brewer's house to hear tidings of the beloved commander, whose gallantry, whose youthful gayety and chivalrous character, made him the prince among our cavalry officers. His life was ebbing out from internal hemorrhage; but his senses were as clear and his mind as calm as noontide. He asked repeatedly for his wife, who, though but fifteen miles away, could not be reached, so completely was the city hemmed in by the enemy. By his side stood our President, who, upon hearing of his situation, had hastened to thank him in the name of his country. 'I have but done my duty,' was the soldier's reply.[147] And near him was the minister of God, good Mr. Peterkin, of whose church (Episcopal) General S[tuart] was a member. He asked for his favourite hymn, and joined his feeble voice with the touching words: 'I would not live always.' From time to time, he turned his head to ask, 'Is she come?' But she, for whom his loving heart so yearned, came not till that heart was stilled forever. At the funeral—at the head of his coffin—sat the soldier who had rescued him, all battle-stained and soiled; and near by, the members of his staff, who all adored him. Upon the coffin lay a sword, formed of delicate white flowers, a cross of white roses, and above these the heavenly crown, symbolized by one of green bay-leaves. We followed him to the church, where, after appropriate ceremonies, attended by many persons, his body was taken to Hollywood Cemetery. No martial pomp, no soldier's funeral, but—

> Slowly and sadly we laid him down,
>   From the field of his fame fresh and gory;

We carved not a line, we raised not a stone,
But we left him alone with his glory.

Everybody was struck with the resemblance to the funeral so beautifully
described in the lines just quoted. As we passed, in slow procession—

"We knew by the distant and random gun,
That the foe was sullenly firing.[148]

These guns were his funeral knell, sounding at intervals the solemn peal,
with which, in the haste and uncertainty of the time, it was impossible for
us to honour him."

One of the morning papers has some lines on the same subject, more
poetic, though not so graphic, as the account given by my friend:

J. E. B. STUART.

We could not pause, while yet the noontide air
Shook with the cannonade's incessant pealing,
The funeral pageant, fitly to prepare,
A nation's grief revealing.

The smoke above the glimmering woodland wide,
That skirts our southward border with its beauty,
Marked where our heroes stood, and fought and died,
For love, and faith, and duty.

And still what time the doubtful strife went on,
We might not find expression for our sorrow;
We could but lay our dear, dumb warrior down,
And gird us for tomorrow.

One weary year ago, when came a lull
With victory, in the conflicts' stormy closes,
When the glad Spring, all flushed and beautiful,
First mocked us with her roses—

With dirge and bell, and minute-gun, we paid
   Some few poor rites, an inexpressive token
Of a great people's pain, to Jackson's shade,
   In agony unspoken.

No wailing trumpet, and no tolling bell,
   No cannon, save the battle's boom receding,
When Stuart to the grave we bore, might tell
   With hearts all crushed and bleeding.

The crisis suited not with pomp, and she,
   Whose anguish bears the seal of consecration,
Had wished his Christian obsequies should be
   Thus void of ostentation.

Only the maidens came, sweet flowers to twine
   Above his form, so still, and cold, and painless,
Whose deeds upon our brightest records shine,
   Whose life and sword were stainless.

We well remember how he loved to dash
   Into the fight, festooned from summer bowers
How like a fountain's spray, his sabre's flash
   Leaped from a mass of flowers.

And so we carried to his place of rest,
   All that of our Paladin was mortal;
The cross, and not the sabre, on his breast,
   That opes the heavenly portal.

No more of tribute might to us remain;
   But there will come a time when freedom's martyrs
A richer guerdon of renown shall gain
   Than gleams in stars and garters.

I claim no prophet's vision, but I see,
   Though coming years now near at hand, now distant,

My rescued country, glorious and free,
    And strong and self-existent.

I hear from out that sunlit land which lies
    Beyond these clouds which darkly gather o'er us,
The happy sounds of industry arise,
    In swelling, peaceful chorus.

And mingling with these sounds, the glad acclaim
    Of millions, undisturbed by war's afflictions,
Crowning each martyr's never-dying name
    With grateful benedictions.

In some fair, future garden of delights,
    Where flowers shall bloom, and song-birds sweetly warble,
Art shall erect the statues of our knights,
    In living bronze and marble.

And none of all that bright, heroic throng
    Shall wear to far-off time a semblance grander,
Shall still be decked with fresher wreaths of song,
    Than the beloved commander.

The Spanish legends tell us of the Cid,
    That after death he rode erect and stately
Along his lines, e'en as in life he did,
    In presence yet more stately.

And thus our Stuart at this moment seems
    To ride out of our dark and troubled story,
Into the region of romance and dreams,
    A realm of light and glory.

And sometimes when the silver bugles blow,
    That radiant form in battle reappearing,
Shall lead his horsemen headlong on the foe,
    In victory careering.[149]

May 26—We are now anticipating a fight at Hanover Junction. General Lee fell back to that point on Sunday last, for some good purpose, no doubt. Our army is in line of battle on the Cedar Hill plantation. The ladies of the family have come to Richmond to avoid the awful collision about to take place. That house, I sadly fear, is to be another sacrifice. Our successes have been wonderful, and evidently, I think, directed by God. We have, however, just met with a sad reverse in Charles City County.[150] General Fitz Lee, commanding two brigades, fought a much larger body of men, who were strongly fortified, and was of course repulsed. Alas, alas, for our gallant army! Bravery cannot always contend safely against overwhelming numbers. We are very uneasy about our dear ones who were in that fight. Strange stories are told of the wounded having been bayoneted. It is difficult to believe that men of human hearts could do such things; and while I feel unhappy about the rumour, I cannot credit it.

May 27—News from Fitz Lee's fight; it was not disastrous as at first reported; many were wounded, many captured, and but four killed. But four desolated homes by this stroke! But four widows, or broken-hearted mothers, in addition to the bereaved of the land! God be with them to comfort them! Nothing farther of the bayoneted wounded: I trust that it was all a fabrication.

We returned to the office yesterday, which had been closed for a week. It is pitiable to see how the rations are being reduced by degrees. The Government is exerting itself for the relief of the soldiers. God have mercy upon and help us!

June 4—There has been skirmishing for some days. One day a fight at Ashland, another at Cold Harbor; but yesterday the heaviest cannonading I ever heard continued all day, until after dark.[151] The fighting was between Bethesda Church and Cold Harbour. We were well fortified, and General Lee reports great success to our arms. "It is the Lord's doings, and it is marvellous in our eyes."[152] We went to church this evening and returned thanks.

June 5—Our daughter-in-law, Mrs. Dr. [McGuire],[153] came from Charlottesville this evening. The regular communication being cut off, she went up to Lynchburg, taking that route to Richmond; but the Government having impressed the cars, she was obliged to take a freight-train, and was fortunate in finding a friend coming down in the same way, who acted as her escort.

At Burkeville (shall I record it of a Virginia house of any degree?)[154] she was treated with such inhospitality, that she was compelled to pass the night in a car filled with bags of corn, which the gentlemen fixed so carefully as to give her *almost* a comfortable resting-place. When she returned from her unsuccessful application for quarters, one of the soldiers said to her (she was the only lady in the company,) "Lady, where are you from?" "The Valley of Virginia," was her reply. He instantly sprang up: "Boys, we must burn that house!" he exclaimed; "they won't take in this lady from the 'Valley,' where we have been treated so kindly." Of course he had no idea of burning the house, though he seemed highly indignant. She came to us looking well after a three days' journey, having borne her difficulties with great cheerfulness.

11th—Just heard from W[estwood] and S[ummer] H[ill]. Both places in ruins, except the dwelling-houses. Large portions of the Federal army were on them for eight days. S[ummer] H[ill] was used as a hospital for the wounded brought from the battle-fields; this protected the house. At W[estwood] several generals had their head-quarters in the grounds near the house, which, of course, protected it. General [Gouverneur K.] Warren had his tent in the "shrubbery" for two days, General [Ambrose E.] Burnside for a day or two, and those of lesser rank were there from time to time. General Grant was encamped at S[ummer] H[ill] for a time. Dr. [John White] B[rockenbrough] was at home, with several Confederate wounded from the battle of "Haw's Shop"[155] in the house. Being absent a mile or two from home when they arrived, they so quickly threw out pickets, spread their tents over the surrounding fields and hills, that he could not return to his house, where his wife and only child were alone, until he had obtained a pass from a Yankee officer. As he approached the house, thousands and tens of thousands of horses and cattle were roaming over the fine wheat fields on his and the adjoining estate (that of his niece, Mrs. N[ewton],) which were now ripe for the sickle. The clover fields and fields of young corn were sharing the same fate. He found his front porch filled with officers. They asked him of his sentiments with regard to the war. He told them frankly that he was an original Secessionist, and ardently hoped to see the North and South separate and distinct nations now and forever. One of them replied that he "honoured his candour," and from that moment he was treated with great courtesy. After some difficulty he was allowed to keep his wounded Confederates, and in one or two instances the Federal surgeons assisted him in dressing their wounds. At S[ummer] H[ill] the parlour was used for an amputating room, and Yankee blood streamed through that beautiful apartment and the adjoining passage. Poor M[ary Newton] had her stricken heart sorely lacerated in every way, particularly when her little son came running in and nestled up to her in alarm. A soldier had asked him, "Are you the son of Captain Newton, who was killed in Culpeper?" "Yes," replied the child. "Well, I belong to the Eighth Illinois, and was one of the soldiers that fired at him when he fell," was the barbarous reply.

On these highly cultivated plantations not a fence is left, except mutilated garden enclosures. The fields were as free from vegetation after a few days as the Arabian desert; the very roots seem eradicated from the earth. A fortification stretched across W[estwood], in which were embedded the fence rails of that and the adjoining farms. Ten thousand cavalry were drawn up in line of battle for two days on the two plantations, expecting the approach of the Confederates; bands of music were constantly playing martial airs in all parts of the premises; and whiskey flowed freely. The poor servants could not resist these intoxicating influences, particularly as Abolition preachers were constantly collecting large crowds, preaching to them the cruelty of the servitude which had been so long imposed upon them, and that Abraham Lincoln was the Moses sent by God to deliver them from the "land of Egypt and the house of bondage," and to lead them to the promised land. After the eight days were accomplished, the army moved off, leaving not a quadruped, except two pigs, which had ensconced themselves under the ruins of a servant's house, and perhaps a dog to one plantation; to the other, by some miraculous oversight, two cows and a few pigs were left. Not a wheeled vehicle of any kind was to be found; all the grain, flour, meat, and other supplies were swept off, except the few things hid in those wonderful places which could not be fathomed even by the "Grand Army." Scarcely a representative of the sons and daughters of Africa remained in that whole section of country; they had all gone to Canaan, by way of York River, Chesapeake Bay, and the Potomac—not dry-shod, for the waters were not rolled back at the presence of these modern Israelites, but in vessels crowded to suffocation in this excessively warm weather. They have gone to homeless poverty, an unfriendly climate, and hard work; many of them to die without sympathy, for the invalid, the decrepit, and the infant of days have left their houses, beds, and many comforts, the homes of their birth, the masters and mistresses who regarded them not so much as property as humble friends and members of their families. Poor, deluded creatures! I am grieved not so much on account of the loss of their services, though that is excessively inconvenient and annoying, but for their grievous disappointment. Those who have trades, or who are brought up as lady's maids, or house servants, may do well, but woe to the masses who have gone with the blissful hope of idleness and free supplies! We have lost several who were great comforts to us, and others who were sources of care, responsibility, and great expense. These particulars from W[estwood] and S[ummer] H[ill] I have from our nephew, J. P.,[156] who is now a scout for General W. H. F. Lee. He called by to rest a few hours at his uncle's house, and says he would scarcely have known the barren wilderness. The Northern officers seemed disposed to be courteous to the ladies, in the little intercourse which they had with them. General Ferrara,[157] who commanded the negro troops, was humane, in having a coffin made for a young Confederate officer who died in Dr. B[rockenbrough]'s house, and was kind in other respects. The surgeons, too, assisted in attending to the Confederate wounded. An officer one morning sent for Mrs. N[ewton] to ask her where he should place a box of French china for safety; he said that some soldiers had discovered it buried in her garden, dug it up and opened it, but he had come up at this crisis and had placed a guard over it, and desired to know where she wished it put. A place of safety of course was not on the premises, but she had it taken to her chamber. She thanked him for his kindness. He seemed moved and said, "Mrs. N[ewton], I will do what I can for you, but I cannot be too thankful that my wife is not in an invaded country." She then asked him how he could, with his feelings, come to the South. He replied that he was in the regular army, and was obliged to come. Many little acts of kindness were done at both houses, which were received in the spirit in which they were extended. *Per contra:* On one occasion Miss D., a young relative of Mrs. N[ewton]'s, was in one of the tents set aside for the Confederate wounded, writing a letter from a dying soldier to his friends at home. She was interrupted by a young Yankee surgeon, to whom she was a perfect stranger, putting his head in and remarking pertly, "Ah, Miss D., are you writing? Have you friends in Richmond? I shall be there in a few days, and will with pleasure take your communication." She looked up calmly into his face, and replied, "Thank you, *I* have no friends in the Libby [Prison]!" It was heard by his comrades on the outside of the tent, and shouts and peals of laughter resounded at the expense of the discomfited surgeon. The ladies frequently afterwards heard him bored with the question, "Doctor, when do you go to the Libby?"

12th—I am grieved to say that we have had a reverse in the "Valley," and that General Jones, of the cavalry, has been killed, and his command repulsed.[158] They have fallen back to Waynesborough, leaving Staunton in the hands of the enemy. General Johnston is doing well in Georgia.[159] Oh, that he may use up Sherman entirely! We are getting on well at home; everybody looks as calm as if there were no belligerent armies near.

24th—I have been much occupied nursing the sick, not only in the hospital, but among our own friends; and a sad, sad week has the last been to us. We have had very little to think of public affairs, but now that the last sad offices have been performed for one very, very dear to us, with sore hearts we must go back to busy life again. It is wonderful to me that we retain our senses. While the cannon is booming in our ears from the neighbourhood of Petersburg, we know that Hunter is raiding among our friends in the most relentless way; that the Military Institute has been burnt,[160] and that we have nothing to hope for the West, unless General [Jubal A.] Early and General [John C.] Breckinridge can destroy him utterly.

July 18—Since the last note in my diary we have been pursuing our usual course. The tenor of our way is singularly rough and uneven, marked by the sound of cannon, the marching of troops, and all the paraphernalia of grim-visaged war; but we still visit our friends and relatives, and have our pleasant social and family meetings, as though we were at peace with all the world. The theme of every tongue is our army in Maryland. What is it doing? What will be the result of the venture? The last accounts are from the Washington papers. Early, they say, is before Washington, throwing in shells, having cut the railroads and burnt the bridges.[161] We are of course all anxiety, and rumour is busier than ever. The army, it is said, has driven innumerable horses, beeves, etc., into Virginia. I trust so; it is surmised that to supply the commissariat is the chief object of the trip. Grant still before Petersburg, sending transports, etc., with troops to defend Washington.

24th—Amid all the turbulent scenes which surround us, our only grandchild has first seen the light, and the dear little fellow looks as quiet as though all were peace.[162] We thank God for this precious gift, this little object of all-absorbing interest, which so pleasantly diverts our troubled minds. His father has left his far-off military post to welcome him, and before he returns we must by baptism receive him into the Church on earth, praying that he may be a "member of Christ, a child of God, and an inheritor of the kingdom of heaven." This rite thus early administered, bringing him into the Episcopal Church, seems to belong to him by inheritance, as he is the grandson of a Presbyter on one side, and a Bishop on the other.

The city looks warlike, though the inhabitants are quiet. Troops are constantly passing to and fro; army wagons, ambulances, etc., rattle by, morning, noon, and night. Grant remains passive on the Appomattox [River], occasionally throwing a shell into Petersburg, which may probably explode among women and children—but what matters it? They are rebels—what difference does it make about their lives or limbs?

July 27—General Early has returned from Maryland, bringing horses, cattle, etc. While near Washington, the army burned Mr. Montgomery Blair's house,[163] which I cannot persuade myself to regret, and spared the residence of his father, by order, it is said, of General Breckinridge. I know that General B[reckinridge] was right, but I think it required great forbearance, particularly in the soldiers, who have felt in their own persons and families the horrors of this cruel war of invasion. It seems to our human view that unless the war is severely felt by those in high authority, it will never cease. Hunter has just passed through the upper part of the Valley of Virginia, his pathway marked by fire and sword; and [Gen. Philip H.] Sheridan has followed Early into Virginia. With no very gentle intent, I fear. I am glad that Maryland was spared as a general thing, particularly as our friends might have suffered with our foes, for it would have been difficult to discriminate; but I cannot avoid thinking that if other places, besides General [Augustus W.] Bradford's house and the town of Chambersburg, had been burnt, it would shorten the war. Yet God has said, "Vengeance is mine, I will repay;"[164] and I hope that Christian principles will ever be observed by our commanders. There seems to be no touch of pity in the hearts of many of the Federal generals. Women and children are made homeless at midnight, and not allowed to save any thing, even their clothes. When houses are not burned, they are robbed of every thing which a rapacious soldiery may desire. The last barrel of flour, the last ham, is taken from store-rooms; and this is done, not in

Virginia only; nor are Hunter, Sheridan, [Judson] Kilpatrick, or [George] Stoneman the only men who do it; but every State in the Confederacy has felt the heel of the despot. North and South Carolina have suffered on their eastern borders most severely; the same of Georgia and Florida. Alabama has had much to bear. The Mississippi country in Louisiana, Arkansas, and the State of Mississippi, has been ravaged and desolated; Tennessee has perhaps had more to bear than any of them. But poor old Virginia has been furrowed and scarred until her original likeness is gone. From the Potomac to the Roanoke, from the seaboard to the Kentucky boundary, including the down-trodden Eastern Shore, she could scarcely be recognized by her sons. Marked by a hundred battle-fields, and checkered by fortifications, almost every spot is classic ground. From the beginning she has acted her part nobly, and has already covered herself with glory; but when the war is over, where shall we find her old churches, where her noble homesteads, scenes of domestic comfort and generous hospitality? Either laid low by the firebrand, or desecrated and desolated. In the march of the army, or in the rapid evolutions of raiding parties, woe betide the houses which are found deserted! In many cases the men of the family having gone to the war, the women and children dare not stay; then the lawless are allowed to plunder. They seem to take the greatest delight in breaking up the most elegant or the most humble furniture, as the case may be; cut the portraits from the frames, split pianos in pieces, ruin libraries, in any way that suits their fancy; break doors from their hinges, and locks from the doors; cut the windows from the frames, and leave no pane of glass unbroken; carry off house-linen and carpets; the contents of the store-rooms and pantries, sugar, flour, vinegar, molasses, pickles, preserves, which cannot be eaten or carried off, are poured together in one general mass; the horses are of course taken from the stables; cattle and stock of all kinds driven off or shot in the woods and fields. Generally, indeed, I believe always when the whole army is moving, inhabited houses are protected. To raiders such as Hunter and Co. is reserved the credit of committing such outrages in the presence of ladies—of taking their watches from their belts, their rings from their fingers, and their ear-rings from their ears; of searching their bureaux and wardrobes, and filling pockets and haversacks in their presence. Is it not then wonderful that soldiers whose families have suffered such things could be restrained when in a hostile country? It seems to me to show a marvellous degree of forbearance in the officers themselves, and of discipline in the troops.

Notes

1. Laura and Isabelle ("Bella") were daughters of Mrs. McGuire's close friend Cordelia Stuart of Chantilly. See June 1, 1861, diary entry; 1850 Virginia Census—Fairfax County.

2. Sarah Brockenbrough Colston was the mother of the Second Virginia's Capt. William B. Colston.

3. Then in her mid-sixties, Caroline Thornton was a widow of considerable means. 1860 Virginia Census—Rappahannock County; Matthew Page Andrews, ed., *The Women of the South in War Times* (Baltimore: Norman, Remington, 1920), 182.

4. A German revolutionist who fled to America in the 1850s, Franz Sigel had a reputation as a skillful teacher and musician. He became a brigadier general largely because of his success in recruiting Germans into the Union armies.

5. The quotation is from Charles Carroll Sawyer's poem "Weeping Sad and Lonely," which became a favorite song on both sides in the Civil War. Mrs. McGuire bemoaned the fact that war narratives like hers would be the only surviving remnants of Confederate civilization. A Winchester matron felt the same way. Writing after the war, Cornelia McDonald observed: "I have seen so much of real suffering, of conflict, danger and death, that for years I could read neither romance [n]or history, for nothing equaled what I had seen and known." Cornelia Peake McDonald, *A Woman's Civil War: A Diary with Reminiscences of the War from March 1862,* ed. Minrose C. Gwin (Madison: University of Wisconsin Press, 1992), 231.

6. "For all our days are passed away in thy wrath: we spend our years as a tale that is told." Psalms 90:9.

7. Flavia K. Daniel was the wife of Fredericksburg attorney Samuel Greenhow Daniel. Andrews, *Women of the South,* 184; 1860 Virginia Census—Spotsylvania County.

8. An expedition of 400 Union infantry and three gunboats proceeded up the York River to destroy a foundry some ten miles above Walkerton. For more on the June 4–5 raid, see U.S. War Department, *War of the Rebellion: A Compilation of Official Records of the Union and Confederate Armies* (Washington, D.C.: Government Printing Office, 1880–1901), series 1, vol. 27, pt. 2, 777–84 (hereafter cited as *OR*).

9. James Roane had a sizable estate along the Mattaponi River. Mrs. McGuire's account of the Union raid is included in Dorothy Francis Atkinson, *King William County in the Civil War: Along Mangohick Byways* (Lynchburg, Va.: H. E. Howard, 1990), 88–89.

10. The date of this entry is in error. On June 9, a Union cavalry force equal in strength to Gen. Jeb Stuart's mounted corps made a surprise attack on the Confederates at Brandy Station. This became the largest cavalry battle in the history of the Western Hemisphere. Fighting ended in a draw. The Union withdrawal left Stuart to claim a victory, but the cavalryman came under severe criticism from the press and the public.

11. Lee's army was now beginning a second invasion of the North. On June 14, two divisions of Ewell's Second Corps attacked Union defenses at Winchester. Gen. Jubal Early's division managed to seize one of the earthworks and severely threaten the main forts guarding the town.

12. Tardy at moving to safety, Union general Milroy had to fight his way through the constricting Southern positions. Union casualties were 95 killed, 348 wounded, and 4,000 captured. Meanwhile, Confederate general Edward Johnson had conducted a movement on Berryville and Martinsburg that resulted in the capture of five cannon, 200 prisoners, and "quartermaster's and subsistence stores in some quantity." *OR*, series 1, vol. 27, pt. 2, 53, 442.

13. On June 15, elements of Gen. Alfred Jenkins's cavalry brigade occupied Chambersburg, Pennsylvania. Confederates the next day destroyed railroad and telegraph lines, gathered supplies, and repulsed a small Union cavalry force. With Federal reinforcements on the way, Jenkins's troopers retired to Hagerstown, Maryland. Robert J. Driver Jr., *14th Virginia Cavalry* (Lynchburg, Va.: H. E. Howard, 1988), 20–21.

14. During June 23–28, the Eleventh Pennsylvania Cavalry heavily damaged railroads in the vicinity of North Anna and South Anna rivers. The cavalrymen were under strict orders that "no pillaging or destruction of private property" was to occur. *OR*, series 1, vol. 27, pt. 2, 795–99.

15. Because Lee was moving his army swiftly and secretly through northern Virginia, tight security measures had been implemented.

16. For Stuart's report of skirmishes he waged near the railroad during June 24–26, see *OR*, series 1, vol. 27, pt. 2, 692–94.

17. A two-story brick structure, Hickory Hill remains one of Hanover County's most historic homes. William Fanning Wickham built the residence in 1820 for his wife, Anne Carter of Shirley. It stands along the Pamunkey River, three miles from Hanover Court House. Robert Bolling Lancaster, *Old Homes of Hanover County, Virginia* (Hanover, Va.: Hanover County Historical Society, 1983), 85.

18. Gen. William Henry Fitzhugh Lee, the second son of Robert E. Lee, had been wounded in action at Brandy Station. He was captured while recuperating at the family home of his wife, the former Charlotte Wickham. Federals took

"Rooney" Lee to a military hospital for further treatment. In March 1864, he was exchanged.

19. This statement may seem callous and harsh, especially from Mrs. McGuire. However, Northern civilians had not faced enemy soldiers at their front doors, or seen homes burned, livestock slaughtered, food and personal property stolen. Such pillage and suffering became common sights in the wartime South.

20. A few miles north of Ashland was Hanover Junction (now Doswell). There the Richmond, Fredericksburg & Potomac Railroad intersected with the Virginia Central line. The nearby RF&P bridge spanning the South Anna River was a prime target for Federals and hence heavily fortified.

21. During July 1–3, Gen. John A. Dix sent a large raiding party to destroy the South Anna bridge and to disrupt communications between that point and Richmond. At Ashland, where the McGuires were living (and as Mrs. McGuire reported in her July 6 entry), Federals did extensive damage.

22. General Orders No. 73, issued June 27, 1863, by Lee to his army at Chambersburg, Pennsylvania, has been called "the finest model of military restraint known to history." Robert E. Lee, *The Wartime Papers of R. E. Lee*, ed. Clifford Dowdey (Boston: Little, Brown, 1961), 533–34; Andrews, *Women of the South*, 384.

23. "Dearly beloved, avenge not yourselves, but rather give peace unto wrath; for it is written, Vengeance is mine, I will repay, saith the Lord." Romans 12:19. On this date, Rev. McGuire wrote one of his favorite former students who was about to enter the army. "I cannot wish you success without some misgiving," the minister stated. "So many of my personal friends have already fallen in this dreadful war." However, "no sacrifices are too great, no devotion too extreme, for our glorious cause. It is but to serve God, Who has a right to all, and then our country next to Him." Arthur Barksdale Kinsolving, *The Story of a Southern School: The Episcopal High School of Virginia* (Baltimore: Norman, Remington, 1922), 57.

24. Confederates under Gen. D. Harvey Hill had a brush with Federal cavalry on July 2 and managed to force their withdrawal from the vicinity of White House on the peninsula. *OR*, series 1, vol. 27, pt. 2, 858–59.

25. Gen. George W. Getty commanded the Union soldiers who struck Ashland. Ordered to "destroy depot, tracks, buildings, houses, and property of the enemy," Getty reported that the assignment was done "in a very thorough and creditable manner." Ibid., 838.

26. Maj. Gen. John F. Reynolds was commanding the Union I Corps on July 1 at Gettysburg when a Confederate sharpshooter killed him. One of

Reynolds's brigadiers, Gabriel Rene Paul, went down from a bullet that entered the right temple and passed out through the left eye. Paul survived but was permanently blind.

27. On July 4, after six weeks of besiegement and starvation, the Confederate garrison of 29,000 men surrendered Vicksburg to Federal forces under U. S. Grant.

28. William W. Loring's only victory in the West was to elude entrapment at Vicksburg. He and his division served thereafter in the Army of Tennessee.

29. Richard Taylor's efforts to slash Grant's supply lines on the left bank of the Mississippi River during the Vicksburg campaign failed. Taylor then launched a series of forays into lower Louisiana. In June 1863, he captured Brashear City and $2 million in supplies.

30. Confederate losses at Gettysburg were officially put at 2,592 killed, 12,709 wounded, and 5,150 captured. *OR,* series 1, vol. 27, pt. 2, 346.

31. Mrs. McGuire here presents the only known account of the actual death of Garnett. His body disappeared on the battlefield and has never been found. Robert K. Krick, "The Parallel Lives of Two Virginia Soldiers: Armistead and Garnett," in Gary Gallagher, ed., *The Third Day at Gettysburg and Beyond* (Chapel Hill: University of North Carolina Press, 1994), 122–23.

32. Jefferson Phelps, Mrs. McGuire's nephew, was then serving on the CSS *Chicora,* one of two ironclad rams guarding Charleston harbor. Although manned by an excellent crew, the vessel was too cumbersome and slow to be a real threat to Union ships.

33. The 7,500 Confederate defenders of Port Hudson, Louisiana, on the Mississippi River, also underwent besiegement by a Union army. The Southerners were reduced to eating mules and rats when word came of the fall of Vicksburg. On July 9, the Port Hudson garrison surrendered. "Now," a happy Lincoln exclaimed, "the Father of Waters runs unvexed to the sea."

34. James Rawlings Maupin left the University of Virginia in 1861 to enlist in the Albemarle Artillery. He transferred to the Richmond Howitzers the following year. In 1866, Maupin's body was removed from Gettysburg to the family burial ground at the university. Lee A. Wallace Jr., *The Richmond Howitzers* (Lynchburg, Va.: H. E. Howard, 1994), 144.

35. A student at Episcopal High School and 1860 graduate of Virginia Military Institute, James Keith Marshall was colonel of the Fifty-second North Carolina when killed at Gettysburg.

36. William Westwood McCreery Jr., had graduated in 1860 from West Point. He was a captain in the Twenty-sixth North Carolina during the Pickett-Pettigrew charge at Gettysburg. The color-bearer fell; McCreery seized the

flag and advanced but a few steps before he too was killed. *Southern Historical Society Papers* 35 (1907): 320.

37. Lt. Valentine W. Southall of the Twenty-third Virginia was wounded and captured. He died on July 20 from the effects of his injuries.

38. Benjamin Harrison McGuire, a lieutenant in the Twenty-second Virginia Infantry Battalion, fell in the first day's fighting at Gettysburg.

39. Austin Brockenbrough of the Fifty-fifth Virginia fell injured at Chancellorsville but had returned to duty in mid-June. On July 2, he was killed by a Union sniper. Richard O'Sullivan, *55th Virginia Infantry* (Lynchburg, Va.: H. E. Howard, 1989), 107.

40. Elizabeth Randolph Cocke, a widow of considerable means, lived fifty-five miles west of Richmond at Oakland. The 155-acre estate was on the south side of the James River and extended across Cumberland and Powhatan counties. In June 1865, Mrs. Cocke provided a temporary home for Gen. Robert E. Lee and his family at Derwent, the Powhatan portion of the estate. Margaret Randolph Dickins copy of McGuire, *Diary of a Southern Refugee,* annotated in 1868 by Judith McGuire, in private collection; Douglas Southall Freeman, *R. E. Lee: A Biography* (New York: C. Scribner's Sons, 1934), 4:209, 211.

41. Mrs. Cocke's two oldest sons both led Company E (Black Eagle Rifles) of the Eighteenth Virginia. Capt. William Fauntleroy Cocke was killed July 3, 1863, at Gettysburg. Lt. (later Capt.) Edmund Randolph Cocke remained with the regiment until his April 6, 1865, capture at Sailor's Creek. James I. Robertson Jr., *18th Virginia Infantry* (Lynchburg, Va.: H. E. Howard, 1984), 46.

42. Robb served in the Ninth Virginia Cavalry. On June 9, he went down from a wound at Brandy Station and died sometime thereafter. An official muster roll listed his death as occurring on August 24, but Mrs. McGuire was writing in mid-July. Robert K. Krick, *9th Virginia Cavalry* (Lynchburg, Va.: H. E. Howard, 1992), 95.

43. Resentment against conscription and blacks combined to trigger four days of rioting (July 13–17), largely by Irish workingmen and -women. Homes and businesses were damaged, and at least six blacks were lynched before police with several regiments of soldiers restored order.

44. On July 16, two Confederate cavalry brigades under Gen. Fitzhugh Lee struck a force of Federals near Bunker Hill and drove them to within a mile of Shepherdstown. Most of the fighting was done on foot because of uneven terrain. Federals abandoned the field under darkness. *OR,* series 1, vol. 27, pt. 2, 706.

45. After a brutal pounding of Fort Wagner, South Carolina, by mortars, ironclads, and artillery, 6,000 Federals charged across the open beach in a full-

scale attack. Over 1,500 were killed or wounded in the July 18 assault. Confederate losses were 174 men. This failure caused an abandonment of all Union efforts to take Charleston by land attack. Thereafter, Union forces employed siege tactics.

46. James Johnston Pettigrew was the best educated and most intellectual of all Confederate general officers. In the beginning months of the war, he commanded the Twenty-second North Carolina. Pettigrew led a brigade at the time of Gettysburg and was conspicuous during two days of the action. On July 14, in a rearguard contest at Falling Waters, he was shot in the stomach. Pettigrew died three days later.

47. Pettigrew's first action in the Civil War was at Seven Pines, where he was seriously wounded. Mrs. McGuire's account of his capture is somewhat garbled. No mention of a soldier named White appears in Pettigrew's biography. See Clyde N. Walton, *Carolina Cavalier: The Life and Mind of James Johnston Pettigrew* (Athens: University of Georgia Press, 1990), 164–69.

48. Actually, Mrs. Lee traveled to Hot Springs in a futile attempt to help improve the health of her daughter-in-law, Charlotte Wickham Lee (see note 18). John Perry, *The Lady of Arlington: The Life of Mrs. Robert E. Lee* (Sisters, Ore.: Multnomah, 2001), 266–67.

49. Among the many wartime duties of Dr. Alexander Yelverton Peyton Garnett was his position of supervisor of Robertson Hospital, where Sally Tompkins held forth. Garnett was also President Davis's personal physician.

50. Albert Jenkins commanded an all-Virginia brigade of cavalry.

51. Robert Burns, *Tam O'Shanter.*

52. Three days before the battle of Gettysburg exploded, Lincoln replaced Hooker at the head of the Army of the Potomac with George Gordon Meade. He and Lee had been close friends in the prewar years.

53. Fear of battle and its consumption of life haunted many women with loved ones in service. In December 1861, a Lynchburg, Virginia, wife and mother commented: "I would welcome two feet of snow, for I would be sure there would be no fighting under such circumstances. My spirits always rise when I think the weather too bad for military operations." Charles Minor Blackford and Susan Leigh Blackford, eds., *Letters from Lee's Army; or, Memoirs of Life in and out of the Army in Virginia during the War between the States* (Lincoln, Neb.: Bison, 1998), 106.

54. No report exists of any action occurring at this time near Brandy Station. Most of the opposing cavalry were contesting the passes through the Blue Ridge Mountains.

55. These two powerful commerce raiders played havoc with merchant

marine vessels. In the course of their brief existence, the *Florida* and the *Alabama* together sank or captured more than 100 American merchant ships.

56. Catherine R. Peyton was then in her late thirties. She and her husband Jefferson were a farm family with six children ranging in age from three to thirteen. Dickins copy; 1860 Virginia Census—Amelia County.

57. John Randolph Tucker became a distinguished member of the Virginia bar. He served a term as state attorney general and, after the war, was one of the attorneys selected to defend Jefferson Davis against charges of treason.

58. Charles C. Stuart was the eldest son of Cornelia Stuart and in his late thirties when the Civil War began. The reference here is to the third Stuart son, Arthur Lee, cited earlier in Mrs. McGuire's diary. Edward T. Wenzel, Vienna, Va., to editor, July 22, 2004.

59. In Greek mythology, Pandora was the first mortal woman. She carried a box containing all of the powers that could bring about the ruin of man. "Consumption" was then the popular term for tuberculosis.

60. Late in the afternoon on July 18, 1863, a Union force of some 1,000 men raided Wytheville in an effort to destroy the nearby railroad and lead mines. The town suffered serious damage. A good account of the action is in Mary B. Kegley, *Wythe County, Virginia: A Bicentennial History* (Wytheville, Va.: Wythe County Board of Supervisors, 1989), 195–98.

61. Following several days of random firing at Fort Sumter, Federal guns on August 17 unleashed a concentrated bombardment that lasted six days and included 5,009 artillery rounds fired at the fort. Sumter became a mass of wreckage and rubble, but Confederates there remained defiant.

62. Insufficient manpower, desertion, and lack of supplies were giving Lee far more concern during that time. See Freeman, *Lee,* 3:162–65.

63. Jackson Hospital, located near Hollywood Cemetery on the west side of Richmond, had four divisions and contained mostly South Carolina, Georgia, and Louisiana soldiers. Dr. Francis Woodson Hancock was in charge of the hospital. Wyndham B. Blanton, *Medicine in Virginia in the Nineteenth Century* (Richmond: Garrett and Massie, 1933), 303–4.

64. The Confederate Army of Tennessee was in need of reinforcements. With a lull in Virginia, President Davis dispatched James Longstreet's corps to Tennessee.

65. Maj. Kensey Johns and Lt. John Johns Jr. received new assignments. Bishop Johns was seldom there because of diocesan obligations. That left Rev. McGuire as the only male at the Ashland home.

66. Mrs. McGuire later identified this individual as Dorsey, the daughter of statesman James Murray Mason. However, the two eldest daughters of Mason

were named Laura and Gertrude. Both were in their twenties during the war. Dickins copy; 1860 Virginia Census—Frederick County.

67. The three-day bloodbath at Chickamauga, Georgia, was all the more confused because neither Bragg nor Rosecrans was ever certain where the other side was. Longstreet's corps punctured the Union line, but Bragg vacillated in going for complete victory until it was too late. Each side suffered 28 percent losses in a contest that strategically accomplished little.

68. William Norwood was the first rector of St. Paul's Episcopal Church in Richmond.

69. In a skirmish with Federals at Raccoon Ford, Captain Newton was leading his company forward when he was killed by a bullet to the head. A fellow officer stated that Newton was "one of the noblest offerings Hanover County laid on the altar in the army of Lee." His men wept openly at the news. Kenneth L. Stiles, *4th Virginia Cavalry* (Lynchburg, Va.: H. E. Howard, 1985), 37.

70. John Alexander Nelson and Lomax Tayloe, both of the Third Virginia Cavalry, died of wounds from the October 11 action at Raccoon Ford. John Vivian Towles of the Fourth Virginia Cavalry was killed May 9, 1864, at Spotsylvania.

71. William Colston Robinson was only sixteen when he enlisted in the Sixth Virginia. He was wounded at Second Manassas in August 1862, and killed October 14, 1863, at Bristoe Station. Michael A. Cavanaugh, *6th Virginia Infantry* (Lynchburg, Va.: H. E. Howard, 1988), 121.

72. "And let us not be weary in well-doing: for in due season we shall reap, if we faint not." Galatians 6:9.

73. Many beleaguered Confederates consoled themselves with stories of their forefathers' greater hardship in the other war for independence.

74. Angela Moreno Mallory was the Spanish wife of the Confederate secretary of the navy. She and Mrs. McGuire were the same age. The secretary's wife hated the Civil War and had no love for the Southern cause. Her wartime letters reveal consistent expressions of gloom and wretchedness. Joseph T. Durkin, *Stephen R. Mallory: Confederate Navy Chief* (Chapel Hill: University of North Carolina Press, 1954), 218, 308.

75. Newton married Alice Thomas of Fauquier County. Brockenbrough Family Records, Museum of the Confederacy, Richmond.

76. "None but the brave deserves the fair" is from John Dryden, "Alexander's Feast."

77. Louisa Gardner Brockenbrough, the daughter of John White Brockenbrough, was then engaged to Thomas M. Semmes. Genealogical chart in the Brockenbrough Papers, MOC.

78. Lucius Bellinger Northrop served as commissary general of the Confederate armies. Perhaps his sole responsibility of providing adequate food for the armies was an impossible task. Nevertheless, he became the most unpopular officer in the entire Confederacy. That did not stop President Davis from appointing him a brigadier general late in 1864. Davis did not forward the nomination for confirmation by the Senate, where it surely would have been rejected.

79. Francis Gildart Ruffin had been a planter in Albemarle and Chesterfield counties prior to his appointment as assistant to Commissary General Northrop. The colonel resigned February 26, 1865, in the face of a court-martial "for conflict of interest." Robert E. L. Krick, *Staff Officers in Gray: A Biographical Register of the Staff Officers in the Army of Northern Virginia* (Chapel Hill: University of North Carolina Press, 2003), 258.

80. Although she was a refugee, Mrs. McGuire was also middle-aged, well educated, and the wife of a well-known minister and educator. It had never occurred to her that she might someday have to apply for remunerative employment, and she resented having to demonstrate proficiency in simple mathematics.

81. Long one of the most respected members of the Richmond bar, John Alexander Meredith would be part of the delegation that surrendered the capital to Union troops in April 1865.

82. Grant was then strengthening his forces and approaching Chattanooga for a full-scale offensive against Bragg's Confederates, who were partially besieging the supply center.

83. Gen. Thomas Lafayette Rosser then commanded the Laurel Brigade of cavalry and throughout this period was skirmishing with Union detachments. However, no record exists of any capture of ninety-three ammunition wagons. William N. McDonald, *A History of the Laurel Brigade* (Baltimore: Sun Job, 1907), 202–4.

84. The November 27 action at Payne's Farm was but part of the Mine Run campaign in which the armies of Lee and Meade jockeyed for position in the area south of the Rappahannock River near Culpeper. Confederates suffered 545 casualties in repulsing the disjointed Union probes. *OR*, series 1, vol. 29, pt. 1, 846–48.

85. Colston had been wounded at Seven Pines and Winchester prior to losing his leg on November 17, 1863, at Payne's Farm. The limb was amputated below the left knee. Colston died December 23 in a Charlottesville hospital and was buried on Christmas Day. Dennis E. Frye, *2nd Virginia Infantry* (Lynchburg, Va.: H. E. Howard, 1984), 90.

86. William Brockenbrough Colston of the Second Virginia received

battle injuries at Kernstown and Fredericksburg. Although he escaped injury at Payne's Farm, Colston retired from active service in April 1864 because he was "disqualified for marching." Ibid.

87. John Barbee Minor was a distinguished professor of law at the University of Virginia. His wife was the former Anne Fisher Colston.

88. During November 22–23, combined Union forces under generals Grant and William T. Sherman assailed Bragg's positions to the east and south of Chattanooga. The battles of Lookout Mountain and Missionary Ridge preceded an attack on the Confederate center. Not only did the Southern line break, Confederates fled the field in near panic. What was left of the Army of Tennessee retreated to Dalton, Georgia. This campaign ended Bragg's career in the West.

89. Early in September, Gen. Ambrose Burnside and 24,000 Federals had occupied Knoxville. The move severed rail connections between Richmond and the western Confederate army. Bragg detached a third of his army under Longstreet to retake Knoxville. Burnside repulsed the weak Confederate jabs. When Grant sent reinforcements to the city, Longstreet retired to a safe locale.

90. Largely because of service in the Mexican War, John Seddon received appointment in May 1861 as a captain in the First Virginia. He served a brief stint as a staff officer and was a major in the First Virginia Battalion when he resigned from service. Seddon was a member of the Virginia General Assembly when he died on December 5, 1863.

91. Thomas Moore served as minister at Richmond's First Presbyterian Church.

92. A native of Georgia, Samuel Blount Brewer was a major and clerk in the Commissary Department from early June 1863 into 1865. Krick, *Staff Officers*, 82.

93. Accelerating the scarcity of food was galloping inflation. Many Richmond refugees had to sell cherished valuables to stay alive. It was not unusual to see black servants peddling family heirlooms on the sidewalks. Sallie Brock Putnam, *Richmond during the War: Four Years of Personal Observations* (1867; repr., Lincoln: University of Nebraska Press, 1996), 253.

94. "Blessed are the pure in spirit: for theirs is the kingdom of heaven." Matthew 5:3.

95. The Right Reverend Henry Champlin Lay was Episcopal bishop of Arkansas.

96. John Staige Davis enjoyed a long career as professor of anatomy at the University of Virginia. His colleague James Lawrence Cabell was chief surgeon of Charlottesville General Hospital.

97. It is strange that in citing all who grieved the death of Colston, Mrs.

McGuire made no mention of the colonel's wife, the former Gertrude Powell of Richmond. Perhaps she is the "one dearer still" mentioned.

98. General Jackson did not believe it was good for morale to single out officers for high praise. No record exists of his favoring Colston over other regimental commanders in the Stonewall Brigade. Nevertheless, soldiers in the Second Virginia had high regard for the lieutenant colonel. Frye, *2nd Virginia,* 59–60.

99. "Thus saith the Lord; A voice was heard in Ramah, lamentations, and bitter weeping; Rachel weeping for her children refused to be comforted for her children, because they were not." Jeremiah 31:15.

100. The eighteenth century Jacobite poet John Byrom composed these lines.

101. The basis for Mrs. McGuire's statement was: "The Lord reigneth; let the earth rejoice; let the multitude of isles be glad thereof." Psalms 97:1.

102. At the time, Charles F. M. Garnett was a commissioner for collecting railroad iron for the C.S. Engineer Department. *OR,* series 1, vol. 30, pt. 4, 496; 33:1116.

103. Petersburg's Sarah Pryor made shoes for her children from an old carpet, then lined the shoes with flannel. Sarah Agnes Pryor, *Reminiscences of Peace and War* (New York: Books for Libraries Press, 1970), 229.

104. The 1860 census for Spotsylvania County contains no entry for a Brown family fitting Mrs. McGuire's description. In all likelihood, Mr. Brown was a transient laborer and entered the army while temporarily working in Fredericksburg.

105. Sometimes called "Butchertown," this area was on the eastern side of Shockoe Valley. It was the site where hogs and other livestock were slaughtered for sale in the markets. Henri Garidel, *Exile in Richmond: The Confederate Journal of Henri Garidel,* ed. Michael Bedout Chesson and Leslie Jean Roberts (Charlottesville: University of Virginia Press, 2001), 95.

106. During February 28–March 2, some 3,500 Union cavalry under Gen. Judson Kilpatrick and Col. Ulric Dahlgren dashed at Richmond from north and west. Local citizens went into near panic. However, lack of cohesion and determination caused the raid to collapse in failure. When evidence came forth that the Federals had intended to free Union prisoners of war in Richmond and to kill President Davis, anger in Richmond was high and long lasting.

107. William Henry Chase Whiting proved to be too cautious and pessimistic for field command. He then was in charge of fortifications in the Wilmington, North Carolina, area. Robert Ransom Jr., had just assumed command of the Department of Richmond. John Pegram was leading an infantry brigade in the Second Corps of Lee's army.

108. During Christmas 1863, the Lee family rented a Greek Revival home at 707 East Franklin Street in the downtown area. There the family would live for the remainder of the war.

109. Willoughby Newton had considerable land holdings in Westmoreland County. For a portion of the war, his wife was a refugee at Summer Hill in Hanover County. Mary Newton Stanard, *Richmond: Its People and Its Story* (Philadelphia: J. B. Lippincott, 1923), 193.

110. Abel Parker Upshur had been a member of the Virginia Supreme Court and a secretary of state. In 1844, while serving as secretary of the navy, Upshur was killed by the bursting of a cannon aboard a naval vessel. His widow was the former Elizabeth Ann Brown.

111. The party to which Mrs. McGuire referred was likely a December 2, 1829, affair. Willie T. Weathers, "Judith W. McGuire: A Lady of Virginia," *Virginia Magazine of History and Biography* 81 (1974): 104.

112. Beginning on April 17, Confederate land forces and the newly finished ram CSS *Albemarle* attacked Plymouth, North Carolina, for three days. The *Albemarle* did extensive damage to naval vessels and forced the Union garrison to surrender. Confederates seized 2,800 prisoners and a large amount of supplies. This was the first Southern naval success along the Atlantic coast in months.

113. Mrs. McGuire referred to the February 20 Confederate victory at Olustee, Florida. This largest battle fought in the state during the war enabled Southerners to reclaim (albeit temporarily) much of the Florida interior. In mid-March, Union general Nathaniel P. Banks led a joint army-navy expedition from New Orleans up the Mississippi and Red rivers. Although Shreveport, Louisiana, was the major objective, Alexandria was as far as the mismanaged offensive got.

114. By early 1864, the Treasury Department had over 1,000 employees. Someone in the Confederate bureaucracy developed the idea of transferring much of the clerical force elsewhere in order to relieve the overpopulation crunch in Richmond. Robert G. H. Kean, *Inside the Confederate Government: The Diary of Robert Garlick Hill Kean,* ed. Edward Younger (New York: Oxford University Press, 1957), 145–46.

115. Matthew 6:34.

116. Mary McGuire Johns was the wife of a Richmond-based inspector of field transportation. Krick, *Staff Officers,* 171.

117. Juliana Johns often accompanied her bishop father on his travels through the Virginia Episcopal diocese.

118. For a revealing narrative of Confederate efforts in eastern North Caro-

lina at the time, see John G. Barrett, *The Civil War in North Carolina* (Chapel Hill: University of North Carolina Press, 1963), 218–25.

119. For Ransom, see note 107. James Lawson Kemper of Madison County, Virginia, had advanced from colonel of the Seventh Virginia to brigade command. Wounded at Gettysburg and imprisoned for a time, Kemper was incapacitated for field service. He then commanded the Virginia reserves.

120. Four-year-old Joseph Emory Davis was his father's favorite child. On April 30, the youth fell headfirst from a balcony twenty feet above the brick pavement. His grief-stricken parents buried their son the following day.

121. Throughout April, Union general Benjamin F. Butler assembled a 30,000-man force called the Army of the James. Its mission was to ascend the James and threaten both Richmond and Petersburg. The movement began on May 5, when 120 vessels at Hampton Roads began transporting Butler's army upriver.

122. The Richmond chapter of this highly active wartime agency stood at Franklin and Fourth streets in downtown Richmond. Robert Beverly Munford Jr., *Richmond Homes and Memories* (Richmond: Garrett and Massie, 1936), 164; Stanard, *Richmond*, 184.

123. Dr. Charles Henry Read was the longtime pastor at Grace Street Presbyterian Church.

124. Richmond's prestige hotel, the Ballard House stood at the corner of Fourteenth and East Franklin streets near the Capitol.

125. The intent of U. S. Grant's 1864 campaign was to push southward toward Richmond and pound Lee's army into submission. The May 5–6 battle of the Wilderness was the first major contest. Grant's army suffered 17,600 casualties, including generals Alexander Hays and James S. Wadsworth killed, three other generals officers wounded, and two captured. Confederate losses were 7,500 soldiers.

126. William Welford Randolph attended the University of Virginia and was lieutenant colonel of the Second Virginia when he was mortally wounded in the head during the first day's fighting in the Wilderness. He was the last and youngest colonel of the regiment. Frye, *2nd Virginia*, 61–62, 125.

127. In 1863 Colonel Randolph had married Ada Stewart of King George County. His sister-in-law was Margaret Stewart.

128. The side-wheel steamer USS *Commodore Jones* mounted six guns. In midafternoon on May 6, the vessel struck a mine near Deep Bottom. The ship blew apart; sixty-nine crewmen were killed. Herbert M. Schiller, *The Bermuda Hundred Campaign* (Dayton, Ohio: Morningside, 1988), 99–100.

129. Port Walthall, three miles south of the James River, was the junction

of two branches of the Richmond & Petersburg Railroad. On May 7, Butler attacked the 2,700 Confederates there with 8,000 Federals. Union forces briefly broke the line, then retired. Ibid., 84–98.

130. George Woodbridge was rector of Monumental Church. Rev. James T. Johnston preached on that occasion.

131. The North's Army of the James was large enough to accomplish much along the weak Richmond-Petersburg line. Yet orders were confusing, and Butler himself displayed a consistent indecisiveness throughout the campaign. Uncoordinated attacks occurred at Chester Station, Port Walthall, and elsewhere.

132. As part of the grand Union offensive in Virginia that spring, Grant dispatched Gen. Philip H. Sheridan and 10,000 horsemen on a raid deep in Lee's rear. The cavalry dismantled miles of railroad, burned supply depots, severed communication lines, and won a number of clashes with outnumbered Confederate units. Sheridan drove to the outskirts of Richmond.

133. It was the cavalry brigade of Gen. Williams C. Wickham, not troops under Gen. Lunsford L. Lomax, that drove Federal cavalry from Ashland. Robert J. Driver Jr., *2nd Virginia Cavalry* (Lynchburg, Va.: H. E. Howard, 1995), 116.

134. Theodore Stanford Garnett Jr. had enlisted in the Ninth Virginia as a private. In late January 1864, he received appointment as aide de camp to General Stuart.

135. Dr. Charles Brewer's home was on East Grace Street.

136. During May 9–10, Grant launched several probes against Confederate lines at Spotsylvania. Lee reported to the secretary of war that "thanks to a merciful Providence our casualties have been small." *OR*, series 1, vol. 36, pt. 2, 982–83.

137. Sheridan's Union cavalry, riding east of Richmond in an attempt to unite with Butler's Army of the James, had sharp fights with Confederates at Meadow Bridge, Mechanicsville, Strawberry Hill, Brook Church, and points along the outer defenses of Richmond.

138. Former law student Robert Randolph went from lieutenant in the Black Horse Troop (Company H) of the Fourth Virginia Cavalry to lieutenant colonel of the regiment. He was killed in the May 12 fighting at Meadow Bridge. Stiles, *4th Virginia Cavalry*, 49, 132.

139. This was obviously one of Mrs. McGuire's favorite biblical verses. See note 115.

140. The seventeen hours of fighting in the rain at Spotsylvania on May 12 may have been the most vicious combat of the Civil War. Lee managed to repulse Grant's repeated assaults, but the cost to both sides was terrible. Thirteen days of sporadic fighting at Spotsylvania resulted in 12,000 Federal casualties and

18,400 Confederate losses. Noah Trudeau, *Bloody Roads South: The Wilderness to Cold Harbor, May–June 1864* (Boston: Little, Brown, 1989), 213, 341.

141. Drewry's Bluff was a strategic hill on the south bank of the James River between Richmond and Petersburg. Confederates turned it into the river's principal defense. During May 11–16, Southerners launched attacks from there against Butler and the lead elements of Grant's army. See Daniel W. Barefoot, *General Robert F. Hoke: Lee's Modest Warrior* (Winston-Salem, N.C.: John F. Blair, 1996), 173–84.

142. In the May 16 fighting at Drewry's Bluff, Gen. Charles Adam Heckman was captured, along with many soldiers in his brigade of Massachusetts and New Jersey troops. William Glenn Robertson, *Back Door to Richmond: The Bermuda Hundred Campaign, April–June 1864* (Newark: University of Delaware Press, 1987), 183, 186, 218.

143. Willoughby Newton Brockenbrough of Lexington served in the Rockbridge Artillery prior to joining the Baltimore Light Artillery. In the postwar years he was an attorney in Columbia, Missouri. Robert J. Driver Jr., *The 1st and 2nd Rockbridge Artillery* (Lynchburg, Va.: H. E. Howard, 1987), 61.

144. The inept Butler positioned his army on the Bermuda Hundred peninsula. Confederates promptly drew a fortified line across the base of the peninsula; and in Grant's words, Butler was as much out of action as if he had been in a tightly corked bottle.

145. Sheridan had 10,000 horsemen on the Richmond raid. Stuart had no more than 4,500 cavalrymen to meet the threat. Emory M. Thomas, *Bold Dragoon: The Life of J. E. B. Stuart* (Norman: University of Oklahoma Press, 1986), 288.

146. A native of Hanover County, John Boursiquot Fontaine had been a medical student at New York University before his enlistment in the Fourth Virginia Cavalry. He became a brigade surgeon in December 1862, and Stuart's staff surgeon shortly thereafter. On October 1, 1864, Fontaine was mortally wounded at Petersburg while ministering to the dying Gen. John Dunovant. Stiles, *4th Virginia Cavalry,* 110.

147. Mrs. McGuire was reporting hearsay observations. For Stuart's several statements on his deathbed, see Thomas, *Bold Dragoons,* 294–95.

148. These verses are from Charles Wolfe, "The Burial of St. John Moore at Corunna."

149. John R. Thompson, who had immortalized Captain Latane in verse back in 1862, was the author of this poetic tribute to his friend and fallen hero.

150. On May 24, two of Gen. Fitzhugh Lee's cavalry brigades made a brief

attack on Federals posted at Kennon's in Charles City County. Supposing that they outnumbered their adversaries, the Southerners found themselves facing 2,500 Federals, two gunboats, and more Federals immediately across the James. Lee's men fell back after suffering sixty casualties. James L. Nichols, *General Fitzhugh Lee: A Biography* (Lynchburg, Va.: H. E. Howard, 1989), 70–71.

151. Grant's persistent drive southward suffered a severe setback on June 3 at Cold Harbor, a crossroads near the Chickahominy River. A series of frontal assaults against Lee's strongly entrenched line failed with frightful losses. The exact number of casualties remains controversial. Gordon C. Rhea, *Cold Harbor: Grant and Lee, May 26–June 3, 1863* (Baton Rouge: Louisiana State University Press, 2002), 386.

152. "This is the Lord's doing; it is marvellous in our eyes." Psalms 118:23.

153. On February 16, 1864, Dr. James Mercer Garnett McGuire had married Bettie Holmes McGuire, daughter of Dr. William D. McGuire. Allyne Garnett Pearce, comp., *You Must Give Something Back: Some Descendants of John Garnett, Gloucester County, Virginia* (Abilene, Tex.: privately published, 2001), 223.

154. Burkeville was the X-formed intersection of the Southside and the Richmond & Danville railroads. A Union soldier would later describe the village as "a sort of tank station with an apology for a hotel; two log barns and a rough station near the watering tank, from which the rickety locomotives took long drinks in passing." Alfred S. Roe and Charles Nutt, *History of the First Regiment of Heavy Artillery, Massachusetts Volunteers* (Worcester, Mass.: Regimental Association, 1917), 215.

155. On May 28, seventeen days after Sheridan's victory at Yellow Tavern, Federals scored another triumph at Haw's Shop. The seven-hour fight gave Union troops the area around the blacksmith foundry. Losses on both sides were severe.

156. Jefferson Phelps, first cited in Mrs. McGuire's diary on August 10, 1861, was then a member of the Ninth Virginia Cavalry. See also *OR*, series 1, vol. 51, pt. 2, 1010.

157. Gen. Edward Ferrero commanded an all-black division in the Union IX Corps.

158. William E. "Grumble" Jones had only 5,600 men to stop the Union advance of Gen. David Hunter's 8,500 Federals in the Shenandoah Valley. On June 5, at Piedmont, seven miles southwest of Port Republic, Jones attacked. Charges and countercharges occurred throughout most of the day before Federals routed their outmanned opponents.

159. Joseph E. Johnston and his Army of Tennessee were falling back

through northwest Georgia toward Atlanta in the face of three armies under William T. Sherman. The only battlefield success Johnston had in the long campaign was a June 27 victory at Kennesaw Mountain.

160. Hunter's troops occupied Lexington late on June 11 and the next day destroyed a large portion of the town. The Virginia Military Institute buildings were all set afire; homes, businesses, and churches were wantonly damaged. Robert J. Driver Jr., *Lexington and Rockbridge County in the Civil War* (Lynchburg, Va.: H. E. Howard, 1989), 60–74.

161. In mid-June, Confederates sent Hunter's force in full retreat after brief action at Lynchburg. Gen. Jubal Early, with a corps from Lee's army, moved boldly down the Shenandoah Valley in a counteroffensive that reached the outskirts of Washington. Only a stubborn defense by Federals at Monocacy River in Maryland prevented Early's soldiers from occupying at least a portion of the Northern capital.

162. The grandson, born July 24, 1864, was named John Johns Jr.

163. Confederate stragglers burned the home of Postmaster Montgomery Blair during Early's Washington raid. It is wishful thinking that Southerners could have destroyed the residence of Montgomery Blair's father. The home of Francis Preston Blair Sr., was directly across the street from the White House in downtown Washington.

164. I Corinthians 12:19.

Selected Bibliography

Acts and Resolutions of the First Session of the Provisional Congress of the Confederate States. Richmond, 1861.

Acts of the General Assembly of the State of Virginia, Passed at Called Session, 1863, in the Eighty-eighth Year of the Commonwealth. Richmond: William F. Ritchie, 1863.

Allen, Felicity. *Jefferson Davis: Unconquerable Heart.* Columbia: University of Missouri Press, 1999.

Alley, Reuben E. *History of the University of Richmond, 1830–1971.* Charlottesville: University of Virginia Press, 1977.

Altschuler, Glenn C., and Stuart M. Blumin. *Rude Republic: Americans and Their Politics in the Nineteenth Century.* Princeton, N.J.: Princeton University Press, 2001.

Andrews, J. Cutler. *The South Reports the Civil War.* Princeton, N.J.: Princeton University Press, 1970.

Andrews, Matthew Page, ed. *The Women of the South in War Times.* Baltimore: Norman, Remington, 1920.

Annual Reports of the Rail Road Companies of the State of Virginia, Made to the Board of Public Works. Richmond: Board of Public Works, 1861.

Applebaum, Diana. *The Glorious Fourth: An American Holiday, an American History.* New York: Facts on File, 1989.

Ash, Stephen V. *When the Yankees Came: Conflict and Chaos in the Occupied South, 1861–1865.* Chapel Hill: University of North Carolina Press, 1995.

Atkinson, Dorothy Francis. *King William County in the Civil War: Along Mangohick Byways.* Lynchburg, Va.: H. E. Howard, 1990.

Ayers, Edward L. *In the Presence of Mine Enemies: War in the Heart of America, 1859–1863.* New York: Norton, 2003.

Bagby, George W. *Selections from the Miscellaneous Writings of Dr. George Bagby.* Richmond: Whittet and Shepperson, 1885.

Barefoot, Daniel W. *General Robert F. Hoke: Lee's Modest Warrior.* Winston-Salem, N.C.: John F. Blair, 1996.

Barnes, L. Diane. "Southern Artisans, Organization, and the Rise of a Market

Economy in Antebellum Petersburg." *Virginia Magazine of History and Biography* 107 (Spring 1999).

Bellard, Alfred. *Gone for a Soldier: The Civil War Memoirs of Private Alfred Bellard.* Edited by David Herbert Donald. Boston: Little, Brown, 1975.

Bensel, Richard. *Yankee Leviathan: The Origins of Central State Authority in America, 1859–1877.* Cambridge: Cambridge University Press, 1990.

Berlin, Ira, Barbara J. Fields, Steven F. Miller, Joseph P. Reidy, and Leslie S. Rowland, eds. *Free at Last: A Documentary History of Slavery, Freedom, and the Civil War.* 1992. Reprint, Edison, N.J.: Blue and Gray, 1997.

Black, Robert C. *The Railroads of the Confederacy.* Chapel Hill: University of North Carolina Press, 1998.

Blackford, Charles Minor, and Susan Leigh Blackford, eds. *Letters from Lee's Army; or, Memoirs of Life in and out of the Army in Virginia during the War between the States.* Lincoln, Neb.: Bison, 1998.

Blair, William. *Virginia's Private War: Feeding Body and Soul in the Confederacy, 1861–1865.* New York: Oxford University Press, 1998.

Blanton, Wyndham B. *Medicine in Virginia in the Nineteenth Century.* Richmond: Garrett and Massie, 1933.

Boatner, Mark. *Civil War Dictionary.* New York: David McKay, 1959.

Breeden, James O. "Rehearsal for Secession? The Return Home of Southern Medical Students from Philadelphia in 1859." In Paul Finkelman, ed., *His Soul Goes Marching On: Responses to John Brown and the Harpers Ferry Raid.* Charlottesville: University of Virginia Press, 1995.

Brice, Marshall M. *Conquest of a Valley.* Charlottesville: University of Virginia Press, 1965.

Bridges, Peter. *Pen of Fire: John Moncure Daniel.* Kent, Ohio: Kent State University Press, 2002.

Brinkley, John Luster. *On This Hill: A Narrative History of Hampton-Sydney College, 1774–1994.* Hampton-Sydney, Va.: Hampton-Sydney College, 1994.

Bruce, Philip Alexander. *History of the University of Virginia, 1819–1919: The Lengthened Shadow of One Man.* 5 vols. New York: Macmillan, 1920–1922.

Burton, Brian K. *Extraordinary Circumstances: The Seven Days Battle.* Bloomington: Indiana University Press, 2001.

Butler, Benjamin F. *Autobiography and Personal Reminiscences of Major-General Benjamin F. Butler.* Boston: A. M. Thayer, 1892.

———. *Private and Official Correspondence of Gen. Benjamin F. Butler, during the Period of the Civil War.* 5 vols. Norwood, Mass.: Plimpton, 1917.

Campbell, Edward D. C., Jr., and Kym S. Rice, eds. *A Woman's War: Southern*

Women, Civil War, and the Confederate Legacy. Charlottesville: University of Virginia Press, 1996.

Cappon, Lester J. *Virginia's Newspapers, 1821–1935: A Bibliography with Historical Introduction and Notes.* New York: Appleton-Century, 1936.

Carmichael, Peter S. *The Last Generation: Young Virginians in Peace, War, and Reunion.* Chapel Hill: University of North Carolina Press, 2005.

Catalogue of the Medical College of Virginia, Session of 1863–1864; Announcement of Session 1864–1865. Richmond: Chas. H. Wynne, 1864.

Cavanaugh, Michael A. *6th Virginia Infantry.* Lynchburg, Va.: H. E. Howard, 1988.

Chesson, Michael B. "Harlots or Heroines? A New Look at the Richmond Bread Riot." *Virginia Magazine of History and Biography* 92 (April 1984).

Clark, John E., Jr. *Railroads in the Civil War: The Impact of Management on Victory and Defeat.* Baton Rouge: Louisiana State University Press, 2001.

Coles, David J. "Richmond, the Confederate Hospital City." In William C. Davis and James I. Robertson Jr., eds., *Virginia at War, 1862.* Lexington: University Press of Kentucky, 2007.

Conrad, James Lee. *The Young Lions: Confederate Cadets at War.* Mechanicsburg, Pa.: Stackpole, 1997.

Cooper, William J., Jr. *Jefferson Davis: American.* New York: Knopf, 2000.

Couper, William. *One Hundred Years at V.M.I.* 4 vols. Richmond: Garrett and Massie, 1939.

———. *The V.M.I. New Market Cadets: Biographical Sketches of All Members of the Virginia Military Institute Corps of Cadets Who Fought in the Battle of New Market, May 15, 1864.* Charlottesville: Michie, 1933.

Crenshaw, Ollinger. *General Lee's College: The Rise and Growth of Washington and Lee University.* New York: Random House, 1969.

Crofts, Daniel. "Late Antebellum Virginia Reconsidered." *Virginia Magazine of History and Biography* 107 (Summer 1999).

———. *Reluctant Confederates: Upper South Unionists in the Secession Crisis.* Chapel Hill: University of North Carolina Press, 1989.

Curry, Richard L. *A House Divided: A Study of Statehood Politics and the Copperhead Movement in West Virginia.* Pittsburgh: University of Pittsburgh Press, 1964.

Dabney, Virginius. *Mr. Jefferson's University: A History.* Charlottesville: University of Virginia Press, 1981.

———. *Virginia Commonwealth University: A Sesquicentennial History.* Charlottesville: University of Virginia Press, 1987.

Daly, Robert W., ed. *Aboard the U.S.S. Monitor, 1862: The Letters of Acting Pay-*

master William Frederick Keeler, U.S. Navy, to His Wife, Anna. Annapolis, Md.: U.S. Naval Institute, 1964.

Daniel, Frederick S. *The Richmond Examiner during the War; or, The Writings of John M. Daniel, with a Memoir of His Life*. New York: Arno, 1970.

Daniel, W. Harrison. "Old Lynchburg College, 1855–1869." *Virginia Magazine of History and Biography* 88 (October 1980).

Davenport, Alfred. *Camp and Field Life of the Fifth New York Volunteer Infantry*. New York: Dick and Fitzgerald, 1879.

Davies, Samuel D. "Observations of Our Literary Prospects." *Southern Literary Messenger*, October 1863.

Davis, William C. *The Battle of New Market*. 1975. Reprint, Baton Rouge: Louisiana State University Press, 1983.

———. *Jefferson Davis: The Man and His Hour*. New York: HarperCollins, 1991.

———. *Look Away! A History of the Confederate States of America*. New York: Free Press, 2002.

———. "Richmond Becomes a Capital." In William C. Davis and James I. Robertson Jr., eds., *Virginia at War, 1861*. Lexington: University Press of Kentucky, 2005.

———. "The Virginian Wartime Scrapbook: Preserving Memories on Paper." In William C. Davis and James I. Robertson Jr., eds., *Virginia at War, 1863*. Lexington: University Press of Kentucky, 2008.

Driver, Robert J., Jr. *The 1st and 2nd Rockbridge Artillery*. Lynchburg, Va.: H. E. Howard, 1987.

———. *14th Virginia Cavalry*. Lynchburg, Va.: H. E. Howard, 1988.

———. *Lexington and Rockbridge County in the Civil War*. Lynchburg, Va.: H. E. Howard, 1989.

———. *2nd Virginia Cavalry*. Lynchburg, Va.: H. E. Howard, 1995.

Dubbs, Carol Kettenburg. *Defend This Old Town: Williamsburg during the Civil War*. Baton Rouge: Louisiana State University Press, 2002.

Dunaway, Wayland Fuller. *The History of the James River and the Kanawha Company*. New York: Longmans, Greens, 1922.

Durkin, Joseph T. *Stephen R. Mallory: Confederate Navy Chief*. Chapel Hill: University of North Carolina Press, 1954.

Dyer, Frederick. *A Compendium of the War of the Rebellion*. 3 vols. New York: Thomas Yoseloff, 1959.

Engs, Robert F. *Freedom's First Generation: Black Hampton, Virginia, 1861–1890*. New York: Fordham University Press, 2004.

Escott, Paul D. *After Secession: Jefferson Davis and the Failure of Confederate Nationalism*. Baton Rouge: Louisiana State University Press, 1978.

Everson, Guy R., and Edward H. Simpson Jr., eds. *"Far, Far from Home": The Wartime Letters of Dick and Tally Simpson, Third South Carolina Volunteers.* New York: Oxford University Press, 1994.

Fahs, Alice. *The Imagined Civil War: Popular Literature of the North and South, 1861–1865.* Chapel Hill: University of North Carolina Press, 2001.

Farmville Female College. "The Next Term of This Institution Will Commence Thursday, October 1st, 1863." Broadside in *Confederate Imprints, 1861–1865,* reel 113, no. 3989-1. New Haven, Conn.: Research Publications, 1974.

Fleet, Betsy, and John D. P. Fuller, eds. *Green Mount: A Virginia Plantation Family during the Civil War: Being the Journal of Benjamin Robert Fleet and Letters of His Family.* Lexington: University of Kentucky Press, 1962.

Fox, William F. *Regimental Losses in the American Civil War.* Albany, N.Y.: Albany Publishing, 1889.

Freehling, Alison Goodyear. *Drift toward Dissolution: The Virginia Slavery Debate of 1831–1832.* Baton Rouge: Louisiana State University Press, 1982.

Freeman, Douglas Southall. *Lee's Lieutenants: A Study in Command.* 3 vols. New York: C. Scribner's Sons, 1942–1944.

———. *R. E. Lee: A Biography.* 4 vols. New York: C. Scribner's Sons, 1934.

Frye, Dennis E. *2nd Virginia Infantry.* Lynchburg, Va.: H. E. Howard, 1984.

Gabel, Christopher R. *Rails to Oblivion: The Decline of Confederate Railroads in the Civil War.* Fort Leavenworth, Kan.: Combat Studies Institute, U.S. Army Command and General Staff College, 2002.

Gallagher, Gary W. *The Confederate War.* Cambridge, Mass.: Harvard University Press, 1997.

Gates, Paul W. *Agriculture and the Civil War.* New York: Knopf, 1965.

Godson, Susan H., et al. *The College of William & Mary: A History.* 2 vols. Williamsburg, Va.: King and Queen, 1993.

Goodrich, Carter. "The Virginia System of Mixed Enterprise." *Political Science Quarterly* 64 (September 1949).

Gray, Lewis Cecil. *History of Agriculture in the Southern United States to 1860.* Vol. 2. 1933. Reprint, Gloucester, Mass.: Peter Smith, 1958.

Green, Carol C. *Chimborazo: The Confederacy's Largest Hospital.* Knoxville: University of Tennessee Press, 2004.

Greene, A. Wilson. *Civil War Petersburg: Confederate City in the Crucible of War.* Charlottesville: University of Virginia Press, 2006.

Grimsley, Mark. *The Hard Hand of War: Union Military Policy toward Southern Civilians, 1861–1865.* Cambridge: Cambridge University Press, 1995.

Hattaway, Herman, and Richard E. Beringer. *Jefferson Davis: Confederate President.* Lawrence: University of Kansas Press, 2002.

Hayes, Jack Irby, Jr. *The Lamp and the Cross: A History of Averett College, 1859–2001.* Macon, Ga.: Mercer University Press, 2004.

Heidler, David S., and Jeanne T. Heidler, eds. *Encyclopedia of the American Civil War: A Political, Social, and Military History.* Santa Barbara, Calif.: ABC-CLIO, 2000.

Heuvel, Sean M. "The Old College Goes to War: The Civil War Service of William and Mary Students." *Virginia Social Science Journal* 42 (2007).

Hilliard, Sam Bowers. *Hog Meat and Hoecake: Food Supply in the Old South, 1840–1860.* Carbondale: Southern Illinois University Press, 1972.

Holt, Michael F. *The Political Crisis of the 1850s.* New York: Norton, 1978.

Holzer, Harold. "Virginians See Their War." In William C. Davis and James I. Robertson Jr., eds., *Virginia at War, 1862.* Lexington: University Press of Kentucky, 2007.

House, Ellen R. *"A Very Violent Rebel": The Civil War Diary of Ellen Renshaw House.* Knoxville: University of Tennessee Press, 1996.

Hubbs, G. Ward, ed. *Voices from Company D: Diaries by the Greensboro Guards, Fifth Alabama Infantry Regiment, Army of Northern Virginia.* Athens: University of Georgia Press, 2003.

Jensen, Les. *32nd Virginia Infantry.* Lynchburg, Va.: H. E. Howard, 1990.

Jones, John B. *A Rebel War Clerk's Diary.* 2 vols. Edited by Earl Schenck Miers. 1866. Reprint, Alexandria, Va.: Time-Life, 1982.

Jordan, Ervin L., Jr. *Charlottesville and the University of Virginia in the Civil War.* Lynchburg, Va.: H. E. Howard, 1988.

Richmond: William F. Ritchie, 1861.

Journal of the Senate of the Commonwealth of Virginia, Extra Session of 1862. Richmond: James E. Goode, 1862.

Journals of the Confederate States of America. Washington, D.C.: Government Printing Office, 1904.

Kean, Robert Garlick Hill. *Inside the Confederate Government: The Diary of Robert Garlick Hill Kean.* Edited by Edward Younger. 1957. Reprint, Baton Rouge: Louisiana State University Press, 1993.

Kegley, Mary B. *Wythe County, Virginia: A Bicentennial History.* Wytheville, Va.: Wythe County Board of Supervisors, 1989.

Kennedy, Joseph C. G. *Preliminary Report on the Eighth Census, 1860.* Washington, D.C.: Government Printing Office, 1862.

Kinnear, Duncan Lyle. *The First 100 Years: A History of Virginia Polytechnic Institute and State University.* Blacksburg: Virginia Polytechnic Institute Educational Foundation, 1972.

Krick, Robert E. L. *Staff Officers in Gray: A Biographical Register of the Staff*

Officers in the Army of Northern Virginia. Chapel Hill: University of North Carolina Press, 2003.

Krick, Robert K. *9th Virginia Cavalry.* Lynchburg, Va.: H. E. Howard, 1992.

———. "The Parallel Lives of Two Virginia Soldiers: Armistead and Garnett." In Gary Gallagher, ed., *The Third Day at Gettysburg and Beyond.* Chapel Hill: University of North Carolina Press, 1994.

Lancaster, Robert Bolling. *Old Homes of Hanover County, Virginia.* Hanover, Va.: Hanover County Historical Society, 1983.

Lankford, Nelson. *Richmond Burning: The Last Days of the Confederate Capital.* New York: Viking, 2002.

Lebsock, Suzanne. *The Free Women of Petersburg: Status and Culture in a Southern Town, 1784–1860.* New York: Norton, 1884.

Lee, Robert E. *The Wartime Papers of R. E. Lee.* Edited by Clifford Dowdey. Boston: Little, Brown, 1961.

Lehman, James O., and Steven M. Nolt. *Mennonites, Amish, and the American Civil War.* Baltimore: Johns Hopkins University Press, 2007.

Letcher, John. "Governor's Address to the Virginia Legislature." In *Journal of the Senate of the Commonwealth of Virginia, 1861.* Richmond: James E. Goode, 1861.

———. "Governor's Message," January 7, 1863. In *Journal of the Senate of the Commonwealth of Virginia, 1862.* Richmond: James E. Goode, 1862.

Link, William A. *Roots of Secession: Slavery and Politics in Antebellum Virginia.* Chapel Hill: University of North Carolina Press, 2003.

Longacre, Edward G. *Army of Amateurs: General Benjamin F. Butler and the Army of the James, 1863–1865.* Mechanicsburg, Pa.: Stackpole, 1997.

Maddex, Jack P., Jr. *The Reconstruction of Edward A. Pollard: A Rebel's Conversion to Postbellum Unionism.* Chapel Hill: University of North Carolina Press, 1974.

———. *The Virginia Conservatives, 1867–1879: A Study in Reconstruction Politics.* Chapel Hill: University of North Carolina Press, 1970.

Mahon, Michael G. *The Shenandoah Valley, 1861–1865: The Destruction of the Granary of the Confederacy.* Mechanicsburg, Pa.: Stackpole, 1999.

Manarin, Louis H., ed. *Richmond at War: The Minutes of the City Council, 1861–1865.* Chapel Hill: University of North Carolina Press, 1966.

Massey, Mary Elizabeth. *Ersatz in the Confederacy: Shortages and Substitutes on the Southern Homefront.* 1952. Reprint, Columbia: University of South Carolina Press, 1993.

———. *Refugee Life in the Confederacy.* 1964. Reprint, Baton Rouge: Louisiana State University Press, 2001.

Matter, William D. *If It Takes All Summer: The Battle of Spotsylvania*. Chapel Hill: University of North Carolina Press, 1988.

McDonald, Cornelia Peake. *A Woman's Civil War: A Diary with Reminiscences of the War from March 1862*. Edited by Minrose C. Gwin. Madison: University of Wisconsin Press, 1992.

McDonald, William N. *A History of the Laurel Brigade*. Baltimore: Sun Job, 1907.

McGuire, Judith W. *Diary of a Southern Refugee during the War*. New York: E. J. Hale and Son, 1867.

McPherson, James M. *Battle Cry of Freedom: The Civil War Era*. New York: Oxford University Press, 1988.

Meaney, Peter. *The Civil War Engagement at Cool Spring*. Berryville, Va.: Clarke County Historical Association, 1980.

Miller, J. Michael. *The North Anna Campaign: "Even to Hell Itself," May 21–26, 1864*. Lynchburg, Va.: H. E. Howard, 1989.

Miller, Mark F. *"Dear Old Roanoke": A Sesquicentennial Portrait, 1842–1992*. Macon, Ga.: Mercer University Press, 1992.

Miller, Randal, Harry S. Stout, and Charles Reagan Wilson, eds. *Religion and the American Civil War*. New York: Oxford University Press, 1998.

Minton, Amy R. "Defining Confederate Respectability: Morality, Patriotism, and Confederate Identity in Richmond's Civil War Public Press." In Edward L. Ayers, Gary W. Gallagher, and Andrew J. Torget, eds., *Crucible of the Civil War: Virginia from Secession to Commemoration*. Charlottesville: University of Virginia Press, 2006.

Moore, George Ellis. *Banner in the Hills: West Virginia's Statehood*. New York: Appleton-Century-Crofts, 1963.

Moore, Samuel J. T., Jr. *Moore's Complete Civil War Guide to Richmond*. Richmond: privately published, 1973.

Munford, Robert Beverly, Jr. *Richmond Homes and Memories*. Richmond: Garrett and Massie, 1936.

Murrell, Amy E. "'Of Necessity and Public Benefit:' Southern Families and Their Appeals for Protection." In Catherine Clinton, ed., *Southern Families at War: Loyalty and Conflict in the Civil War South*. New York: Oxford University Press, 2000.

Neely, Mark E. *Southern Rights: Political Prisoners and the Myth of Confederate Constitutionalism*. Charlottesville: University of Virginia Press, 1999.

Nelson, Scott Reynolds, and Carol Sheriff. *A People at War: Civilians and Soldiers in America's Civil War, 1854–1877*. New York: Oxford University Press, 2007.

Nichols, James L. *General Fitzhugh Lee: A Biography.* Lynchburg, Va.: H. E. Howard, 1989.

Niederer, Frances J. *Hollins College: An Illustrated History.* Charlottesville: University of Virginia Press, 1973.

Noe, Kenneth W. *Southwest Virginia's Railroad: Modernization and the Sectional Crisis.* Urbana: University of Illinois Press, 1994.

Osborne, William H. *The History of the Twenty-ninth Regiment of Massachusetts Volunteer Infantry.* Boston: A. J. Wright, 1877.

O'Sullivan, Richard. *55th Virginia Infantry.* Lynchburg, Va.: H. E. Howard, 1989.

Otto, John Solomon. *Southern Agriculture during the Civil War Era, 1860–1880.* Westport, Conn.: Greenwood, 1994.

Pace, Robert F. *Halls of Honor: College Men in the Old South.* Baton Rouge: Louisiana State University Press, 2004.

Paludan, Phillip Shaw. *The Presidency of Abraham Lincoln.* Lawrence: University Press of Kansas, 1994.

Parker, John L. *Henry Wilson's Regiment: History of the 22nd Massachusetts Infantry, the Second Company Sharpshooters, and the Third Light Battery in the War of the Rebellion.* 1887. Reprint, Boston: Butternut and Blue, 1997.

Parrish, T. Michael, and Robert M. Willingham Jr. *Confederate Imprints: A Bibliography of Southern Publications from Secession to Surrender.* Austin, Tex.: Jenkins, 1987.

Perry, John. *The Lady of Arlington: The Life of Mrs. Robert E. Lee.* Sisters, Ore.: Multnomah, 2001.

Phisterer, Frederick. *Statistical Record of the Armies of the United States.* New York: Blue and Gray, 1963.

Pierce, Edward L. "Contrabands at Fortress Monroe." *Atlantic Monthly,* November 1861.

Pryor, Sarah Agnes. *Reminiscences of Peace and War.* New York: Books for Libraries Press, 1970.

Rable, George C. *The Confederate Republic: A Revolution against Politics.* Chapel Hill: University of North Carolina Press, 1994.

Ramsdell, Charles W. "The Confederate Government and the Railroads." *American Historical Review* 22 (July 1917).

Rhea, Gordon. *The Battle of the Wilderness.* Baton Rouge: Louisiana State University Press, 1994.

———. *Cold Harbor: Grant and Lee, May 26–June 3, 1863.* Baton Rouge: Louisiana State University Press, 2002.

Richmond & Danville Railroad Company. *Fourteenth Annual Report of the Richmond & Danville Railroad Company, Embracing the Reports of the President, Treasurer & Superintendant, Together with the Proceedings of the Stockholders.* Richmond: H. K. Ellyson, 1861.

Robertson, James I., Jr. *18th Virginia Infantry.* Lynchburg, Va.: H. E. Howard, 1984.

———. *Proceedings of the Advisory Council of the State of Virginia, April 21–June 19, 1861.* Richmond: Virginia State Library, 1977.

———. *Stonewall Jackson: The Man, the Soldier, the Legend.* New York: Macmillan, 1997.

———. "The Virginia State Convention of 1861." In William C. Davis and James I. Robertson Jr., eds., *Virginia at War, 1861.* Lexington: University Press of Kentucky, 2005.

Robertson, William Glenn. *Back Door to Richmond: The Bermuda Hundred Campaign, April–June 1864.* Newark: University of Delaware Press, 1987.

Roe, Alfred S., and Charles Nutt. *History of the First Regiment of Heavy Artillery, Massachusetts Volunteers.* Worcester, Mass.: Regimental Association, 1917.

Ruffin, Edmund. *The Diary of Edmund Ruffin.* 3 vols. Edited by William Kauffman Scarborough. Baton Rouge: Louisiana State University Press, 1972–1989.

Scanlon, James Edward. *Randolph-Macon College: A Southern History, 1825–1967.* Charlottesville: University of Virginia Press, 1983.

Schiller, Herbert M. *The Bermuda Hundred Campaign.* Dayton, Ohio: Morningside, 1988.

Sears, Stephen W. *Landscape Turned Red.* New York: Houghton Mifflin, 1983.

Selby, John G. *Virginians at War: The Civil War Experience of Seven Young Confederates.* Wilmington, Del.: Scholarly Resources, 2002.

Shade, William G. *Democratizing the Old Dominion: Virginia and the Second Party System, 1824–1861.* Charlottesville: University of Virginia Press, 1996.

Shanks, Henry T. "Conservative Constitutional Tendencies of the Virginia Secessionist Convention." In Fletcher Green, ed., *Essays in Southern History Presented to Joseph Gregoire de Roulhac Hamilton, Ph.D., LL.D., by His Former Students at the University of North Carolina.* Chapel Hill: University of North Carolina Press, 1949.

———. *The Secession Movement in Virginia, 1847–1861.* 1934. Reprint, New York: AMS, 1971.

Sheehan-Dean, Aaron. *Why Confederates Fought: Family and Nation in Civil War Virginia.* Chapel Hill: University of North Carolina Press, 2007.

Stackpole, Edward J. *From Cedar Mountain to Antietam.* Harrisburg, Pa.: Stackpole, 1959.

———. *Sheridan in the Shenandoah.* Harrisburg, Pa.: Stackpole, 1961.

Stanard, Mary Newton. *Richmond: Its People and Its Story.* Philadelphia: J. B. Lippincott, 1923.

Stevenson, George J. *Increase in Excellence: A History of Emory and Henry College.* New York: Appleton-Century-Crofts, 1963.

Stiles, Kenneth L. *4th Virginia Cavalry.* Lynchburg, Va.: H. E. Howard, 1985.

Sutherland, Daniel E. *Seasons of War: The Ordeal of a Confederate Community, 1861–1865.* Baton Rouge: Louisiana State University Press, 1995.

Thomas, Emory M. *Bold Dragoon: The Life of J. E. B. Stuart.* Norman: University of Oklahoma Press, 1986.

———. *The Confederate State of Richmond: A Biography of the Capital.* Austin: University of Texas Press, 1971.

———. *Robert E. Lee: A Biography.* New York: Norton, 1995.

Travers, Len. *Celebrating the Fourth: Independence Day and the Rites of Nationalism in the Early Republic.* Amherst: University of Massachusetts Press, 1997.

Trexler, Harrison A. "Davis Administration and the Richmond Press, 1861–1865." *Journal of Southern History* 16 (May 1950).

Tripp, Steven Elliott. *Yankee Town, Southern City: Race and Class Relations in Civil War Lynchburg.* New York: New York University Press, 1997.

Trudeau, Noah. *Bloody Roads South: The Wilderness to Cold Harbor, May–June 1864.* Boston: Little, Brown, 1989.

———. *The Last Citadel: Petersburg, Virginia, June 1864–April 1865.* Boston: Little, Brown, 1991.

Tunnell, Ted. "Creating 'the Propaganda of History': Southern Editors and the Origins of *Carpetbagger* and *Scalawag.*" *Journal of Southern History* 72 (November 2006).

Turner, Charles W. "The Virginia Central Railroad at War, 1861–1865." *Journal of Southern History* 12 (November 1946).

Turner, George Edgar. *Victory Rode the Rails: The Strategic Place of Railroads in the Civil War.* Lincoln: University of Nebraska Press, 1992.

U.S. War Department. *War of the Rebellion: A Compilation of Official Records of the Union and Confederate Armies.* 128 vols. Washington, D.C.: Government Printing Office, 1880–1901.

Valentine, Mrs. Mark. "A Girl in the Sixties in Richmond." *Confederate Veteran* 20 (1912).

Vance, L. J. "Dixiana." *Bachelor of Arts,* December 1895.

Vickery, Dorothy Scovil. *Hollins College, 1842–1942: An Historical Sketch*. Hollins College, Va.: Hollins College, 1942.

Virginia Central Railroad Company. *Correspondence between the President of the Virginia Central Railroad Company and the Postmaster General, in Relation to Postal Service*. Richmond: Ritchie and Dunnavant, 1864.

———. *Twenty-eighth Annual Report of the President and Directors of the Virginia Central Railroad Company, to the Stockholders, at Their Annual Meeting, November, 1863*. Richmond: M. Ellyson, 1863.

———. *Twenty-ninth Annual Report of the President and Directors of the Virginia Central Railroad Company, to the Stockholders, at Their Annual Meeting, November, 1864*. Richmond: M. Ellyson, 1864.

Wallace, Lee A., Jr. *The Richmond Howitzers*. Lynchburg, Va.: H. E. Howard, 1994.

Wallenstein, Peter. *Cradle of America: Four Centuries of Virginia History*. Lawrence: University Press of Kansas, 2007.

Watters, Mary. *The History of Mary Baldwin College, 1842–1942: Augusta Female Seminary, Mary Baldwin Seminary, Mary Baldwin College*. Staunton, Va.: Mary Baldwin College, 1942.

Weaver, John R. *A Legacy in Brick and Stone: American Coastal Defense Forts of the Third System, 1816–1867*. Missoula, Mont.: Pictorial Histories, 2001.

Wilson, Clyde N. *Carolina Cavalier: The Life and Mind of James Johnston Pettigrew*. Athens: University of Georgia Press, 1990.

Index